The Woodhaerst Reunion

Book 2 of The Woodhaerst family drama trilogy

Patricia M Osborne

White Wings

Books

Published 2024 in Great Britain

by White Wings Books

ISBN 978-0-9957107-5-7

All rights reserved.

No part of this publication may be reproduced, stored in a retrieval system, or transmitted in any form or by any means, electronic, mechanical, photocopy, recording or otherwise, without prior written permission of the copyright owners. Nor can it be circulated in any form of binding or cover other than that in which it is published and without similar condition including this condition being imposed on a subsequent purchaser.

British Cataloguing Publication data:
A catalogue record of this book is available from the British Library

This book is also available as an ebook

In Memory of

my dearest mum,

Lila (1932-2014)

and

Sister,

Heather (1956-2009)

Two courageous and inspiring women

A light went out in my heart when you both left this world

Chapter One

Rachel

March 1977

Almost blinded by the sun, I drove on to the housing estate, turned into Springfield Road and parked outside number seven.

My legs shook as I climbed out of the car. Why was I so nervous? Was it because Linda's letters had dried up about six months ago and she'd avoided me when I came home at Christmas? I took a deep breath, locked up the car, made my way through the garden gate, down the path and tapped the knocker.

Mrs Smith opened the front door with a cigarette dangling from her mouth. 'Hello, Rachel, I thought it was you getting out of the car. When did you get back?'

'Last night.'

She looked out at the Mini. 'Driving. When did that happen?'

'I started learning a while back but passed my test last November. Is she in?'

'She is. Come on in.'

When I stepped onto the carpet it was like walking on air. 'Ooh, I love this.'

'It's beautiful, isn't it? Do you mind taking your boots off, love?'

'Course not.' I unzipped my platforms and left them neatly by the door. 'Feels gorgeous underfoot.'

'The salesman called it a shag pile. It's got a thick underlay which gives it an extra spring.'

'Cool.' I peered around at the matching coffee and cream walls. 'I love your colour scheme.'

'Thank you. I thought it was time we decorated now we're both earning a little more. She's in her room. Go on up if you like. I'll put the kettle on.'

'Cheers, Mrs Smith.' I headed upstairs and gave a tap on the bedroom door before walking in. Linda was lying on her bed facing the wall. I touched her shoulder.

She jumped. 'Bloody hell, Rach, where did you come from?'

'Your mam told me to come on up.'

'Did she now? What are you doing here, anyway?'

'I thought you'd be a little more pleased to see me. What's going on, Lind? And why did you stop writing? And then avoiding me last Christmas? Have I done something wrong?'

'No, of course not. It's not you, it's me.' She broke down in tears.

Mrs Smith padded in with two cups of coffee and placed them on the bedside cabinet. 'Still black, no sugar, Rachel?'

'Yes, ta. You didn't need to come up though.'

'It's good exercise. Right, I've got some washing to peg out so I'll leave you girls to catch up.'

'That was tactful of your mam.' I perched on the edge of the bed and rested my fingers on Linda's arm. 'What is it?'

'I can't tell you.' She sobbed. 'You'll hate me.'

'No, I won't. I could never hate you. What is it?'

'I' – she sniffled – 'I had... you're going to hate me but, nope, I can't tell you. I can't even say the words.'

'Just tell me.'

'I had… Sorry, I can't.'

'Course you can. Just spit it out.'

'Okay. But you're going to hate me. I had an abortion.' She sniffled. 'There, now you know.'

'And I don't hate you. But how come? What happened? And why didn't you tell me?'

She sat upright, wiping her eyes with the back of her hand. 'Remember I told you about the new girl, Anna, at Woolies?'

'Yep. I was pleased to hear you had a new friend.'

'Well, one day she suggested I went to a party with her.'

'Stu too?'

'No, just me. He was having a boys' night so it seemed the obvious thing to go out with Anna. The problem was I didn't know anyone else so when she went off with some chap I was left alone with his mate. I'm so ashamed cos I got really drunk and agreed to let this guy take me home.' She pulled at her lips. 'I never fancied him. And I wasn't interested in him, but I didn't want to walk home on my own.'

'That's understandable and very wise.'

'Unfortunately, not so wise on this occasion. He came on to me and I tried…' She whimpered.

'What are you saying?'

She turned away from me.

'Linda' – I squeezed her hand – 'did he rape you?'

She nodded.

I took a clean hanky from my pocket and dabbed her eyes. 'Did you report him?'

'What was the point? No one would've believed me. It's not like he forced me to get into his car.'

'Even so…' I stroked her wet cheek. 'You poor thing.'

She spluttered. 'It gets worse' – she blew her nose – 'I only got bloody pregnant.'

'Gawd. Did you decide on the abortion because you couldn't face having the baby?'

'No. I thought if I had an abortion Stu would forgive me.'

'Forgive you for what, Lind? You'd done nothing wrong.'

'That's what he said, afterwards, but he couldn't forgive me for having an abortion.'

'What? Why?'

'Turns out he's a Catholic. Did you know that?'

'That's the first I've heard of it.' I sighed. 'So, you had to go through this on your own then?'

'No, me mam was brilliant, sorted everything, and came with me to you know. But now I feel so bloody guilty about the whole thing.'

'Are you still seeing your counsellor?'

'I wasn't but after this I started seeing her again. I'm not sure how much she's helping though because I can't get rid of the thought that I killed a little life inside me.'

'You can't think like that, Lind. Most women in your position would have done the same.'

'Would you?'

I brushed her fingers. 'I don't know. Probably. Come here.' I hugged her. 'I'm so sorry about what you've had to go through. You've had such a rotten time and I wish I'd been here to support you. Stick with the counselling, and now I'm here to help too.'

She looked up and smiled.

'How about Woolies?'

'What about it?'

'You still happy there?'

She shrugged. 'Not really. I now know what you meant about being bored. Same old thing every day. I'm so bored.'

I patted her hand. 'Have you thought about doing something else?'

'Like what?'

'I'm not sure. Look, I can't do anything about what's happened but I could help you look for a new job or hobby. Something to give you purpose.'

'Doing what?'

'Have you got a copy of *The Echo*?'

'Yeah, downstairs. Why?'

'You'll see. Come on.' I picked up my coffee, left the bedroom, and hurried downstairs with Linda in tow. On reaching the sitting room I said, 'I love what you and your mam have done in here.'

'Cool, isn't it?'

'Sure is.' I put my cup down on the occasional table, grabbed the newspaper from the armchair and kneeled on the soft pile, spreading the newspaper open. 'We want the classifieds.' I flicked through to the job ads. 'Here, how about this? Freeman Hardy and Willis are looking for a manager. You could do that. What with all your experience at Woolies, and you know how much you love shoes. This would be perfect. You'd be the boss.'

She got down on the carpet next to me. 'Maybe. Not sure how I feel about being around men's sweaty feet all day though. What else is there?'

'Here' – I pointed – 'a new boutique opening in the High Street want a manageress.'

'Now you're talking. I think I'd like that.' She grabbed a blue biro from the coffee table and circled the position.

'Oh, I almost forgot' – I got up from the carpet and took a seat on the brown velour sofa – 'Mum and Dad have invited you and your mam over to lunch today.'

'Really?'

'Yes. All their idea. I think they want to make my homecoming a little special as Jen's not back yet. What do you think?'

'Well, we've not started cooking...' Linda shouted, 'Mam, you back in?'

Mrs Smith peeped her head around the door. 'I was giving you girls a bit of time. Is it safe to come in now?'

'Sure,' I said. 'I was just saying to Linda that my parents have invited you both over for lunch today. I've got the car so no need to worry about buses, and I'll bring you back this evening.'

Mrs Smith touched the turquoise chiffon scarf on her head. 'I'll have to take these curlers out first and put on a clean frock.'

'Is that a yes then?'

'If Linda would like to. Yes. Are you two okay?'

'Yep. Rachel's been helping me find a new job. 'Linda picked up the newspaper. 'Look there's this one in a boutique opening next month. I think I'd be good at that.'

Mrs Smith turned to me, smiled and mimed thank you.

At least it had stopped raining. I gazed up at the cerulean blue sky. A beautiful spring day but it still felt far too cold.

'This is a bit of all right.' Linda patted the roof of my Mini. 'I love the dark green. How did you afford it?'

'A present from Mum and Dad for passing my exams.'

'Lucky cow.' Linda chortled.

'I know. I now really appreciate what wonderful parents they are after, well you know... Look you get in the back, and let your mam sit in the front.' I pulled the driver's seat forward.

'This is nice, Rachel,' Mrs Smith said smoothing down her camel-coloured coat.

'Thanks. Hope you're not too squashed. That's the only trouble with a Mini.'

I turned the ignition and pushed the long gearstick into first.

Linda ruffled my hair. 'Actually, Rach, there was another reason I stopped writing to you.'

'Oh aye?'

'Never mind. It can wait until we get to yours.'

I switched the gear into neutral and turned the ignition off. 'No tell me now. What is it?'

'It's Joe. He's been seeing someone.'

My heart beat faster. Joe, my Joe, had found someone else. 'Oh well I suppose it was bound to happen sooner or later.' It had been over four years so I couldn't have expected him to stay celibate forever. I turned on the ignition again, pushed the gearstick into place and drove off.

'Did you meet anyone while you were away, dear?' Mrs Smith asked.

'Nope. I didn't have the time. I had to commute to London from Croydon every day. If truth be told I was too tired to do anything. But now that I'm back, Lind and I are going to have some fun. We've found her a new job, fingers crossed, now we need a hobby. How about photography? Or painting?'

'Hell.' She chortled. 'I can't draw for toffee.'

'Embroidery? Dressmaking?'

Mrs Smith craned her neck to speak to Linda. 'Photography sounds good, dear.'

'Yeah, I suppose it does. And you say we'll do this together, Rach?'

'Sure. And another thing, you should learn to drive.'

'Oh, I don't know about that.'

I stopped at the red traffic lights. 'You too, Mrs Smith. Think about it, you'll save money by getting a weekly shop and you'll be able to pile all the groceries straight into the car. And it'll be easier for you to get to and from work so you don't have to catch the bus. I'm sure Adam will be able to pick you up a nice runabout. You could always buy one car to share?'

'That's not a bad idea, Mam,' Linda said. 'What do you think?'

'Possibly but I think I'm maybe a little too old to start learning now.'

'Rubbish,' I said as the lights turned green and I pulled away. 'You're only what, forty? Forty-one? They say life begins at forty. And isn't it time you got yourself a boyfriend?'

Mrs Smith put her hands to her face. 'Don't, Rachel, you're making me blush.'

'It's true though, you're still a young woman. Time you started to live a little. Don't you agree, Lind?'

'Yep. She's right, Mam. Let *operation get mam a man* begin.' Linda giggled.

I drove into the drive. 'Here we are.'

My best friend and her mam peered up at the house. 'Bloody hell,' Linda said, 'you didn't tell us that you lived in a mansion.'

'Sorry. I thought you knew we had a big house.' It was wrong of me not to have warned them but I hadn't actually seen it as a problem. But in reality, I should've realised they'd be alarmed comparing it to their tiny terrace. I tried to make light and laughed. 'It's big but definitely not a mansion.' I stepped out of the car and pulled the seat forward.

Mrs Smith gasped. 'What a gorgeous garden. So many flowers. What are they all called? I recognise the daffs and crocuses in the lawn but not the others?'

'The yellow bushes over there are forsythia, the deep pink on the right are camellias, that tree there's a magnolia, I love that, and the gold and purple blooms under the window are wallflowers. Mum's favourites.'

'Mum, Dad.' I peeped into the kitchen. 'Something smells good.' I opened the oven door. 'Looks like we've got roast beef. I wonder where they've gone.' I turned to the fridge and spotted a note on the door held by a magnet.

Gone for a quick stroll. Back soon.
Mum and Dad

'Tea? Coffee?' I asked Mrs Smith and Linda as they followed me in.

'Coffee would be lovely.' Linda's mam wandered over to the pine dresser in the dinette area. 'Beautiful flowers everywhere.' She sniffed at the mixed vase of daffodils and tulips.

'Yep, my mum loves flowers.' I'd forgotten how much Mum loved having flowers in the house and I'd also forgotten how they gave me hay fever.

'Would you like some help making the coffee?' Mrs Smith asked.

'No, it's okay. You two take a seat at the table and I'll pop the kettle on.' I gave it a shake to check there was enough water before flicking the switch.

Linda ran her fingertips across the smoked glass. 'You mentioned Adam might be able to get us a car. Have you seen much of him?'

'Nope. Not seen him since I moved away. Peggy met up with me a few times when I came home for visits but Adam never showed.' I added a spoon of Nescafé to each of the cups, poured out the boiling water and put the drinks on the table.

Mrs Smith stirred her beverage. 'Have you managed to adjust to Peggy being your real mother?'

'I suppose so.' I pulled out a chair to sit down. 'You know, if anyone had told me five years ago that my life could have changed in one year, I'd have laughed at them. There I was a normal teenager, then I discover my mum and dad aren't my real parents and then' – I took a deep breath – 'then find out my fiancé was my half-brother.' I shook my head. 'I've not seen Joe since I left for Sheffield at the beginning of 1973 when I went off to start the pre-entry course. Maybe when I do, I'll see him differently and he won't make my heart race.'

Mrs Smith clasped her fingers over mine. 'It's been tough for you, dear. Not that it's stopped you. Look at you now, a journalist, and a very attractive one too.'

'Now you're making me blush,' I said as the front door slammed. 'That'll be Mum and Dad. In here,' I called.

Dad entered first. 'Ah, good afternoon, Mrs Smith. Wonderful to see you again after all this time.' He gave her a kiss on the cheek.

'Sandra please.'

'Sandra. And you must call me Charles, and my wife Rosalind. Isn't that right, Rosalind?' Dad said to Mum as she came in.

'Absolutely. Thank you for coming, Sandra. And Linda, how are you doing? You're looking very grown up.'

'I'm well, thanks, Mrs Webster. Rachel was suggesting I get myself a new job.'

'Always good to have a change. Rachel, dear, do show our guests through to the dining room. Lunch will be ready shortly. Take your coffees through with you.'

'Thank you' – Linda's mam picked up her cup and saucer – 'but are you sure I can't help with something?'

'No. It's fine. It's just the case of getting everything served into dishes. Please, go through as it's warmer in there.'

I led Linda and her mam into the dining room. 'Sit wherever you like.'

'The table looks lovely,' Linda said. 'Does your mam always set it like this?'

'No' – I laughed – 'only when we have guests.'

'It must be wonderful to have Rachel back home?' Linda's mam said when we retired to the lounge after lunch.

'It is' – Mum poured coffee from the pot into the cups – 'although we've not really seen her yet. It was late evening when she arrived yesterday and she was still in bed this morning when we left for church.' She handed Linda's mam a Royal Doulton china cup and saucer.

'What about your other daughter? Jenny, isn't it?'

Dad passed Mrs Smith the onyx cigarette box. 'Smoke? We're expecting Jennifer home next week.'

'Thank you.' Sandra helped herself to a Marlboro.

Dad flicked a lighter and leaned across and ignited her ciggie. 'Jennifer starts work as a staff nurse at the hospital in a couple of weeks. She's been waiting for her papers to come through to confirm she's qualified. We're all very proud of her. The house is going to be very different after over three years with just Rosalind and me.'

'But Rachel's been away longer?'

'Yes, just over four years since she first left. I'm sure Rosalind's already noticed the difference with the workload. Rachel never was the tidiest.'

'That's not fair.' I laughed.

'All right, maybe it wasn't.' Dad winked at me.

Over lunch Mum and Dad had been chatting to Sandra like old friends. I used to think they were snobs and their reasoning for not wanting me to see Linda was because she was working class. How wrong I had been. It was because Linda had swayed me to leave college and work at Woolies full-time. Nothing to do with class at all.

I rose from the couch. 'Do you mind if Linda and I go up to my room for a proper catch-up?'

'Not at all. You girls go and have some fun.' Mum crossed her slender legs. She still had a good figure for a woman in her late fifties and her hair had turned a lovely platinum colour.

'Rachel,' Dad said, 'you're looking a bit tired. If you like, I'll drive Sandra and Linda home later to save you going out again.' He turned to Mrs Smith. 'Shall we say around seven?'

'Thank you, Charles, that's very kind of you. Seven o'clock is perfect. It'll give us time to get things sorted for work in the morning.'

I flopped onto my bed and Linda curled up next to me. 'How do you feel about going into work tomorrow?' she asked.

'A little nervous. I think I'll be under John, unless he's moved on, and I never really had much to do with him before so no idea what kind of boss he'll be. It'll be nice to see everyone though, especially Betty and Mel. While I was at Sheffield, I lived in a shared house so I always had company, but once I'd finished the pre-entry journalism and moved to Croydon for the main course I was isolated. I joked to everyone about the nightlife but in truth I was too tired most nights to go out and even if I wanted to, I had no one to go with. It was a lonely life but I kept myself busy with study.'

Linda clasped my fingers. 'Well, you're home now and you've got me. How about you help me write an application letter for that boutique.'

'Sure.' I sat up and reached to a drawer in my bedside cabinet and took out a lined notepad and black biro. 'You write and I'll dictate. Dear…'

Chapter Two

Rachel

The windscreen wipers swung back and forth as I drove into the car park behind the newspaper premises. I parked next to a white Triumph 2000 and wondered who it belonged to. It made me think of Joe, as he and his dad had worked at a British Leyland garage. *Stop it.* I grabbed my bag and brolly from the passenger seat and stepped out of the car into the pouring rain. With the brolly over my head, I hurried to the office, taking a deep breath before opening the door.

I was greeted by Mr Strange, 'Good morning, Miss Webster. Glad to have you back on board. The team have missed you. You did extremely well in your exams and we're all very proud of you. As you know Mr Smythe will be your immediate line manager.'

Lizzie beamed on Reception. She waved. 'Look at you all grown up and a reporter now too. Betty's in the back.'

'Cheers.'

'Come and say hello to everyone.' Mr Strange ushered me through to the back office which appeared pokier than I'd remembered.

Before I knew what was happening Betty was smothering me. 'Look at you. No longer that cocky teenager but a classy young lady. We've missed you, pet.' She held me at arm's length.

'Let me look at you. How are you? Are you looking forward...' She took a breath. 'Listen to me not letting you get a word in edgeways.'

'That's okay, Betty.' I smiled. 'I'm fine. Feeling a little strange being back after four years and knowing I shan't be in here typing letters, answering the switchboard, or on the telex.' I gazed over to where I used to sit and spotted a young redhead.

'That's Verity, our new trainee,' Betty said. 'The last girl didn't work out. Verity's been with us for two months now.'

'Hi Verity,' I said.

She peered up from the typewriter. 'Hi there, Rachel. I've heard all about you.'

'All good I hope.'

'Yes.' She giggled. 'Rachel did it like this. Rachel did it like that.'

'Oops. Sorry. Are you enjoying the job?'

'Yes, I love it, although I'm hoping to get trained up as a journalist like you did.' She turned to the boss, smiling.

'In time, Miss West. In time. Let's learn to walk before we run.' He turned back to me. 'Miss Webster, get yourself a cup of tea and we'll pop into my office for a quick briefing before you start.'

'Yes, sir.'

'Good luck,' I said to Verity as I poured a mug of tea and added a dash of milk. 'I'll catch up with you all at lunchtime.'

'If you manage a break before then,' Betty said, 'come and tell me all about what you've been doing.'

'Will do.' I picked up the mug and followed Mr Strange into his office.

༺

It was weird being upstairs with John and away from the others.

'Are you happy to do that on your own?' he asked.

'Yep. Think I can manage. Now?'

'Unless you've got anything better to do?'

'No, of course not.' I patted my bag. 'My notepad and pen are in here ready.'

'Next Saturday evening you'll attend the gig when Alan, our photographer, will meet you down there. Now back to today, you need to ask for the manager. Paul Avery.'

'Okay. Cheerio then.' I hurried downstairs, smiling. An assignment on my first day, and with a rock band at that. As I darted past the back office I called, 'Bye, Betty. I'll see you tomorrow. I'm out on a job and you'll be gone by the time I get back.'

'All right, pet.' She held up her crossed fingers. 'Good luck.'

'Thanks.'

༺

Was this building even safe? I put my fist up to tap on the cracked wooden door but before I got a chance to knock someone opened it. 'Hiya, you must be the reporter from The Echo?'

'Yes' – I held out my hand to shake – 'Rachel Webster.' My heart was doing double-unders as I peered up at this tall chap with short ginger hair and round-rimmed glasses. I mustn't mess this up.

'I'm Paul.' His fingers almost crushed mine. 'Come and meet the guys.' He slammed the dilapidated door closed and made his way down the narrow corridor with me in tow. 'In here.'

As I followed him into a much brighter, bigger space, music stopped playing. DARK CHAOS was printed on the face of the bass drum. The drummer put his sticks down on the cymbal and came over. 'Hi babe' – he looked me up and down – 'that old guy, Smythe, didn't let on he'd be sending a gorgeous chick.'

I sensed myself blushing at this sexy bloke. 'You lot are my first story so please be kind.' I chortled.

'Course they will. Boys, find Rachel a seat and I'll get her a cuppa.' Paul patted the top of my arm. 'You'll be fine. Just get to know them and then print us a great story so we get lots of punters next Saturday.'

Today had been unexpected. It was wonderful meeting Dark Chaos. The drummer, Steve, was rather handsome. He reminded me of Joe with his long dark hair but instead of brown eyes he had the loveliest electric blue. Paul had given me a couple of free gig tickets for my friends. It was a shame I hadn't had the chance to catch up with Betty or Mel at work but there was always tomorrow. I drove up the drive and turned off the engine.

Mum was on the phone as I stepped into the hallway. She glimpsed up and mimed, 'Good day?'

'Fabulous.'

'Sorry love, yes, it's your sister. Would you like to speak to her?' Mum turned to me. 'It's Jennifer, she'd like a quick word.' She passed the handset to me.

'Hiya. You never were great on timing. I've literally just come through the door. I've not even had a chance to take my coat off.'

※

'Come and get warm by the fire.' Mum almost dragged me into the lounge. It was strange being back here, and even stranger without Jen. At least she'd be home next week.

Dad plodded in and kissed me on the cheek. 'How was your first day?'

I grinned. 'Better than I'd hoped. I got to interview a rock band who are performing at the village hall a week on Saturday. Tomorrow I'll be in the office typing up the story to help them get a sell-out.' Still grinning, I took a seat on the sofa. 'The job's brilliant. I thought John would have me doing boring stuff to start, but no, he let me have this.' I rubbed my hands. 'I was a bit nervous when I got to their rehearsal digs though. It looked derelict from outside but once I got inside it was fine. In fact, it was huge inside and reminded me of a tardis.'

'That sounds interesting.' Dad eased himself on to the sofa next to me.

'Yes, it was. The guys were lovely too. I think I might just be cut out for this reporter lark after all.'

'We never doubted you,' Mum said from the doorway. 'Now get yourself warmed up while I serve dinner.'

Dad held the lighter flame over the bowl of his pipe. 'How are you feeling about being back in Woodhaerst?' He took short puffs.

'The job's great, but I do have mixed feelings about being back. It's been nice not having to worry about bumping into you know... London was fabulous though,' I lied, 'our Jenny would love it. The nightlife is to die for.'

'Hmm, yes. I've a feeling Jennifer and her fellow nurse friends know how to party from what she's said in her letters.'

'Rachel,' Mum called from the kitchen. 'Would you mind setting the table, please?'

'Sure.' I headed into the dining room, took the cutlery and mats from the drawer and placed them neatly on the table. The last four years had given me a lot of time to appreciate my parents. Sometimes you didn't know what you had until it was almost snatched away. My heart was still empty. It didn't matter how hard I tried I still loved Joe, despite knowing I couldn't have him. I was going to need to face him soon. That is unless he no longer lived in Woodhaerst. Peggy had avoided talking about him but she'd mentioned that Kate, my half-sister, was doing well and looking forward to meeting me.

Chapter Three

Peggy

Adam peered up from his bacon and eggs. 'Curlers? Off out somewhere?'

'Yes' – I patted my head – 'meeting Rachel later. Remember I told you?'

He buttered a slice of toast. 'I can't say I do. When did she get back?'

'Last Saturday. Look, why don't you join us?'

'Sorry, love, but the MOTs are packed solid. I may even have to work late and once I get in, well, I reckon I'll need a rest. Do give her my love though.'

'She'll think you don't want to see her as you've never bothered coming with me for the last four years.'

'That's ridiculous. I thought as they were only short meetings and happened rarely that you'd appreciate the time on your own. Look why not invite her over to tea?'

'Really? I was going to ask you about that idea. I thought I'd invite our Sheila too. That way Rachel can get to meet Kate and her aunty. What do you think?'

'That sounds like a good idea. Tell you what, invite Miranda over too. The sooner Rachel sees that Joe's moved on the better for all of us.'

'If you like.' I wondered how Rachel would take it, or Joe for that matter. 'Do you think it's wise though, you know…'

'What?'

'Supposing Joe's still holding a torch for her?'

'He's with Miranda now.'

'Yes, but have you looked at her?'

'What do you mean?'

'Her likeness to Rachel. It's almost like he went looking for her twin.'

'You're reading too much into things, Peg. Invite Rachel and we'll get Miranda around too. Time to move on. There's no way I want to go back to where we were four years ago.'

Once the curlers were out my hair fell in soft waves brushing my shoulders. I wondered whether I should be getting it cut short now I'd turned forty-one. The weight was piling on around my waist too. I needed to put myself on a diet without Kate noticing, and increase the exercise. Must've been going through the change as my periods had stopped around four months ago. I slipped into my denim skirt but struggled to fasten it. I'd heard menopause could cause weight gain. First thing Monday morning I'd book an appointment with the doctor.

Thankfully the increase in weight hadn't put Adam off me. Things were back as they used to be before Rachel came into our lives. He was still a sexy man.

I rummaged through my wardrobe trying to find something decent to wear and settled for a pair of brown ski pants with a long, green baggy jumper. The elasticated waist on the trousers was a relief.

Rachel waved as I hurried through the pub car park.

'Hello, love.' I kissed her on the cheek. 'You look well.' In fact, she looked better than well. She'd always been a bit of a looker but now there was something different. What was it? Had she changed her hair? Make-up? She was stunning. I bet she had all the men flocking over her.

'Thanks. I'm good.' She shivered. 'It's bloody cold. Shall we go inside?'

'Of course.' I headed for the bar. 'What would you like to drink?'

'Just a coke please as I'm driving.'

I pulled a fiver from my purse and held it up to attract the bar person's attention.

'What can I get you, love?' a grey-haired man asked.

'Just two cokes, please. Are you serving food?'

'Yes but we stop serving at two, so if I were you, I'd get your order in before the herd stampedes.' He handed me a menu. 'Tell you what, pop yourselves by the fire and I'll be over in a min to take your order while we're quiet.'

'Thanks. That's kind of you.'

He flicked the lids off the bottles. 'Straws or glass with ice and lemon?'

'Glasses please but without the ice and lemon. It's too cold.' I folded my arms. 'That wind's biting.'

'Here you go, duckie. You'll soon warm up by the fire.'

'Thanks.' I picked up a bottle and glass and Rachel did the same and we made our way over to a couple of armchairs by the glowing flames. 'This is nice,' I said. We'd not been in this pub before, or at least I hadn't. I perused the menu. 'Ploughman's?'

'Sounds good.' Rachel crossed her legs showing off her black, knee-length boots.

'They must take you an age to lace up.'

'Not so long now I've got used to them. They're suede. Do you like them?'

'I love them. I'd quite like a pair myself but I think I'd look like mutton dressed as lamb.'

'Not at all. Tell you what, I'll buy you a pair if you like as I missed your birthday last week.' She laughed and I joined in knowing exactly where she was going, reminding me of the pair of boots I'd bought for her when we first met.

The barman came across. 'You two look like you've made up your minds.' He winked at me.

'Yes, thanks. Two ploughman's.'

'Do they come with chips?' Rachel asked.

'They don't but I can add a bowl or two?'

'Yes please. One will do. We'll share. Should I come up to the bar and pay now?' I asked.

'No, you're all right. You look like a lady I can trust.' He grinned before going back behind the bar.

'You've pulled,' Rachel said.

'What?'

'He fancies you.'

I screwed up my face. 'Do you mind? Have you forgotten I'm a happily married woman?'

'Everything's all right now between you two?'

'Yes, better than all right. Really good. We're back on a nice smooth front' – I glared at her – 'and we'd like to stay that way. Right?'

'Of course. I'm not here to rock the boat. I'd like to meet my kid sister though.'

'She'd like that too. And that's why I, we, Adam and I, wondered whether you'd like to come over for your tea on Sunday?'

'Tomorrow?'

'No, I meant a week tomorrow.'

'Er that should be okay. I've got to cover a gig on the Saturday but I don't think I have anything planned. Our Jen's coming home sometime next week so can I let you know on Monday? I should know more by then.'

The pub started to fill up. A group of men crowded around the bar, and a party of women bustled in taking up the three tables behind us.

I glanced around. 'He wasn't kidding about the crowds coming in.'

Rachel chuckled. 'I still reckon he fancies you.'

A young lad came over to us with two plates. 'Ploughman's?'

'Yes thanks.' I sat back in the chair so he could put the lunch down.

'Chips are coming.' He wiped his hands down the blue apron before leaving us to it.

I spread the French bread with Anchor butter. 'I haven't had a ploughman's for ages.'

'Me neither.' Rachel put her knife down. 'Are we going to mention the elephant in the room?'

'I'm not sure what you're talking about.'

'Come off it, Peggy. Joe. How is he? Is he still living in Woodhaerst? Just because you don't mention him doesn't mean I'm not thinking about him.'

I coughed. 'You're right. I shouldn't have avoided the subject but when you never brought him up, I thought it was easier for you that way. I was trying to protect you. Although…'

'What?'

'He's still living at home and he'll be there for tea when you come.'

She gave a half smile. 'That's great. Linda told me he has a girlfriend.'

'Yes, he does. Miranda. She'll be there too, and Sheila, my sister, as well as Kate, naturally,' I said hurriedly.

'Great.' She nibbled her bread in silence.

'Is she coming?' Adam unwrapped the fish and chips and popped them on plates.

'Yep. I think so. Mmm, they smell good. Are the kids in?'

'Our Kate is but Joe's gone out.'

'I'll give her a yell.' I wandered out to the hallway and called upstairs.

'Coming.' She hurried downstair in a pair of black corduroy straight-legs and a sky-blue V-necked T-shirt. They suited her. She had a gorgeous figure, slim but not too skinny. Adam and I still watched her in case she had a setback with the anorexia nervosa but she'd learned to be open with us when she was struggling.

'We've got fizz 'n pips.' I smiled, recalling an old memory.

'Goodie. I'm starved.' Kate picked up a plate and carried it over to the table. 'So have you been to see Rachel today, Mam?'

'Yes, and I've asked her over to tea next Sunday so you'll be able to meet her. I think you'll like her.'

She shoved a chip into her mouth. 'These are yummy.'

It was wonderful to watch her eat without worrying.

'I hope so,' she said. 'I've always wanted a big sister, not that I'd want to do without my big brother as he's the best. Does she look like me?'

'Maybe the same smile.' I glimpsed at Adam and he winked at me.

Chapter Four

Rachel

Fairy lights illuminated the outside of the village hall. We click-clacked up the steps in our four-inch-heel platform shoes. A huge queue formed at the closed door.

'Come on,' I said to Mel and Linda, 'let's to go around the back and I'll show my press card.' We hurried around the side of the building and knocked on the door. Paul answered with a beaming smile.

'Rachel. Fab you made it. And brought some friends too, I see.'

'Yes, this is my best friend, Linda, and Mel is my friend from work.'

'Come on in, girls.' Paul couldn't take his eyes off Linda.

The last time I'd been in this hall was for a village fete. What a transformation. Coloured lights circled the ceiling giving a dance hall effect. A temporary stage had been built at the front where the band was practising. Steve stopped drumming. 'Hang on, boys.' He jumped down from the platform and swaggered towards me. 'Rachel, babe. Thanks to you we've got a full house. That was an awesome full page spread you did. We're looking forward to your write-up after tonight.'

I sensed myself blushing. 'Why thank you, kind sir. Our photographer, Alan, will be along shortly.' Mind you, I hadn't met Alan yet. John said I'd recognise the short man in glasses.

'Cheers. Hang about. Here they come. Catch you later, babe. See you at the end.'

The crowd came flowing in and the band climbed back up onto the stage. Steve sat behind the drums and the others picked up electric guitars. Paul whispered something to them before taking to the microphone. 'Laddies and lassies, you're in for a treat this evening as Dark Chaos make their debut appearance. Let's see you all up on the dance floor and if you get thirsty, there's a bar in the lobby. Without further ado, give a big hand to Steve on the drums, Greg on guitar, Simon on bass guitar, and our lead singer, Ray.' Paul started clapping and the audience joined in with the applause as the lights went lower.

They opened up with Deep Purple's, 'Black Night'. Linda and I lined up next to each other and went straight into a dance of matching moves. Mel watched but as she caught the steps joined in. An involuntary tear escaped from my eye as the dancing brought back memories of Joe and I when we used to go to the bikers' dances at the Methodist Hall. When Dark Chaos finished everyone clapped which subsided as they started their next song, T. Rex, 'I love to Boogie'.

'Gosh, aren't they fab?' I shouted to Mel and Linda.

'Groovy.' Linda swayed her hands in the air.

'I'll go and get us a drink,' Mel said. 'What would you like?'

'Half a cider for me, please,' Linda said.

'I think they're only allowed to sell soft drinks,' I said, 'so a diet coke for me, please.'

'You're joking.' Linda frowned. 'If I'd known I'd have brought a bottle of my own.'

'I'm sure you can manage without. Anyway' – I poked her on the arm – 'a soft drink is much better when we're dancing.'

She screwed up her face. 'Suppose so.'

'Right. Three diet cokes then. I shan't be long.' Mel swayed out to the foyer.

She and Linda had hit it off straight away. What a shame I hadn't thought of introducing them before I left Woodhaerst, although I wasn't in the right mind then. It was good for Mel to be here as Lizzie from work mentioned she'd barely gone out since the break-up with Sam all those years ago. We'd all been hurt one way or another. No wonder we got on so well.

Paul was back up on the stage. 'Dark Chaos will now play their own composition, a ballad, 'When She Left Me'.

Steve came off drums and took the microphone as he opened up the song with, 'My world was full but then you left, leaving me in the cold darkness, you broke my heart...'

Linda and I were smooching when someone patted my shoulder. I pulled away to see who it was and a short chap with glasses peered up at me.

'You, Rachel?'

'Who's asking?'

'I'm Alan. The photographer.'

'Sorry, Alan, I didn't mean to be so abrupt.'

'That's okay. Good to finally meet you. The band seem a bit of all right.'

'They're tops. I reckon they'll get a record deal in no time and to think it will be you and me with our article that'll put them there.'

After playing more songs by The Sweet, Bee Gees, Eagles and Rod Stewart, the lights went up and the audience applauded. Following shouts of 'Encore Encore' from the crowd the lights dimmed and the band struck the strings with the T. Rex single, 'Ride a White Swan'. They finished with 10cc's 'Donna' where Steve was back on the microphone singing in a high-pitched voice.

As the lights went up for the final time a team of cleaners tackled the clearing up straight away. Alan and I headed up to the stage to speak to the band.

'You were amazing,' I said. 'No one would believe this was your debut concert. I reckon you'll get a recording contract in no time at all. I loved your composition. Who wrote that?'

'That would be me,' Steve said as I jotted down some notes.

'And who founded the band?' I continued.

'Again, that would be me.'

'And has it always been you four from the beginning or what?'

'Always us four. We got the band together at school when we were in the third year, so around fourteen. All thanks to a fab music teacher who taught us how to play and then allowed us the music room at lunchtimes to rehearse. We used to play for school functions but this is our very first public paying event.'

'That's brilliant. I think I've got enough to do a nice write up. Alan's just going to take a few shots now, if that's okay.'

'Cool,' Steve said.

'It shan't take long as I've already taken quite a few during your performance,' Alan said, 'but it would be nice to have a group picture and also an individual of each of you. And how about a snap with your lovely reporter, Rachel?'

'Awesome.' Steve ushered me up to the stage and Alan took a photo of me with the band, and then one with Steve's arm around me.

'That's about it.' Alan gathered his photography equipment together. 'I'll be off now. Good to meet you guys. Hope you're back here again soon.'

'Cheers, Al.' Paul jumped down from the stage and followed Alan out to the lobby.

Steve took me to one side. 'Do you fancy coming out with me for a drink one night?'

I wasn't sure but then Joe was moving on so why shouldn't I? 'If you like.'

'Next Thursday. I'll pick you up.'

'Sure. I'll write down my address.'

Before I could stop him, he kissed me full on the lips. 'Till then, darlin.'

As we wandered out of the hall and around to the car park, Linda said, 'You pulled then?'

'It seems so.'

'Me too.' She grinned. 'I had Paul and Greg after me but I said I'd go out with Paul.'

'How about you, Mel?'

She shook her head. 'Nope. No one asked me.'

I put my hand on her shoulder.

'It's okay. I'm not worried. I didn't really fancy any of them, well except the one you bagged. That Steve is something else.'

Chapter Five

Rachel

Jen spread out *The Echo* on the dining table. 'This article is impressive, Rachel. And look at you in the photo with the drummer. He's a bit of all right.'

'I must admit I'm rather pleased with it. John and Mr Strange were impressed too and they said I'll be getting some bigger jobs. What about you? Are you ready to start work next Monday?'

'I sure am. Really looking forward to it. I wonder if I'll know anyone else who works there.'

'Be good if you do.'

'Yeah. It's lovely being back home again though, don't you think?'

'I suppose so, although, I'm finding it a bit of a struggle knowing Joe only lives a short drive away.'

'Must be difficult. Have you seen him yet?'

'Not yet. I was supposed to go to tea at Peggy's last Sunday but put it off until this week.'

'Will he be there then?'

'Yep. And his girlfriend.'

'Yikes.' She patted my shoulder. 'What about this pop star?'

'Steve?'

'Yeah.'

'He's supposed to be ringing me but I've not heard from him yet. Never mind that, anyway, I wanted to ask your advice.'

'That's a first.' She chuckled.

I ignored her. 'I'm thinking of getting this cut.' I lifted my hair.

'What?'

'I want a new me.' I passed a magazine featuring Liza Minnelli. 'I'm thinking like hers.'

'Wow. That's quite a difference. Are you sure you want that much off?'

'I'm sure. I've made an appointment with the new hairdresser down the road. Fancy coming with me?'

'What time?'

'Half past two. Maybe you could get yours done too.'

'I don't want mine cut short like that. Perhaps a trim.'

Mum was in the hallway as I unlocked the front door. 'Get yourselves ready girls, your dad's taking us out to dinner to celebrate being back home together.' She glared at me with her mouth wide open. 'What the devil...?'

'Do you like it?' I stroked the side of my head.

'Er. It looks... but you... Let me see it properly under the light.' She flicked the light switch and came closer. 'Have you had a colour put on it?'

'Just a few auburn highlights.'

'You certainly look glamorous. More mature too but...'

'What?'

'It's just... you don't look like our Rachel. You look more like a movie star.'

'Good. That's what I want.'

Mum shrugged. 'Go and get changed as the table's booked for half an hour. Your father's just finishing off his shave.' She turned to Jenny. 'Thankfully you didn't get your gorgeous locks cut off too.'

'No. Just a little trim.' She flicked back the long blonde, straight hair that hung down her back.

After charging upstairs, I slipped out of my jeans and T-shirt into a black cheesecloth maxi skirt and a white gypsy blouse. I added a bit of nude make-up and blush, a small amount of eye liner and a light-brown lipstick giving me a natural look that I knew Mum and Dad would approve of. Finally, I inserted a pair of pearl studded earrings into my lobes which accentuated my new hairstyle.

※

Lizzie gave a wolf whistle as I entered the newspaper office. 'Wow. It looks like we've got a new girl. You were gorgeous before but now well... I've never noticed how striking those dark brown eyes of yours were before. What made you do it?'

'I needed a change.'

'Betty's in already. Pop in and show her before going upstairs. Are you in the office today or out on a job?'

'Think I'm in. I believe John wants to go through some training with me.'

'Surprised there's anything left to teach you after you produced that wonderful article last week. What was the band called? Hot Chaos?'

'Nearly right. Dark Chaos. I'd best go through if I'm going to have time to get a cuppa before going up.' I hurried along the corridor and into the back office. 'Morning, Betty.'

'Morning, pet.' She glanced up from the post. 'Good God, we've got a new girl. Is that really you, Rachel?'

'You like it?'

She came closer and patted each side of my head. 'I do. Where did you get it done?'

'In the hairdresser's that's opened up close to my house. I thought I'd run it through John about me doing a full page spread with a paid advert.' I filled the kettle and placed it on the gas ring. 'Fancy a cuppa?'

'Go on, if you're making one. My hubby was very impressed with your article on the band. Couldn't believe it was the same young girl that was working under me four years ago. I always knew you'd go far.'

The kettle whistled. I took it off the stove, added the boiling water to the teapot, gave it a stir, and poured out two mugs of tea.

'Leave mine there, pet. I've got sweeteners.' She patted her stomach. 'We've booked a holiday to Spain in June so I want to lose some of this before showing myself off in a swimming costume.'

'Good on you.' I stirred my tea and left the spoon on the tray. 'I'd best make my way upstairs.'

Linda was waiting at the clock tower. 'I didn't realise it was you,' she said. 'You look amazing. Do you think that style would suit me?'

'I don't see why not,' I said as we strolled arm in arm over to the Wimpy bar. 'But never mind that, how did your interview go?'

She crossed her fingers. 'He seemed to like me. Said he'll let me know by the weekend as he wants to open the first week in April.' Linda pushed the café door open and I followed her in. 'It's lovely there, Rach. Beautiful décor. All bright reds and yellows on the walls, and the clothes... you'll love them. Gypsy blouses, tiered maxi skirts. And he said I'll get twenty percent staff discount.'

'I hope you get it.'

A young waitress came to our table. 'What can I get you?' she asked chewing the top of a biro.

'Two Wimpy specials please' – I passed her the menus – 'and two black coffees.'

'Won't be long.' She strode over to the counter.

'If I get the job,' Linda said, 'I'm going to get my hair cut like yours. Where did you go?'

'A new place near me. I'm going to run a full page spread for them in return for a weekly ad for the next six weeks. They're offering a ten percent discount to anyone who quotes the advert. Shall I make you an appointment?'

'I'll only be able to make Wednesday afternoon unless they do an evening.'

'That's okay. They close Mondays so open all day on Wednesdays.'

'Cool. Oh look, here comes our lunch.'

The chef placed a plate of burger, fries, frankfurter, tomato and fried egg in front of each of us. 'Enjoy your meal.'

'This looks yummy.' Linda dipped a golden chip into the yolk. 'So,' she said with her mouth full, 'have you heard from Steve yet?'

The waitress came over. 'Two coffees.'

'Thank you.' I leaned back in my seat so she could put them down. Once she'd left our table, I said, 'Yep. Got a call last night. He wants me to go out with him tomorrow evening.'

'Did he say where? And did you say yes?'

'One question at a time.' I took a sip from my cup. 'No, he didn't say where but I did say yes, although I'm not sure about it. I didn't particularly like the way he kissed me full on the lips like that at the dance. I've a feeling he may expect more from me than I'm prepared to give.'

'He seems a nice chap and not one that won't take no for an answer.'

'True. He reminded me of Joe. In looks I mean, not personality.'

She cut into her burger. 'I suppose there was a likeness. Paul came into Woolies and asked me out too.'

'Really? What did you say?'

She laughed. 'Yes, of course. Not that I fancy him but he seemed an okay guy.'

'When are you seeing him?'

'Tomorrow evening. I'm thinking, maybe we could try and meet up?' Using her serviette she wiped ketchup from her lips.

'Oh yes, please. I'd feel much easier if we went out together.'

'He gave me his phone number so I'll give him a ring when I finish work. Talking of work, we should get back. And don't forget to book my hair appointment.'

'I won't.' I checked the bill. 'This is on me. I dropped two pounds and a fifty pence piece onto the tray. 'That should cover a tip too.'

'Thanks,' Linda said, hooking her arm in mine as we left the restaurant. 'My treat next time. I'll ring you later after I've spoken to Paul.' She crossed the road to Woolies and I turned right to The Echo.

※

Steve met me at the end of my road. He held the passenger door open to his yellow Capri.

'Thanks.'

He climbed into the driver's seat, started the engine and bombed along. My feet were braking on the floor. I wanted to ask him to slow down but thought that might make him go even faster.

'We're meeting Paul and your mate Linda at the Black Horse.'

'Great.' I felt more at ease knowing I wouldn't be alone with him.

'Your write-up was terrific. We've got so many more bookings. We've even been booked for a street party on fourth of June to celebrate the silver jubilee. Do you think you'll be able to cover it?'

'I'll make a point of it. I think we've got quite a lot of silver jubilee celebrations coming up around that time. Let me know the address and I'll ask my line manager if he minds me doing it, and I'll get Alan on board too.'

'That'll be cool.' Steve pulled into the pub car park.

※

We had a fairly pleasant evening but it was too reminiscent of our times with Stu and Joe. Although Linda said she didn't fancy Paul she was cuddling up to him a lot.

At the end of the evening Steve was supposedly driving me back home when he pulled into the parking area of Maple Park.

'I thought it would be nice if we had a bit of time on our own.'

'Oh, okay.' I wasn't sure what he was expecting.

He moved closer and kissed me full on the lips. When I responded he stuck his tongue down my throat and moved his fingers across my breast. I pushed his hand away. The next thing his hand was inside my coat and up my jumper.

'Don't.'

'I think you're a real cool babe.' He kissed me some more but it wasn't long before his hand wandered up my skirt.'

'Don't.' I shoved him away.

He took hold of my hand and placed it on his trousers.

I pulled away. 'For God's sake.'

'What's the matter with you?'

'What do you mean, what's the matter with me? I don't bloody know you and you expect me to...'

'Most girls would give their right arm.'

'Well, I'm not most girls. Look, Steve, you might be a nice chap and all that but I'm just not into this. I think it's best if you find yourself a groupie who'll be up for whatever you're after.'

After straightening up and fixing his clothes he said, 'Your loss, babe.' He started up the engine and drove me home in silence. At the end of my road, he reached across and opened the passenger door. 'See you then, babe.'

'Night.' I got out and closed the door behind me.

He drove off with his foot full on the throttle, without even bothering to see if I got into my house okay like Joe always did. My dad had always warned me that business and pleasure shouldn't be mixed. I should've listened to him. What a disaster. I hoped Linda's evening was going better than mine.

Chapter Six

Peggy

Plates of sandwiches with various fillings from ham, to cheese and cucumber, and egg mayonnaise filled the kitchen table. A sherry trifle topped with strawberry Angel Delight, and Dream topping held the centrepiece along with a Black Forest gateau which I'd purchased from Bejam's. Bread cobs spiked with sausages on sticks and cheese and pineapple resembled hedgehogs. I stood back to admire the spread.

'It looks lovely, mam.' Kate hugged me. 'Is there anything you'd like me to do?'

'No thanks, love. I think that's about it. Oh, I've just remembered, if you could grab the French bread and the bowl of salad. They're over on the worktop.'

The table was set for six. Adam, me, Kate, Rachel, Joe and Miranda. Unfortunately, Sheila and Malc were unable to make it. My stomach curdled from nerves not knowing how this tea was going to pan out with Joe and Rachel being together in close proximity.

Kate placed the salad and bread basket down on the table. 'It'll be all right, Mam. I'm sure we're going to like each other.' She had no idea about Joe and Rachel's history. 'I'll just go upstairs and finish off getting ready.'

The doorbell rang. Adam hurried downstairs. 'I'll get it.' When he opened the door he asked, 'Is that you, Rachel?'

Why would he ask that? I rushed to the hallway. 'Rachel? It is Rachel. You've had your hair cut?'

'Just a bit.' She laughed.

'Come in, come in.' I ushered her into the lounge. 'We're just waiting on the others. Joe's gone to collect Miranda, and Kate's upstairs getting ready. She'll be down in a minute.'

Rachel smiled. My goodness she looked even more gorgeous than she had before. How was Joe going to cope with her looking like this?

Adam took a seat on the sofa next to Rachel. 'You look so grown up. Of course, it's been a while.'

'Over four years. I was beginning to get a complex as you never came along with Peggy to see me.'

He squeezed her fingers. 'That's because I didn't want to intrude on the short time you had together. Anyway, I hear congratulations are in order. Passing all your exams and now a qualified journalist.'

'Yes. I had my first big job last Saturday. That's why I had to put Peggy off until now. I wanted to start writing it up while it was fresh in my head.'

'We saw it.' He got up from the sofa and pulled a newspaper out of the magazine rack. 'See.' He opened it up. 'You've still got your hair long here though so you can see why we were shocked.'

She laughed. 'It was an impulsive decision but not one I regret. I was fed up of being me so decided to have a change.'

The front door slammed shut. 'That'll be them now,' I said. 'Excuse me for a moment.' I left the room. 'Hello Miranda, dear. Joe, Rachel's here.' I'd already briefed him and Rachel to pretend that they'd not met each other before.

'Rachel,' I said, on heading back into the lounge, 'this is my son, Joe, and his girlfriend, Miranda.'

She held out her hand to Joe. 'Hi, Joe, it's good to finally meet you.' They held each other's hand far too long for my liking.

'And this is Miranda,' I said to break the moment.

'Hi, Miranda.'

'Hi.' Miranda turned to the door as Kate charged in. 'Kate.' She turned around and hugged her.

Rachel took a few steps closer and kissed her half-sister on the cheek. 'I'm pleased to finally meet you, Kate.'

'Let's go and have tea.' Adam signalled for everyone to follow him into the kitchen.

'Wow. What an awesome spread,' Rachel said, 'you shouldn't have gone to all this trouble.'

'Nonsense.' Adam pulled out a chair next to his seat. 'You're here, Rachel.'

⁂

Rachel insisted on washing up while I dried. 'Joe seems happy,' she said.

'He is. Miranda's a nice girl.'

'She seems nice enough but...'

I dried the tea plate and placed it on top of the others. 'What?'

'Come on, Peggy, you can't tell me you haven't noticed.' She rinsed the soapy dish before placing it on the draining board.

'Notice what? Just what is it you're getting at Rachel?'

'She looks like me.'

'Maybe a little.'

'A bit more than a little. Suppose she's his sister too?'

'Don't be so bloody stupid. I'd know if I'd had another baby.'

'But would you know if Mike had? Who's to say he hasn't got a dozen illegitimate kids all over the world?'

'Now you really are being stupid. You look like me, not Mike, so let's not have any more rubbish like that spouting from your mouth. Remember what I said, we don't want you rocking the boat. Especially now...'

'Now what?'

'Nothing.'

'Tell me.'

'Tell her what,' Adam said.

'Nothing. I was just saying that we'd bought her a present and she wanted to know what it was but I've told her she has to wait until we give it to her. Can you get it?'

'Sure.'

'Please, Rachel. Behave.'

⊰⋆⊱

'Well, that seemed to be a success,' Adam said once everyone had gone home or was in bed.

'Yes.' Although I wasn't sure about that. Kate had taken well to her half-sister but it was clear there was still magnetism between Joe and Rachel. Joe had barely taken his eyes off her all evening. And Rachel's comments about Miranda were clearly out of jealousy.

'Penny for them.' Adam stroked my cheek.

'There's something I need to tell you.'

'What? You're not leaving me for the milkman, are you?' He chortled.

'No, of course not.' I snuggled up to kiss him. 'There's only one man for me and he's right here next to me but there is something I should tell you and I don't know how you're going to take it.'

Adam sat upright. 'Just tell me then.'

'You must've noticed I've gained a little weight.'

'Yeah, sure. It suits you.'

'Well, there's a reason for it.'

'You've been eating too many pies.' He laughed.

'That probably hasn't helped but no, that's not the prime cause. I went to see the doctor the other day.'

'You're not ill, are you?'

'No, but I thought perhaps I was going through the change.'

'You're a bit young for that, aren't you?'

I shrugged. 'It does happen to some women around forty and I'm forty-one.'

'So, are you? Can the doctor help?'

'That's just it' – I took his hand – 'I'm not going through the change. I'm...'

'What? Peg, are you ill?'

'No,' I whispered, 'I'm expecting.'

He jolted back. 'For a moment there I thought you were going to say that you're pregnant.'

'You're not listening, Adam. That is what I said. I'm not only pregnant but five months.'

'Oh my god. You mean we're having a baby?'

'Yes.'

He took me into his arms. 'That's wonderful news. A new baby is just what we need. We'll tell the kids tomorrow. We're going to need to get the nursery ready if you're that far along.'

It was wonderful he was so pleased while my head was in a turmoil. This was the last thing I wanted, what with still watching to make sure Kate didn't have any setbacks and now Rachel back on the scene. Would our marriage be able to cope?

Chapter Seven

Rachel

'You all set?' I asked Linda.

'Yes, can't wait. Thanks for giving me a lift.'

'Made sense as I was doing the interview for a full-page spread.' I unlocked the Mini. 'Any news on the job?'

She beamed. 'Yes. I can't believe it's mine. I gave my notice in to Mr Peters this morning.'

'How did he take it?' I asked as we climbed into the car.

'He was sorry to see me go but really pleased with my new career choice. Said if it doesn't work out there would always be a place at Woolies for me.'

I started the engine. 'So, tell me about the boutique.'

'It's awesome. I get every other Saturday off. How cool is that?'

'Really? Who'll manage the shop then?'

'Mr Walker's wife, apparently, though I've not met her yet. And he's invited me to have an advanced view of the stock on Friday after work so I can choose three outfits as a sort of uniform.'

I frowned. 'Have you got to buy them?'

'No. He said I can choose them for free as I'll be advertising the goods.'

'I should think so too. Maybe I should contact him to see if he'd like me to write an article for the newspaper.'

'Go for it. Oh no, bloody hell it's only started raining.'

I flicked on the windscreen wipers. 'Don't panic. It's not likely to come to much as the sun's still shining.'

'We may get a rainbow. I love a rainbow but I'd hate to get my hair wet straight after having it done.'

'It'll probably have stopped by then. Anyway, there's a place to park right outside.'

'Yours is still looking good. Is it easy to style?'

'Yep, I just run my fingers through it while using the hairdryer. I wish I'd had it cut years ago. Everyone loves it.'

'You do look gorgeous, Rach.'

'Cheers, Lind. I needed a change.' I slammed my foot on the brake as the pedestrian light suddenly changed to red. 'Bloody hell and there's not even anyone crossing.' The signal flashed amber so I stuck the car back into gear and pulled away.

'How did it go with Joe the other day?'

'I shan't lie, it was hard.'

'Did you see the girlfriend?'

'Yeah, I did. I reckoned she looked just like my double. Well that is before I had my hair cut. Peggy got right narked when I suggested Miranda, that's her name, could be Joe's sister too.'

'You didn't?'

'I did. Of course I knew there was no way but... well you know? I just felt like saying it. She gave me a right what for.' I stopped at the junction for a couple of vehicles to pass before driving over the crossroads. 'Joe's asked me to meet him for a coffee.'

'Are you going to?'

I turned left, pulled on to the parade and parked outside the shop. 'Yes. We need to talk. Somehow, I have to get past this.'

We climbed out of the car and I locked it up. 'You can tell me about Paul on the way back.'

'Oh yes, and you about Steve.'

※

Alan packed up his photography equipment. 'Right, I'm done. It was nice to meet you, Susan.' He shook hands with the owner. He'd taken pictures of the dusky-pink interior with its glazed mirror skirting as well as a before and after of Linda who'd been offered a free haircut for agreeing to be a model.

Once Alan had left, the hairdresser said to Linda, 'I'll just rub something in to hold it in place.' She worked gel through Linda's hair.

'It suits you, Lind,' I said before turning to the owner. 'I'll get the article typed up ready for this Saturday's *Echo* with your advert going in over the following six weeks.'

'Thank you.' Susan rinsed her hands under the tap. 'And thank you, Linda, for being my model.' She passed her a business card. 'That'll get you ten percent off your next booking, that is, if you decide to come back again.'

'Oh yes, I'll definitely be back.'

'And Rachel, yours is looking fabulous. We should've got the photographer to take a picture of you too.' Susan laughed. 'Typical that I've only just thought of it now.' She shook my hand. 'Seriously, thanks for all your help.'

'You're welcome.' As we left the premises an elderly woman hobbled in smiling. I gave Susan a thumbs up before heading over to the car, unlocking it, and climbing into the driver's seat.

Linda stepped into the passenger side. 'At least it's stopped raining.' She peered up at the sky. 'And look, a rainbow. And it's a full arc.'

'Maybe all our dreams will come true.' I got into the car too.

'Do you have to go straight back to work?'

'I should really, but I suppose we can call in for a coffee somewhere first, then I'd best be heading back to get this story typed up. Now tell me about Paul.'

Linda grinned. 'He was the perfect gentleman. Might not be a great looker but wonderful company. Really interesting too.'

'More than can be said about Steve.' I turned right at the junction.

'What happened?'

'Apart from the fact he had hands like an octopus, the bastard only stuck my hand on his pants. Ugh. I felt sick. I mean I never even did that with Joe.'

'So did you do it?'

'No, I bloody didn't. Told him I wasn't in to that and he should go and find himself a groupie. Do you know what he said?'

'No?'

'That it was my loss and I should be grateful he was offering it. Well not those exact words but that's what he meant. Bloody men. I knew I shouldn't have bothered. I'm going to concentrate on work in future.'

The following day I'd promised to meet Joe in Elmo's at lunchtime. He was already there when I arrived so I joined him at the back table. It was almost like old times except now he was my half-brother and not my fiancé.

'Thanks for meeting up with me, Rach. Too difficult to talk at Mam's, what with Kate and Miranda not knowing anything about us.'

'I know what you mean. So, they call you Joe now at home too?'

He grinned. 'Yep, Mam finally got the message thanks to you. I had it changed by deed poll so it's official, Neil is dead and buried. Anyway, what did you make of Miranda?'

I chewed my lip. 'If you don't mind me saying, she looks an awful lot like me.'

'Yes, I suppose she does.'

'On purpose?'

'Yes. I told you I'd have to find another you. She's not you though. She might look like you but not as much fun and…'

'What?'

'I know I shouldn't say this but her kisses don't come close to yours.'

I put the menu up to my face. 'Don't, Joe. You're right you shouldn't say it. Are you just leading this girl on?'

'No, of course not. She's nice and if I can't have you then… mind you Mam and Dad would marry me off tomorrow just so that they could put a line under you and me. Are you seeing anyone?'

I shook my head. 'I had a date the other night with the drummer from this new band I interviewed. Gawd, talk about arrogant. He seemed to think I owed him something for taking me out. I shan't be seeing him again, that's for sure. Not socially anyway. I'll have to see him when I do another article on the band as they've got a gig booked for a street party in June. Is your road doing anything?'

'Not sure. I think Mam was all for sorting something out until…'

'What?'

'I'm not sure whether I should say.'

'You have to now.'

'Well, promise to pretend you don't know when Mam tells you.'

'Promise.'

'We're getting another brother or sister.'

'What?'

He nodded, grinning. 'You heard me.'

'You mean Peggy's...?'

'Yep. Due July apparently. Dad's over the moon but I don't think Mam's that happy.'

'Crikey, I don't blame her with grown-up kids and having to start over again. Yuk. Dirty nappies and sleepless nights.'

Joe screwed up his nose. 'I don't fancy sleepless nights either. Maybe I should get my own place and move out.'

'Changing the subject, it was nice meeting Kate. She's lovely.'

'She's a darling and I reckon she'll be a real little mam to the new baby.'

'I'm looking forward to getting to know her better. I'm planning to arrange a shopping trip with her and Peggy one Saturday.'

Alan positioned Linda, Mr Walker the boutique owner, and the young assistant into focus before taking the shot. 'That's about it.' He packed up his camera equipment. 'Best of luck with the opening,' he said before turning to me. 'I'll see you back at the office.'

'Cheers, Al.' Linda waved.

'That's me done, too.' I put the notepad and pen into my bag. 'Do you mind if I take a quick peep around at the clothes? I know you're not open yet but...'

'No, you must,' Mr Walker said. 'In fact, if anything takes your fancy I'll do you a special price.'

'Thanks.' I browsed the racks. 'Wow. I love this.' I held a white cheesecloth dress with an embroidered bodice up to me.

Linda was at my side. 'Try it on.' She ushered me into the changing room.

After slipping off my trouser suit, I placed the frock over my head, and once I was done, pulled back the curtain. 'What do you think?' I gave a spin.

'Beautiful.' Linda smoothed her hands across my waistline. 'It fits you like a glove. Hang on though, it needs something else.' She charged across to the jewellery section and returned with a necklace. 'You like?'

'It's gorgeous.' I ran my fingers across the shiny maroon beads.

'Here. Let me.' She stood behind me and fastened the chain. I stared at my reflection. The beads rested on my breastbone accentuating the 'V' shaped neckline.

Mr Walker came over. 'Miss Smith is right. The dress is perfect for you. Your dark hair and the white fabric are a great contrast. I'll tell you what, I'll knock off twenty-five per cent.'

'That's very generous, thank you. Look, I don't have my credit card or any cash on me right now but can I leave it here and I'll sort it out with Linda later.'

'That's absolutely fine. You can settle up later. Bag it up, Miss Smith.'

Linda wrapped the dress in tissue, placed the beads in a satin pouch, and popped both packages into a Walker's Boutique carrier bag.

Chapter Eight

Rachel

Stu was outside the newspaper office waiting for me. 'Hi Rach, hope you don't mind me turning up like this but have you got time for a coffee?'

'I suppose so. Everything okay?'

'Yeah, I just wanted a bit of a chat.' He glared at me. 'You look nice.'

'Thanks. Decided I needed a change. Where do you want to go?'

'Elmo's?'

'Sure.'

'Unless that's too painful for you with Joe and that?'

'No. It's closest anyway so we won't get too wet.' I put up my brolly. 'Talk about April showers.'

He linked his arm in mine as we made our way across the road to the café. After pushing the door open, he headed for a seat close to the back. 'How've you been?'

'You mean you care?'

'Don't be like that. Sorry, I know I should've been in touch with you before but...'

'What?'

'I've been a bit cut up about Lind. Did she tell you what she did?'

'Yep. And who are we to judge after what happened to her?'

'If only she'd spoken to me about it first. I'd have stood by her, you know?'

'And how do you think you or she would've felt once the child was born? It would be a constant reminder to you both of what that animal had done to her.'

'But she didn't give me the chance to have my say. Anyway, I've been thinking...'

'Oh yeah.' I glanced up at the waitress. 'Just two black coffees please.'

'Certainly.' The blonde girl hurried over to the counter.

'Thinking what?' I asked.

'I heard she's seeing someone.'

'Joe told you, I suppose?' I sighed.

'He mentioned it in passing, yes. Didn't take her long to get over me, did it?'

'Two coffees.' The girl placed our coffees down before making her way over to a table up at the front.

I gritted my teeth. 'What the hell, Stu? You wanted her to sit around pining after you?'

'No, of course not but I didn't damn well expect her to sleep with the first guy who came along.'

'For your information, not that it's any of your business, she's not bloody sleeping with anyone. What is it with you?'

He surprised me by breaking down. 'I'm sorry, I shouldn't have said that, it's just that I miss her so much.'

'And she misses you but' – I blinked – 'you may well be too late. You know you didn't have to break up with her. Unlike me and Joe, we had no choice. He was my one. I was his. How do you think we felt?'

He squeezed my fingers. 'You're right. Have you managed to move on?'

I shook my head. 'Now you've started me off too.' I dabbed a tissue across my eyes.

'What do you make of Joe's new bird? He said you met her.'

'Okay I suppose. Glad I had my haircut otherwise I could've almost been looking at myself in a mirror.'

'The likeness is uncanny, isn't it? I suppose it's the long dark hair and heart-shaped face. You look different now though.' He stared at me, his eyes twinkling. 'In fact, God, you look damn gorgeous. I'm surprised you haven't got blokes queueing up to take you out.'

'And who said I haven't? I said I hadn't moved on, that doesn't mean I've not had offers.'

'That told me.' He patted the back of his hand. 'Do you think you could have a word with Lind for me? At least see if she's prepared to give me a second chance. You know, like I did with her?'

'And what about you being Catholic?'

'I'm not a practising one. I don't really know why I said that.'

'Okay I'll speak to her but I can't promise.' I took my purse from my bag.

Stu pushed my purse away. 'It's on me. Least I can do.'

'Cheers. I'd best get off otherwise Mum'll have dinner on the table.'

'Sit yourself down, Rachel' – Mrs Smith puffed on a ciggie – 'Linda will be down in a minute.'

'This is nice.' I ruffled the lace tablecloth. 'Is it new?'

'A present from a woman at work. She bought it at a Spanish market. I'm thinking I may go to Spain next year. Saving up my pennies.'

'Sounds cool. Will you go with a mate?'

'Not sure.' She grinned.

'Aye aye. Something you'd like to share?'

'Oh, all right.' She pulled out a chair from the table and took a seat next to me. 'I've met someone. I'm surprised our Linda didn't tell you.'

'No. She didn't. I shall have words.'

Sandra chuckled. 'Don't be cross with her, I told her not to, and for once she's kept her mouth zipped.'

'I'll let her off then. So, what's he like, this guy?'

'Quite a dish. Bit older than me though. In his early fifties. Divorced with three grown-up kids.'

'Have you met them?'

'Not yet. Early days. He's not met our Lind yet either. Although...'

'Although what?' Linda asked as she entered the room.

'I was thinking of asking Keith to tea next Sunday. Will you be around?'

'I'll make sure I am. Can't wait to meet him.' Linda put her arm around Sandra's neck. 'I'm really happy for you, Mam.'

'Right' – her mam got up from the chair – 'I'll leave you girls to it. I'm off for a bath as I've got myself a date this evening.'

'Enjoy,' I said, 'both the bath and your date.' I giggled as she left the room. 'Well, I wasn't expecting that.'

'I know. Nor was I when she told me. She met him at ballroom dancing classes. I'm made up for her.' Linda filled the kettle from the tap. 'Cuppa?'

'Cheers.'

'Why did you have to see me so urgently?'

'Do I need a reason? Wondered how the new job was going for starters.'

'Good. Really good. I love it and Mr Walker just leaves me to it now. He only comes in on a Friday to give us our pay packets.'

'How you getting on with the young girl?'

'Tasha? Yeah, she's lovely and a good grafter. I've got two young Saturday girls now too. But want to tell me why you're really here?'

'You know me too well, Linda Smith.' I folded my arms. 'I saw Stu the other day.'

'Oh yeah. What did he have to say?'

'That he misses you and wonders if you'll give him another chance.'

'You mean he's heard about me seeing someone else and the green-eyed monster has risen.'

I laughed. 'Maybe. He definitely knows about you and Paul. How's that going?'

She shook her head. 'Oh, I don't know. Truth be told, I'm finding him a bit boring. All he does is talk about the band and while at first that seemed interesting it's a bit much now.'

'Have you, you know?'

'Nah. Not interested in him that way. I don't think he fancies me either as he's not even tried it on.'

'Why don't you give Stu another go?'

She sighed. 'I really want to' – she took a deep breath – 'but if I agree then he'd better get around to putting a bloody ring on my finger. We've been together for years now. All I've ever wanted is to settle down with a hoard of kids. I know I had the whatsit and it broke my heart doing that but' – she blew her nose – 'I long to hold a baby of mine and Stu's in my arms.'

'Give him a call.'

Chapter Nine

Peggy

Adam helped himself to the last piece of toast from the rack. 'I'll have to eat on the run today.'

'You're up later than usual.' I ran hot water into the sink.

'Didn't sleep too well.'

Joe hurried into the kitchen. 'Best get used to that, Dad.'

'Ha ha,' Adam said, 'you'd best watch it, mate, otherwise you'll be on baby duty.'

'Not on your life. Right, I'm off. See you tonight, Mam.' Joe kissed me on the cheek before grabbing his bike keys and leaving the house.

'Did you say you're meeting up with Rachel?' Adam asked me.

'Yes. Kate and I are going shopping with her.'

'You going to tell her about the baby?'

I turned around to face him. 'That's the plan although I may not need to' – I glanced down at my stomach – 'as I've suddenly blown up.'

Adam put his hand on my tummy. 'You look beautiful, Peg. I'll be back around one but you'll most likely have gone by then so have a nice time.' He kissed me on the lips before leaving.

I was washing up the dishes when Kate came in. 'Dad and Joe gone?'

'Yes. Just. What would you like for breakfast?' I dried my hands on a towel.

'Cereal and a slice of toast, please. Have you had yours?'

'Yep. Had mine before everyone came down.' I passed her a clean bowl and stuck a slice of bread into the toaster.'

She shook a portion of cornflakes from the box and added semi-skimmed milk. 'Are you looking forward to shopping and seeing Rachel?'

'Yes, it's been weeks since I last saw her. Although I don't think I'll be buying anything from the new boutique, that is unless they do maternity wear.'

'You have got big all of a sudden. Do you think you're having twins?'

'Bloody hell, love. I hope not.' The toast popped up and I passed it to Kate. 'I'll just go and get ready. I told Rachel we'd meet her at eleven.'

⤸

Kate and I sauntered into the café. After peering around the seating area, I spotted Rachel waving at the back. 'There she is.' We headed over to the table.

'Hello love.' I kissed her on the cheek.

'Bloody hell, Peggy,' she said. 'Is there something you wanted to tell me?'

I held my swollen stomach. 'Sorry, Rachel, I hadn't meant for you to find out like this but I didn't want to tell you on the phone. I'm not sure what happened as I woke up this morning huge like this.'

Kate slid in to a chair by the window. 'It's true,' she said, 'Mam seems to have suddenly popped.'

'Sorry I've been remiss in not meeting up,' Rachel said, 'but work's been so busy with the run up to the silver jubilee functions.'

'Never mind. It's good to see you now. I can't believe we're in May. Time's flying by far too quickly.'

'I know. Anyway, congratulations. Rather you than me.'

'Thanks, although it wasn't exactly planned. All a bit of a shock to be honest as I thought I was going through the change.'

I took a seat next to Kate, opposite Rachel.

Rachel reached for my hand. 'Exciting news.'

I touched my bump. 'Yes, it is.'

Rachel turned to Kate. 'Hey, did you get that job?'

'I did, and I started almost immediately. I'm really enjoying it.'

The young male waiter winked at Kate. 'What can I get you?'

'Coffee?' Rachel asked me.

'Gone off it so I'll have a tea. Kate?'

'Coffee please.'

'Two coffees and a tea then.' Rachel smiled at the lad.

He scribbled on his little pad. 'Anything to eat?'

We all shook our heads.

'Shan't be long.' He turned and headed to the counter.

'I think he fancies you,' Rachel said to Kate.

She blushed. 'I doubt it.'

'He's not bad looking,' I said.

Kate blinked. 'I didn't notice.'

'What is it you're doing in the job?' Rachel asked Kate to change the subject.

'Secretary and Personal Assistant to a doctor at the hospital.'

The waiter was back with our drinks. 'Two coffees and a tea.'

'Thanks. I'm the tea,' I said.

He put the drinks down in front of us. 'Can I get you anything else?'

Kate looked up at the lad. 'No, thanks. We're okay.'

'Enjoy your drinks.' He winked at Kate again before making his way to a customer who had his hand in the air.

'That sounds interesting.' Rachel fiddled with one of her gold drop earrings. 'Our Jenny's a nurse at Woodhaerst. Is that where you are?'

'Yes.'

'Which ward?'

Kate ran her tongue over her teeth. 'It's actually a psychiatric ward. I'm working for the doctor who helped me through my illness. I rather like to think that I may be helping others who struggled like me.'

'How are you now?' Rachel took a sip of her drink.

'I'm good' – Kate turned to me – 'aren't I, Mam?'

I squeezed her hand. 'Yes, darling, and we're all very proud of you.'

―⁂―

We ploughed into Walker's Boutique.

Kate's eyes widened. 'What a gorgeous shop.'

Linda came over and hugged Rachel. 'Hi Rach,' she said before turning to me. 'Good to see you again, Peggy.'

'You too. I see Rachel wasn't exaggerating about this place.'

Linda beamed. 'I love it here.' She faced Kate. 'And you must be Kate? I've been looking forward to meeting you.'

Kate squinted.

'Sorry, Kate,' Rachel said, 'this is my best friend, Linda.'

'Ah, yes' – Kate smiled – 'I've heard a lot about you. You must love working here surrounded by this awesome gear.'

'Yeah. I do.' Linda grinned. 'Take a good look round. That rail there' – she signalled ahead – 'is on sale and over here' – she pointed to the right – 'is our new stock. Only came in today. There's something there, Rach, that I think you might want to grab.'

'Cheers, Lind.' Rachel popped over to the rail and picked up an emerald green satin skirt. 'Do you mean this? It's very elegant but no idea where I'd wear it.'

Linda strode over. 'That would suit you but I was thinking of this.' She waved a black-floral, tiered maxi skirt in the air.

'Now you're talking.' Rachel held it up against her. 'I'll need a white gypsy blouse to go with it. Preferably one with an embroidered neckline.' She turned to Linda who was holding up exactly what Rachel wanted.

'You know me too well, Linda Smith.' Rachel took the top off her friend and put it with the skirt. 'That's me sorted, providing they fit. What about you, Kate? Spotted anything you like?'

Kate offered up an orange-flowery tiered skirt that fell just below her knees. 'What do you think, Mam?'

'It's lovely,' I said. 'That will look stunning on you.'

'And I have just the thing to go with it.' Linda hurried over to the other side of the shop and returned with an amber peasant T-shirt. She pulled open the curtains to two changing rooms. 'Go and try them on. Both of you.'

'What about you, Peggy?' Rachel asked as she and Kate popped into the cubicles.

'Unless Linda's selling maternity wear, I fear I must decline.'

Linda turned to me. 'You don't mean you're...'

I unfastened my loose coat. 'I'm afraid so.'

'How far?'

'Around seven months, I think. Due end of July. A shock I can tell you.'

Linda rushed over by the counter and came back with a chair. 'Take a seat. You shouldn't be standing.'

'Thanks, love.' I opened my mouth as my two girls came out of the changing room looking eye-catching. They were so alike yet so different, especially now Rachel had her hair cut short. 'Wow.'

Kate did a twirl. 'What do you think, Mam?'

'I love it.'

'It really suits you,' Rachel said. 'And I'd like it to be my treat.'

'Are you sure?' Kate smiled.

'Is that my girls home?' Adam called out from the lounge before meeting us in the hallway.

'Yes.' Kate wrapped her arms around her dad. She was a real daddy's girl. 'Wait until you see my new outfit.'

'Hope you've not gone mad on spending, Mrs D.'

'No, she hasn't' – Kate took her garments from the carrier – 'Rachel bought them for me. What do you think?'

'Beautiful, but how about you model them for your old dad?'

'If you like.' She hurried upstairs.

'I'll put the kettle on,' I said.

Adam followed me into the kitchen. 'Good day?' He kissed me on the lips.

'Yes. Lovely. Tiring though.'

He pulled out a chair at the table. 'I think you'd better sit down and I'll make the tea.'

'Thanks.' I took the seat.

'Did you tell Rachel about the baby?'

I chuckled. 'There was no need to tell her. It was obvious.' I put my hand over my tummy. 'I mean, look at me. Kate thinks I'm having twins. You don't think I am, do you?'

His face paled. 'Oh my God, I hope not. One baby's going to be hard enough at our age but two?'

'I've got a midwife appointment next week. Maybe she'll be able to tell me something.'

'What day is that? I'll try and get the time off work.'

Kate came into the kitchen donning the new clothes. She twirled. No one would ever know she'd suffered from an eating disorder. Her figure was perfect. I wondered whether I'd ever get mine back after having a child at this age.

Joe slammed the front door and sloped into the lounge. 'Good. You're both here. I need to talk to you.'

'That sounds mysterious.' I patted the seat next to me on the sofa.

Adam lit up a Player's. 'Want one, Joe?'

'No, ta.' He slumped into the cushion.

'What's this about?' Adam puffed on the cigarette.

'Miranda's …'

'Miranda's what?' Adam flicked the ash into the tray.

Joe pinched his lip.

I took his hand. 'What is it? Has she finished with you?'

He shook his head. 'If only.'

'Then what? You know you can tell us anything.' I squeezed his fingers.

'She reckons she's pregnant.'

Adam stumped out the cigarette. 'For God's sake, Joe. Didn't I teach you anything about being careful?'

'You can talk when you got Mam up the duff at her age.'

'That's a bit bloody different. Your mam and I are married. So, what now?'

Joe shrugged his shoulders. 'I suppose I'll have to marry her.'

'No, Joe,' I said, 'you don't have to marry her unless that's what you both want.'

'Your mam's right but you will have to support the baby.'

'No, I'll marry her because it's the right thing to do.'

'Don't make a decision straight away.' Adam got up from the chair. 'Invite the girl and her parents over and we'll talk about the next move. Your timing's lousy though. As if we didn't have enough to worry about without another new baby coming along.' He left the room.

I patted Joe's arm. 'Don't worry, he'll come round. He's just in shock.'

Chapter Ten

Rachel

After finishing an interview at St Margaret's Church, I rushed back to town, parked up the car and hurried over to Elmo's wondering why Joe wanted to see me so urgently. He was going through the door as I reached him.

'Hi there, Rach. Thanks for coming.'

'Couldn't say no really. You had me intrigued.'

'Let's sit down.'

I glanced around the crowded café looking for a spare booth. 'It's busy today.'

'Look, there' – he pointed – 'that couple are leaving.'

We darted over to the cluttered table before anyone else took the seats.

'Are you on your lunch break?' Joe asked.

'Yep.'

'Then you'll need something to eat. What do you fancy?'

'Beans on toast will do' – I pushed the dirty dishes aside – 'but I've not got long as I need to be across to the village hall by half past two.'

'You're always busy these days.'

'Yes. Just the way I like it. How come you're not working today?'

Joe put his hand up to attract a waiter.

The owner came over. 'Hiya there, Joe. How you doing, mate?' He gathered up the used mugs and plates.

'Good thanks, Elmo. Can you do us two beans on toasts and a couple of black coffees please. And any chance we can queue jump as Rachel's got to get back to work?'

'No worries. I'll get that sorted for you.'

Joe turned back to me. 'I had to tell you something before anyone else did.'

A waitress came over and wiped the table clean.

'What's happened? Is it Peggy? Has she lost the baby?'

'Nothing like that.'

'Two coffees.' Elmo placed the cups in front of us. 'One of the guys will bring over your meal in a few minutes.'

'Cheers, Elmo.'

'And don't be such a stranger. We miss your smiling face.' He patted Joe on the back.

'I won't.'

'For God's sake, Joe, put me out of my misery. What is it you've got to tell me?'

Joe ran his fingers through his long hair. 'There's no easy way to say this, Rach, so I'll just come out and say it.'

'Two beans on toast.' The waitress placed the plates on the table. 'Enjoy your meal,' she said before heading over to a young couple.

'You were saying?' I took a sip from my drink.

'Miranda's pregnant.'

'What?' I spluttered, grabbed a tissue from my pocket, and mopped the spilt coffee from my jacket sleeve. 'Well, I wasn't expecting that. You didn't bother waiting with her then?'

He shook his head. 'No, we didn't wait, but it was she who initiated it.'

'So, what now?'

'We're getting married.'

I blinked. 'When?'

'Six weeks. I wanted you to know before it became public knowledge.' He cut into his toast and scooped a piece onto his fork with baked beans.

'Bloody hell, you're not hanging about.' I picked up the cup to hide my eyes.

'We can't. We need to be married before she starts to show. The church is booked for third of July. So a shotgun wedding it is.'

'You're having a white one then? Even though she's, you know?'

'That's what she wants. No one worries about that these days. You will come though. Won't you?'

I took a deep breath. 'You want me to come?'

'Yes. It will look strange if you don't. To Miranda and to Kate. Please.'

I set down my knife and fork. 'Looks like I don't have a choice.'

'Sorry. If only things had been different.'

'If only.' I rushed to the Ladies to throw up.

I pushed the door open to the boutique.

Linda rushed over. 'This is a nice surprise. But what's wrong? You look like you've seen a ghost? Have you had a shock?'

'I kind of have. Not seen a ghost but had a shock.' I flicked through the hangers on the summer range rail.

'Look, I'm due a break. Lunch time was extra busy with the sale on and I've not had a chance to stop all day. We could take a stroll around the park?'

I glanced at my watch. 'If you don't mind, I'd like that, but I must be back at the office by four to type up a story.'

'Tasha,' Linda called, 'I'm going for a break but I'll be back within the hour so if you can keep an eye on the shop.'

The young red-headed girl popped from the back. 'Sure. Take your time.'

We took a seat on the park bench by the pond. A gaggle of Canada geese cackled by our feet.

Linda nudged me. 'Out with it then.'

'Joe's getting married.'

'To Miranda?'

'Yep.'

'Blimey. Is she up the duff? I mean they've only been seeing each other for a short time.'

'She is.'

'Hell.' She put her hand over mine. 'How are you doing?'

I shrugged. 'You know.' I burst into tears.

'Hey.' She put her arm around me. 'I'm so sorry, Rach.'

'Thanks.' I sniffled. 'How are things with you and Stu now?'

'Good. Really good. Oh I'm sorry, Rach, here's me gloating while you're struggling.'

'No. I'm happy for you. Maybe he'll get you a ring for your birthday.'

'Has he said something to you?'

'No, I've not seen him.'

She rested her fingers on my arm. 'Sorry, Rach, I shouldn't be going on about that. Not now.'

'No point in us both being miserable. I told you. I'm happy for you both.'

'Do you think she really is pregnant, or is she trying to trap him into marrying her?'

'Surely not?' I thought about it. Could Linda be right? 'I don't know her well enough to answer that. I mean, why would she? I'm surprised Joe let it happen though. But it's worse than that, Lind. He expects me to be at the wedding.'

'Bloody hell. That's a bit thoughtless.'

'Hmm, that's what I thought at first until he explained how questions would be asked if I'm not there.' I slipped off my suit jacket. 'Bearing in mind that Miranda and Kate know nothing about our past. I don't care about Miranda but there's no way I want to upset Kate.'

'So you came in to the boutique to look for something to wear and not a shoulder to cry on?'

'No, you were right the first time. They've set the date for third of July. Joe said they want to be married before she shows. Poor Peggy's going to find it difficult as she'll be almost nine months.'

'Life can be so hard sometimes. If only things had been different, it would be you walking down that aisle.'

'Oi' – I nudged her – 'don't need to rub it in.'

'Sorry. No one could ever call me tactful, could they?'

'Nope. At least I'll have you and Stu to support me on the day. Joe's bound to ask Stu to be best man.'

'Surprised Stu hasn't mentioned it to me.'

I brushed away a cloud of gnats. 'He probably doesn't know yet. Joe wanted to let me know first.'

'Joe, always the thoughtful one.'

'Yep. Now are you going to help me choose an outfit?'

'Sure. Have you got time to come back with me? I've got just the thing in mind that will be perfect for you and I've an idea for something for me too.'

Chapter Eleven

Rachel

Red, white and blue bunting swung between lampposts and houses. On both sides of the road trestle tables were jam-packed with cakes and sandwiches. People of all ages joined in the fun, elderly men and women, some with walking sticks, mums and dads pushing prams or carrying tots, small kids hiding under tablecloths, and teen girls appearing mesmerised by the upcoming popstars. In the street, a group of adolescents smooched in pairs on the cobbles to the band's slow composition. I wrote my observations down in a notebook ready to write up the article later. Alan followed me around taking shots. I spoke to a gang of youngsters and jotted down their quotes.

> *Dark Chaos are the best*
> *I think I'm in love with the drummer*
> *The best band since the Beatles*

and so many more. When the band stopped for a break, I headed over to speak to them. Steve jumped down from the drums.

'Hi there, Rach. You're looking gorgeous. Are you sure you don't fancy giving us another go? I could do with a chick like you on my arm.'

'No, thanks.'

'You don't know what you're missing. Look at this lot. I could have any one of these dolls.'

'Good for you. I'm here to write a story not to help boost your ego.'

'Suit yourself.' He turned to the guys. 'Ready boys.'

Paul jumped down from the platform. 'Hi, Rach, how are you?'

'Fine thanks. And you?'

He shrugged. 'I've been better. How's Linda?'

'She's okay.'

He looked around. 'Is she here?'

'No.'

'Shame. I really liked her.'

'You know she went back to her ex? They'd been together for years.'

'Yeah. I heard that. Felt kind of used to be honest.'

'She wasn't using you though, she really thought they were finished. I'm sorry if you got hurt. I got the impression from Linda that there wasn't much chemistry between you two anyway.'

'You mean me not trying it on? That was just me being shy.' He rolled his eyes. 'That's me, always the one getting chucked. Unlike him up there?' He signalled to Steve.

'He gets chucked too. He's just too arrogant to care. I don't know what he told you about me and him but I wasn't interested.'

Paul chortled. 'You're kidding?'

'No. Why?'

'According to him you couldn't get enough of him.'

'Well, he's a bloody liar. I told him where to go. I hate blokes like him who think because they're good looking that all the girls are going to run after them. Well not in my case, thank you very much.'

He surprised me by taking me into a hug. 'Thanks. I needed to hear that. Now you look after yourself. Oh, and do the lads a good write-up. I'd best get back up there.'

'I will. I never let personal feelings get in the way of business.'

'How did you get on,' John asked me back at the office.

'Brilliant. I'm going to type up the article now. There was quite a crowd and Alan got lots of cool shots. The band should go far.'

'A little dicky bird told me you went out with one of them. Is that still going on?'

'Bloody hell, no. I went on a date with the drummer and once was more than enough to be around that conceited, arrogant pig.'

'Ooh, that's a bit strong.'

'Sorry but I'm livid. His manager just told me that Steve, he's the drummer, had been saying I was up for everything. How dare he smear my name like that?'

'My apologies. I didn't mean to touch a raw nerve. Fancy a cuppa?'

'Sure. I'll get them. It'll give me an opportunity to calm down while saying a quick hello to the gang downstairs.'

'Make mine milk and two sugars.'

'Righty-o.' I took the steep stairs slowly to ensure I didn't trip. 'Hiya everyone,' I said on reaching the back office. Verity glanced up from the switchboard and waved. Mel was at her desk listening to a Dictaphone tape, typing around sixty words per minute, but caught sight of me, took the earplugs out and darted over.

'It's good to see you,' she said. 'How was the gig?'

'They were amazing. Huge crowds of all ages with the young girls hanging around like groupies.' I put the kettle on the stove to boil and spooned Nescafé into two mugs. 'Want one?' I asked Mel.

'No, ta.'

'Verity?'

She shook her head.

The kettle whistled and I poured water into the mugs and stirred the coffee. I peered around the office. 'No Betty?'

'In with the boss,' Mel answered.

'That's a shame. You free for lunch?'

'I am. Want to do something?'

'Yep, I thought it would be nice to have a catch-up. I've been so busy lately I've barely seen any of you.'

'Can we make it oneish? Only I've a report to finish first.'

'Cool. One is fine.' I added milk and sugar to John's coffee and gave it a stir. 'I'd better get back upstairs with his lordship's cuppa. Hopefully I'll see Betty before she goes home.'

⸻

We wandered across to the park where the maple trees boasted different shades of red, some pinkish while others almost brown. Autumn blaze was my favourite with its fiery appearance which could be seen from a distance. Poppies and violas created a sea of red, white and purple, in a shared flowerbed. Scent from sweet peas climbing on a nearby trellis travelled to my nose, tickling my nostrils.

'What are these?' Mel asked as we approached some low shrubs close to the pond.

'Peonies. Isn't the magenta gorgeous?'

'Yes. My mum has them coming up in her garden but we didn't know what they were.'

'Now you'll be able to tell her. I love the stark white ones over there too,' I said as we approached the bench. 'Let's sit here.' I perched on the slatted wood and in no time at all a trio of ducks waddled over looking for food.

'You're always busy these days,' Mel said taking a seat next to me.

'I know. But I love it.'

'It's good you type up your own articles unlike lazy John who gets me to do his.'

I chuckled. 'Good job he does, otherwise you'd be out of a job.'

'True. Although lately Mr Strange has been handing more of his stuff over to me to lighten Betty's load.'

'How is she?'

'Looking tired. I think she may be ill. You should try and catch up with her.'

I squinted from the blazing sun. 'You're right. I must.'

'But you didn't ask me here for small talk, did you?'

'No. I wanted to tell you Joe's getting married. Got some girl in the pudding club.'

Mel put her hand on mine. 'Sorry to hear that. That must be tough for you.'

'Yep.'

'My sister's getting married next month. She's having a shotgun wedding too.'

'In a church?'

'No. Register office.'

'That's what I thought Joe and Miranda would do but she wants the dress, big wedding, and everything. How about you? Seeing anyone?'

'I was but it didn't work out. Found out he was two-timing me.'

'Oh, Mel.' I stroked her arm. 'You don't have a lot of luck do you?'

She shrugged. 'Such is life. Plenty more fish in the sea.'

'That's the spirit.' I checked my watch. 'We should get back as I've got a job at three. A small gallery the other side of Woodhaerst is opening an art exhibition.'

'Ooh that sounds interesting. Wish I could come.'

'Maybe I'll ask the boss if you can come on a job with me one day. Give you a bit of insight into what it's like for when you're typing up John's stuff.'

'Now that would be cool. Do you think he'll go for it?'

'No idea. But I can ask. Come on, we'd better go.'

'Sure. I'm starving anyway and my sandwiches are at the office. Have you got anything to eat?'

'Yep, a pasty in the fridge to have with a cuppa before setting off.'

Mel clasped her hand in mine. 'If you need to talk at all...'

'Thanks, Mel. You're a good friend.'

I pulled up outside the gallery and was greeted by a blond-haired chap as I got out of the car.

'You must be Rachel from The Echo?' His ice-blue eyes sparkled.

'Yes, I am. And you are?'

'Philip Jordan. The curator. But call me Phil. Come on in. My assistant's making coffee, unless you'd prefer a cold drink in this heat.'

'Coffee is fine thanks. It's gorgeous out. I love summer days like this.' I followed him up four stone steps and through a set of double glass doors. The various picture frames displayed on the freshly painted walls were inviting. My footsteps echoed in the open space as I walked across the cream-tiled floor. I stopped at a painting in a large gilded surround of a wooden bridge with greenery either side. A red admiral hovered over a lilac buddleia and the artist had created a cerulean blue sky. 'Stunning,' I said.

'One of my favourites too. The exhibition opens in a couple of weeks. Hence why we need you to let the public know we're here. Let's get that coffee and go through things.' He showed me into a decent sized kitchen where a small-built woman was filling up a kettle at the sink.

'Hi,' she said, 'I'm Jan. You must be Rachel?'

'Yes. How do you do?'

'Coffee?'

'Black no sugar. Thanks.'

Phil signalled to the couch. 'Do sit down.'

'Thanks.' I sank into the tan leather two-seater.

Jan placed a mug in front of me on the glass coffee table and took the armchair opposite. Phil flopped into another at the side of me.

I got out my notepad and pen. 'Is this your first exhibition?'

'Yes, it is.'

'And what prompted you to host one?'

'Jan here is a new artist, and because she's starting out, she didn't have enough material of her own to fill the area so we thought it would be a good idea to offer space to local artists.'

'That seems like a wonderful opportunity. Were there any stipulations for the exhibits?'

'Only to keep to a specific theme. We opted for nature which offered a variety of choice.'

'Did you go to art school, Jan?'

'Yes. My dad sent me to Paris.'

'Jan's my kid sister.' Phil laughed. 'Our parents never sent me to Paris. Just their favourite child.'

I smiled. 'I'm sure that's not the case.' I coughed. 'How many artists have you got participating?'

'Six,' answered Phil.

'And are they all local?'

'Yes, but some are more experienced than others.'

'Are you able to quote their names?'

'Sure. Hang on.' Phil got up, went over to a mahogany desk at the side of the room, opened a ledger and read out the names. 'John Browning, Ada Claret, Simone Davies, James Snelling, Jan here, and then me.'

'You're an artist too?'

'Yes. The painting you admired is one of mine.'

'You're very talented. But you didn't go to Paris?'

'No. I'm self-taught.'

'Amazing.' I was just about to take a sip from my drink when there was a knock on the entrance door of the building. 'That'll be my photographer. Do you mind if we take a look around so he can get some shots?'

'No. Please do.' Phil rose from the chair and made his way through the gallery to the entrance with me in tow. He opened the door and greeted Alan. 'Come in.'

'Sorry I'm late.' Alan wiped a handkerchief across his forehead.

'No worries. I was just about to show Rachel around. Fancy a cuppa before we start?'

'A glass of cold water would be nice. This heat's too much for me. Hello there, Rachel,' he said on spotting me behind Phil.

'You look hot, Alan,' I said. The sweat poured from his face.

'So would you if you had to hike here in this heat. Bloody car broke down half a mile away.'

'Here you go.' Jan passed him a pint glass of iced water which he downed in one.

He licked his lips. 'Thanks, that's better.' He held out his hand for Jan to shake. 'Alan. And you are?'

'Jan. I'm one of the exhibitors and this is my brother Phil who runs the show.'

'Cool. Maybe we can start with a shot of you both. Perhaps under one of your paintings?'

'Sure.' Phil headed for a picture in a wooden picture frame. A grove of silver birch complemented bluebells sheltering under the trees. Fields in the distance were separated by ranch fencing. 'This is my favourite of Jan's.'

'It is rather lovely,' I said. 'You're both so talented.'

Once Alan had taken a few shots I suggested we move over to the best of Phil's art. After taking photos of other artists' work, and of the gallery interior, Alan packed up his gear and said, 'I'll be off then. Are you finished, Rachel, as I wondered if I could grab a lift back?'

'I'll just get my stuff together.' I headed back into the kitchen and slipped my notebook and pen into the bag. As I was coming out of the room, Phil stopped me.

'I hope you don't think me too forward, Rachel, but do you fancy a drink sometime?' He smiled.

'I'd like that.'

He gave me a thumbs up. 'Cool.' He passed me a card. 'Call me. The sooner the better.'

And without thinking I said, 'How about tomorrow evening?'

'Brilliant. Where?'

'The Black Horse in town. Seven o'clock?'

'I'll be there.' He beamed and I sensed I was beaming too.

Chapter Twelve

Rachel

Kate opened the door and let me in. I kissed her on the cheek. 'How's it going?'

'Good thanks. Mam's in the lounge with her feet up. I'm just on my way out but can get you a cuppa if you like before I leave.'

'No, you're all right. You get off. Is your dad in?'

'He'll be back soon. He popped out to get Mam some chocolate.' Kate picked up her rattan bag and slid it across her shoulder. 'If you're sure there's nothing I can get you, I'll see you later. That is if you're still here.'

'Have a good time.' I closed the front door behind Kate and headed into the lounge to find Peggy sleeping on the couch.

She opened her eyes as I approached. 'Hello there, love.' She moved to sit upright.

'Don't get up.' I lifted her leg slightly. 'Your ankles are swollen.'

'Tell me something I don't know.'

'I'm surprised they've not taken you in. How's your blood pressure?'

'Quite high but the midwife said to rest. She's coming in weekly now to check on me. Doesn't help with the wedding in less than a month.'

'Yes, about that' – I inched myself on to the sofa and put Peggy's feet on top of my lap – 'is she showing yet?'

'No, she's not. Goodness knows where she's hiding it.'

I massaged one of Peggy's feet. 'Supposing she isn't hiding it. Supposing she's been lying and there is no baby.'

She wriggled her foot from my hands and sat upright. 'I thought you'd come here to make me feel better not to make my blood pressure go higher?'

'I have but...'

'No more buts, Rachel. Get over it. Joe's getting married in three weeks. Move on.'

'I have.'

'You have.' She blinked.

'Yeah. Met a new guy. Phil. You'll like him.'

She beamed. 'Thank God for that. So, we'll hear no more about...'

The front door slammed and Adam strode in. 'Hear no more about what?'

'Rachel's got it into her head that Miranda's lying about being pregnant.'

He shook his head. 'You've got to stop this, Rachel. And to come around with accusations like this when my wife needs rest, it just isn't on.'

'I'm sorry. I'll get a bowl for your feet, Peg.' I hurried from the lounge into the kitchen. My heart was banging. I hated confrontation but this wasn't fair. They didn't want to listen to reason. They were so desperate to get me out of Joe's life they'd have him married to anyone. Never mind whether it made him happy or not. I dug out a bowl from under the sink, filled it from the taps, and carried it into the lounge.

'Here you are.' I put the bowl down on the carpet and placed Peggy's feet into the warm water. 'That should help.'

'Thanks, love.' Peggy patted my hand.

'Are you staying for tea?' Adam asked.

'No, I think I'll leave Peggy to rest. I only popped in to see if you were up to a meal out for my birthday next week but having seen... I think it's best you leave it.'

'We'll make up for it once the baby's born,' Peggy said.

'You reckon?' I chortled.

'And we want to meet this new man.' Peggy winked. 'What does he do?'

'He's an artist.'

'Artist? Blimey, Rachel. First a popstar, now an artist. Who's next? A writer?'

'Who knows? Maybe my artist is the one.' I leaned down to kiss Peggy on the cheek.

She grasped my hand. 'I hope he is.'

⋆

Mum placed a serving dish on the dining table and sat down to join the rest of us.

'Did you get to see Peggy?' Dad asked as he spooned a portion of chilli and rice onto his plate.

'Yes. I tried talking to her about Miranda but she wasn't having any of it.' I ate a forkful of chilli. 'Mmm, this is delicious, Mum.'

'It's a new recipe.' She broke off a piece of French bread. 'What do you mean Peggy isn't having any of it?'

'I told you. I don't believe Miranda's pregnant. She's trying to trick him into marriage.'

Dad put down his cutlery. 'Where's this coming from? I thought you were building up a good relationship with Joe as your brother? If not, then you need to stay away.'

'I am, but I'm concerned for him as his sister. He's making a huge mistake. I just know it.'

Dad sighed. 'How was Peggy?'

'Not good. Swollen ankles and high blood pressure.'

'You badgering her about Miranda and Joe isn't going to help her.' Mum shook her head. 'Is it?'

'No, I suppose not. I didn't think. I tried to help by massaging her feet and soaking them in a bowl of water.'

'You're a good girl at heart,' Dad said. 'Your problem is that sometimes you just don't think.'

Jenny helped herself to a chunk of bread from the basket. 'Tell Mum and Dad about your new man.'

'Now this sounds interesting.' Dad's eyes twinkled. 'Maybe he'll distract you from meddling in Joe's affairs.'

'Why not invite him for your birthday dinner?' Mum stacked the dishes. 'Dessert, anyone?'

⋘

The front door slammed. Surely that couldn't have been Mum and Dad back from church. I pulled off the quilt and perched on the edge of the bed with my ears pricked up. 'Hello,' I called out.

Footsteps came upstairs. Was someone in the house? My bedroom door knob turned. My heart raced.

'Happy Birthday, lazy bones.'

I put a hand to my chest. 'For God's sake Jen, you frightened the life out of me. What the hell are you doing home at this time?'

'I ended up doing an earlier shift than planned.' She yawned. 'I didn't think you'd have gone to church with Mum and Dad.'

'No way. They tried to get me there. How was work anyway?'

'Busy. I'm going to get some kip now otherwise I'll be too tired for your birthday meal. Is Phil joining us?'

'Yes.' I laughed. 'He doesn't know what he's in for with you lot to interrogate him. What about you? Anyone new on the scene?'

She grinned. 'I may be seeing one of the doctors but that's all I'm saying for now. And keep it quiet, otherwise Mum and Dad will want to be looking him over.'

'Mum's the word. Have a good sleep. I'm going to see if I can get another hour in. Had a dreadful night. Nightmares and all.'

'Stop worrying about Joe. He's old enough to take care of himself.' She kissed me on the cheek. 'Right catch you later, sis.'

⊰⊱

The taxi pulled up outside Taverna Mythos. Mum, Jenny and I climbed out of the back while Dad paid the driver. I peered up at the flashing lights around the restaurant window. 'This looks a nice place.'

'It's supposed to be,' Mum said. 'It was a struggle for your dad to get the booking with it being their official opening night. Come along now, your dad can follow us in.'

'If you don't mind, I'll wait for Phil.'

'All right. Ah here's your dad now,' Mum said as the cab drove away. 'Rachel's going to wait for her young man.'

'Righty-o. We'll see you in there.' Dad followed Mum and Jenny into the restaurant.

I paced up and down wondering if I'd scared Phil off, inviting him out with the parents, when a car pulled up and he jumped out. 'Cheers, Jan. See you tomorrow.'

'Hello.' I brushed my lips against his. 'For a moment there I thought you were going to be a no show.'

'You can't get rid of me that easy. Happy Birthday by the way.'

'Thanks. The others have gone in.'

'Sorry, I'm not late, am I?'

'Only by a couple of minutes. Come on. Oh and let me apologise for my folks in advance.' I took hold of Phil's hand and pushed open the door. 'There they are.' I pointed to a round table with balloons. 'How embarrassing.'

'Let them spoil you. You're their little girl. My mum and dad are just the same with Jan.' He took a deep breath. 'Let's get this over with.'

As we approached the table, Dad stood up. 'Hello, you must be Phillip?' He shook hands with my boyfriend.

'Hi. Yes. And you must be Rachel's father, mother, and sister.'

'Do sit down.' Mum signalled to the free chair next to her. 'It's good to finally meet you.'

Finally, what was she on about? What would Phil think? We'd only been going out for a few weeks. I took the seat next to Phil with Jenny on my other side. Classical music played in the background.

'Good evening.' A waiter came over. 'Welcome to our opening evening. I highly recommend you try the meze.' He dealt a menu to each of us. 'Drinks?'

'Red or white wine, Phillip?' Dad asked.

'Red but I don't mind white.'

Dad perused the drinks' menu. He smacked his lips. 'We'll have two bottles of the house red.' He glanced around the table. 'Is everyone happy to go with the meze?'

We all nodded. 'And the meze for us all,' Dad told the waiter who I thought was the owner.

A different waiter came along with the wine. He poured a drop into Dad's glass. Dad tasted it. 'That's good. Thank you.'

The waiter poured wine into Mum's, Jenny's and my glass before Phil's and refilling Dad's. 'Your food won't be long.'

Dad raised his glass. 'Happy birthday, Rachel.'

The others joined in.

'We understand you're an artist?' Mum placed the napkin on her lap.

'That's right. Rachel did a piece for our opening exhibition.'

'Oh yes, we saw that. Are you planning any more exhibitions?'

'We thought we'd do another one late autumn.'

'We'll try and make that one. What do you think, Charles?'

The restaurant was jam-packed but plenty of waiters darted from party to party and no one appeared to be left waiting for long. A waiter pulled up a trolley at our table and set down hot and cold snacks. One plate had cucumber slices and green olives, another small chunks of feta cheese with tomato wedges drizzled in olive oil, and dishes of taramasalata and hummus sat amongst plates of hot pitta bread.

We all put a bit of everything onto our plates and dipped bread into the dips.

'What did you get for your birthday?' Phil asked while scooping hummus onto a bit of cucumber.

'I've not had my presents yet.' I laughed.

Mum smiled at Phil. 'We tend to do present opening after dinner.'

We cleared the plates and in no time at all the waiter had set down another course. This time grilled octopus which I wasn't sure about at all but the meatballs and fried potatoes looked inviting.

'Have you ever tried octopus?' I asked Phil.

'I can't say I have but I'm always up for an adventure, as are you, I'm sure being a reporter.'

'Yes.' I gulped. I waited for Mum and Dad to serve some on to their plates and taste. Jenny waited too.

'It's delicious,' Dad said but Mum didn't look convinced.

I piled fried potatoes and meatballs onto my plate and hoped no one would notice if I omitted the octopus. The waiter placed down tiropita, which were layers of buttered filo filled with cheese and cut into triangles, along with a skillet-fried dish called saganaki. I opted for a portion of each and noticed that Jen had done the same. Phil glanced at my plate and surprised me by scooping octopus onto his. He took a bite.

'Mmm, you should try it, Rachel,' he said. 'Tastes a bit like onion rings.'

'I'll take your word for it.'

At the end of the meal, we finished with coffee and loukoumi, otherwise known as Turkish delight. Moussaka had been my favourite dish with the stuffed vine leaves a close second. I'd opted for walnut cake as dessert. Mum and Dad passed me a package. Embarrassed, opening presents in front of Phil, never mind a whole restaurant of people, I tried not to let it show.

'Thanks, Mum and Dad.' I tore off the paper revealing a black leather handbag. 'This is lovely. Thank you.'

Jenny nudged me. 'Open it.'

I unclasped the catch and dug inside. The bag contained more gifts. The first, unwrapped, a matching purse. I opened the purse and inside was a twenty-pound note. 'Wow thanks.'

'Keep going,' Dad said.

I took out a long box covered in glitter paper and ripped it open to find a gold herringbone choker. 'This is gorgeous.'

'Let me.' Phil fastened the necklace around my neck.

'My turn now.' Jen passed me a small parcel in birthday paper.

I tore off the paper. 'A bangle watch. Thanks, Jen. I really wanted one of these.'

'You're welcome.'

Mum, Dad and Jenny turned to Phil, waiting. I sensed myself blushing from embarrassment.

He held his hand in the air to attract a waiter. 'I'm ready now,' he said. The next minute the waiter returned with a huge brown paper package. Phil signalled to the waiter to pass it to me.

'Sorry, it's not in fancy paper,' he said.

'Phil, I wasn't expecting anything.' I didn't know where to turn. In fact, I wished the floor would swallow me up. What was it? Supposing I didn't like it. My face never could lie.

'Open it then,' Jenny said.

Phil squeezed my hand. 'Go on. You'll like it. I'll hold it while you do the business.'

'Okay,' I said, carefully ripping the paper off while Phil held it in place. I stared down at the painting I'd admired at the gallery. 'Thank you so much. This is wonderful, but far too much. I can't accept it. It's your favourite piece.'

He rubbed my arm. 'You must. I'll be offended if you don't.'

'Then I must accept. Thank you.'

Mum and Dad got up from the table to check out the painting. 'You painted this?' Mum asked.

'Yes.'

'You really are talented. Do you take on commissions?' Dad asked.

'Depends what it is?'

'I'd quite like a painting of our house and garden.'

'I'd need to see it.'

'The garden's full of colour,' I said. 'Mum loves flowers. Inside and out. So much so she doesn't even worry about my hay fever.' I kissed Phil lightly on the lips. 'I shall treasure this.'

On the following Saturday evening Phil and I were back in another restaurant but this time with Stu and Linda. Her favourite food was Italian and as it was to be a shared birthday celebration, I suggested she chose the venue.

'Stu took a gulp of water from his glass. 'Rach says you're an artist.'

'Yep, that's right.' Phil twiddled his thumbs. 'Painting is all I've ever wanted to do. Runs in the family too as my little sister has also taken that route.'

'I wish I could paint.' I fanned myself with the menu.

'You do paint,' Phil said, 'you paint pictures with words.'

Linda beamed. 'Aw that sounds so romantic.'

'Thanks, Phil. I'm glad you were happy with the article. Wait until you come around to mine, Lind. Phil's given me the most beautiful picture and Dad's hung it in the hallway. He's commissioned Phil to do a painting of our house and garden.'

'You get on okay with them then?' Stu took another drink of water.

'At the moment but who knows? Maybe they won't like their painting.' He chuckled.

'No fear of that.' I looked up. 'Here comes our food.' At least there was no concern about strange foods here. 'Have either of you ever had octopus?' I asked.

'Ugh, no.' Linda screwed her nose up. 'I don't fancy that. Have you?'

'Nope but they served it at the new Greek restaurant we went to for my birthday. Phil had it though.'

'What was it like?' Stu asked.

'Tasted a bit like onion rings. You should try it.'

'Maybe I will.' Stu peered around the restaurant before getting down on the floor.

'What have you lost?' I got up to help and spotted him on one knee in front of Linda with a ring box. Before he had the chance to say anything Linda clapped her hands and beamed a smile as she watched him.

'Linda Smith' – Stu opened the box and brought it up higher – 'will you do me the honour of becoming my wife?'

'Yes. Yes.' Linda held her hand out for Stu to put the ring on her finger.

Chapter Thirteen

Rachel

We arrived at St Margaret's just before three o'clock. I held Phil's hand as we made our way to the third pew behind Peggy and Adam.

Adam turned to us. 'Glad you could make it.'

Peggy stared at Phil and gave me a nod of approval but I was drawn to Joe standing next to Stu on the front row. Joe glanced across and winked at me. They looked like twins in ivory colour suits with red carnations pinned to their jackets and both sporting ponytails. Why did he have to be my brother? And why was it taking me so long to get over him? He'd moved on. Why couldn't I?

Phil squeezed my hand, reminding me that I hadn't introduced him to Peggy and Adam.

'This is Phil,' I said. 'Phil this is Peggy and Adam. The groom's mam and dad.'

'How do you do?' Phil whispered as the organ kicked in with *Here comes the bride*.

Miranda walked down the aisle on the arm of her father, a tall man with a paunch. Her pink rose and white gypsophila bouquet hung low emphasising her smallframe in the full-length empire-line gown and the lace bodice that shaped her tiny waist.

Three young bridesmaids in matching dresses followed Miranda and behind the attendants came Kate as maid of honour. Her frock flowed to the floor, showing off her trim figure, and the deep rose colour accentuated her dark hair and eyes. After settling the girls onto a pew, she moved closer to the bride. Miranda turned, offering a frontal view, and passed her bouquet to Kate. I gasped at Miranda's flat stomach. Had Linda been right? Was Miranda lying about being pregnant? Surely, she should've had at least a slight swelling. What was it to me, anyway? It didn't make any difference as it wasn't like Joe could ever be mine. I turned to Phil and smiled. Maybe I could make a go of things with him.

'Who's that?' Phil whispered.

'That's Kate, my half-sister.'

'She takes after you for her beauty.'

'Don't.' I held the order of service to my face. 'You'll make me blush,' I said as the vicar made his way to the front of the altar.

'Dearly beloved, we are gathered here today in the sight of God, and in the face of this congregation, to join together this man and this woman in holy matrimony...'

I wished I could close my ears. There was my Joe marrying someone else. That should've been me. *Stop it, Rachel.*

'...that if either of you know any impediment, why they may not be lawfully joined together in matrimony, they do say so now.'

I hoped someone would stand up and say something to stop this wedding. ***You can't marry her, Joe. She's tricking you.*** I forced myself to think about Phil while Joe and Miranda spoke their wedding vows but I couldn't block out Joe's *I will* and when he slid the ring on to her finger, I hurried from the pew and once outside in the churchyard I threw up.

Phil found me at the side of the building. 'Want to tell me what that was about?'

'I get claustrophobic and everything was closing in on me.'

'That must be tricky in your profession.' He put his arm around me. 'Now would you like to tell me the truth? Are you ill?'

'No. I'm not ill.'

'Do weddings always have that effect on you?'

'Not normally.'

'Because he's your brother then?'

'Yes. No. Look, I think there's something you should know.'

'That sounds a bit ominous.'

Phil deserved an explanation. 'Let's sit over there.' I stroked his hand. 'I really like you, Phil, which is why I want to tell you something.' We perched on a wall adjacent to the graveyard and took in the warm sunshine. 'Did I mention that I was adopted?'

'Nope. Not that it matters.'

'I was eighteen when I first found out. Before that I had a boyfriend, a fiancé. I was in love and had everything I ever wanted.'

'What happened?'

'I tracked down my real mother, Peggy. And later discovered my fiancé and half-brother were one and the same.'

'So, Joe, your brother who's getting married right now, was your fiancé?'

'Yes. We hadn't committed incest or anything like that. But we were in love, and when we found out the truth our whole world collapsed. That was five years ago and it's behind us but sometimes, like when he was saying those vows, I find it raw.

And,' I added hurriedly, 'I don't trust that Miranda. I think she's lying to him. She's supposed to be pregnant but did she look like she was expecting to you?'

'Well no.'

'Exactly. If she was, I'm sure she'd have worn a looser gown but...'

'Hey don't upset yourself.' Phil took me in his arms and kissed me full on the lips. 'Are you ready to go back inside? Or if you'd rather not...'

'No, you're right. We should go back in.'

The bridal party was positioned at the top table with Joe next to Miranda's mother, and Miranda adjacent to Adam. Adam and Peggy beamed with pride. Kate as a maid of honour sat the other side of Peggy. Thankfully I'd been placed on a round table with Linda, her mam, Aunty Sheila, Uncle Malc, and my plus one, Phil.

'You look gorgeous.' Linda ruffled the puffed sleeves on my off-the-shoulder dress. 'I knew that mauve cheesecloth would be perfect for you. Don't you think so, Phil?'

'Yes, I've already told her she looks stunning.'

'She certainly does. Takes after Peggy for that.' Sheila fluttered her eyelashes at Phil. 'And who's this?'

'Phil. My boyfriend.'

Sheila and Malc stretched across to shake Phil's hand in turn echoing, 'Pleased to meet you.'

'Phil's an artist,' I said.

Malc picked up his small fork. 'And what sort of paintings do you do?'

'Landscape, mostly. Although I have been known to dabble in life drawing.'

'Really. It sounds fascinating.' Sheila tittered.

I spooned my prawn cocktail. 'Phil and his sister run a small gallery in Smithdown Road. You should pop in.'

Sheila nudged Malc. He nodded. 'Yes, we sure will.'

Waitresses busied around the dining room placing plates of roast chicken, potatoes and veg in front of the guests while waiters poured wine into crystal goblets.

Linda reached for my hand under the table and whispered, 'Are you okay?'

'I just want it to be over.'

'I know.' She squeezed my fingers.

Chatter was loud. Cutlery scraped on plates and I forced myself to eat a bit of food before pushing the remainder to the side to look like I'd eaten plenty.

Stu did his best man's speech, telling guests how he and Joe had been friends for most of their lives. He had everyone laughing at the tales about the boys going scrumping or playing knock down ginger, and they smiled when they heard how the boys bought their first motorbikes at the exact same time. Toasts were given first by Stu followed by the bride's father, and I drank far more champagne than I should have. It was time for Joe to get up and do his speech. Phil clasped my hand, leaning in to me and kissing my cheek. To onlookers we would've been seen as a couple in love.

'Thank you for coming everybody.' Joe blew his nose. 'I think I'm supposed to do a lot of thank yous. So here goes. Thank you to Miranda's parents for organising this fabulous spread, to the bridesmaids, in particular my gorgeous sister Kate, to my mam and dad for all their support and finally to Miranda for making me a happy man.' He picked up his champagne glass. 'Please join me in a toast to my wife. To Miranda.'

The guests picked up their glasses. 'To Miranda.'

The guests retired to a lounge and sank into comfy chairs drinking coffee and eating wedding cake which the waitresses had distributed. A woman around fifty played background music on a harp in a corner of the room. Presents galore of various shapes and sizes were piled high on a couple of trestle tables. I looked across at Joe fidgeting. Was today as tough for him as me? Part of me wanted him to struggle while the other part didn't want him to suffer. He deserved happiness. We both did but was Miranda the right woman to make him happy?

'It looks like the champagne's gone to your head,' Phil said as we strolled up the road to get a cab. 'Tomorrow, I'm sure, you'll feel better about things. If you'd rather not be on your own, you can always stay at mine tonight.'

Should I? He certainly gave me butterflies when we were close, but if I went home with him, would he expect me to go further than I wanted? It was as though he read my mind.

'We can just curl up together. We don't have to do anything.'

'Okay. So long as you're not expecting anything more.'

We cuddled on a wall by the taxi rank enjoying the warm evening and peering up at the stars. 'That there is Orion's Belt.' I pointed.

'An astronomer too?'

'Not really. I don't know much about the constellations but I know that one.'

A cab pulled up.

'Come on, let's get you home to mine.' Phil pulled me up and helped me into the back seat.

Chapter Fourteen

Peggy

Leaning on Adam, I managed to hobble in-between contractions to the entrance of the maternity unit.

'Can I get some help here, please?' he called.

A nurse hurried over with a wheelchair and assisted me into it. 'What's your name, dear?'

'Margaret Davies but I prefer Peggy.'

'All right, Peggy, we'll just get you down to the labour ward. Can you tell me how far apart the contractions are coming?'

Before I could answer, Adam said, 'Every five minutes. I've been timing them.'

'Okay, let's get you settled and we can take a look.' She pushed me into a side room. 'Is Dad coming too?'

Adam held my hand. 'Yes. Try and keep me away.'

'Can you get up onto the bed, Peggy?' the midwife asked.

'I think so.' I bent over in agony.

She took my arm. 'Let the contraction pass first, dear.'

Once it had passed, I was able to get on the bed to be examined.

'How many weeks are you?'

'Thirty-nine.'

'Has your midwife had any concerns about you carrying a big baby?'

'No, but she did rule out twins as I'm much bigger with this one than any of my others.'

She flicked through the notes. 'Geriatric mother and this is your fourth pregnancy.'

I went into another contraction.

'Coming closer. That was only two minutes. I think we need to get you down to the delivery ward.' She peered out of the door and called someone. The next minute another nurse was at her side.

'Not long now, Mrs Davies,' the new nurse said. 'We're just going to wheel you into the delivery room. Doctor's been notified to be on standby in case we need him. We're just a little concerned that you may need an emergency caesarean section.'

'Adam.' I stretched out my hand.

'It's all right, love. I'm here.'

The nurse pushed the cot close to my bed. 'Fancy giving the feeding a go?'

'I'm not sure. I thought with my age I might bottle-feed instead.'

'Baby's not worried how old you are. Why not give it a try?' She picked up the baby and placed him to my breast.

My toes curled as he latched on. I gritted my teeth.

'It'll ease soon. Did you feed your other children?'

'The youngest two but that was a long time ago. My youngest is almost twenty-one.' I squinted.

'You're in pain? Is it the feeding?'

'No, although that does hurt, it's more down there.'

'I'll get you some meds for that.' She took the baby and put him on the other side. 'Now try here.'

Completely worn out, all I wanted to do was lie back and sleep. I was too bloody old for this. Geriatric mother they'd called me. That would be right. Unlike when Rachel was born. And now twenty-four years later I'd given birth to another child. One I was allowed to keep. I stared into his dark eyes. Not that I'd let anyone take him away. I was in love with him already. Somehow, I'd find the strength to take care of him.

The nurse lifted the baby from my arms and placed him back in the cot. 'You did well, dear. I'll get those painkillers and then you can try and rest before visiting time.'

'Thank you.'

※

Adam, Kate, Joe and Miranda gathered around my bed. A nurse wandered in. 'You do know two is the maximum visitors at one time?'

I tried to sit up. 'Can they all stay for a few minutes?'

'Ten minutes and then two of you outside.'

Adam looked up at the nurse and smiled. 'Thank you.'

'Don't forget. Ten minutes or Matron will have my guts for garters.' She hurried to the nurses' station.

I rested my head back on the pillow. 'Have you seen your baby brother?'

'Yes. He's gorgeous,' Kate said, 'but he looks enormous next to the other babies.'

'He is rather. Nine pound ten ounces.'

A nurse wheeled a cot down the ward and stopped at my bed. 'I thought you'd like Baby Davies close now he's stopped that screaming.'

'Thanks,' Adam said. 'He's certainly got a good set of lungs. I'll give him that.'

I peered through the transparent crib at the small bundle with his mop of dark hair which reminded me of Rachel. 'Rachel,' I said. 'Where is she?'

Kate looked at Adam. Adam looked at Joe.

'Has no one phoned her? She'd want to be here.'

'Sorry, love'– Adam caressed my hair – 'I completely forgot, what with letting your Sheila, and Joe know. I'll phone her in a few minutes.'

'Yes. Yes, you must. She wouldn't want to be left out.'

Kate leaned over the cot and stroked the baby's cheek. Adam patted her shoulder. 'Don't wake him up. Your mam needs her rest.'

'I won't. He's beautiful. Has he got a name yet?'

'Not yet,' I said, 'but I have one in mind and wanted to run it past Joe first.'

Adam jerked forward. 'Joe? Why?'

'Because I don't want history repeating itself. That's why.'

Adam frowned. 'Fair enough. Let's have it then.'

'I'm thinking Benjamin Adam Davies. He can be known as Ben. What do you think, Joe?'

'I'd say that's a real cool name, Mam, one I'm sure Ben will be proud to have.' He kissed me on the cheek. 'Miranda and I will go and phone Rachel so you can have a bit of time with Dad and Kate before Aunty Sheila and Uncle Malc arrive. We won't come back in as, like Dad says, you need your rest.' Joe waved as he and Miranda left the ward.

'Adam for a middle name, eh?' Adam leaned into the cot. 'Hello Benjamin Adam Davies.' He turned back to me. 'I like it.'

I smiled. 'How about you, Kate? Do you think it suits him?'

'Deffo and I love the name Ben. Look, why don't I go and get some coffees or teas to give you and Dad a few minutes alone?'

'If you're sure you don't mind. Thanks love.' Adam dug into his pocket and passed Kate a few coins. 'Coffee for me.' He glanced across at me. 'Peg?'

'Yes, a hot drink sounds nice.'

Once Kate had gone, I asked Adam, 'Is Joe okay? He didn't seem his normal bouncy self.'

'Probably terrified that this will be him and Miranda before long.'

'Yes. That's probably it.' Miranda still showed no signs that she was having a child. Although neither did I in the first few weeks when I was expecting. I pushed Rachel's words out of my head. She was just being paranoid.

Rachel hurried towards me. 'Sorry, Peg. I came as soon as I heard.' She kissed me on the cheek. 'How are you feeling?'

'Tired.' I rubbed my eyes.

'Not surprising. Adam said you had a long labour.'

'Compared to the others yes. It was hit and miss for a while whether they were going to do an emergency caesarean section but in the end with the help of a bit of cutting, I was able to push him out. Nearly ten pounds. Can you believe it? Imagine having a sack of spuds coming out of you. No wonder I'm so bloody tired. He's gorgeous though. Take a peep.'

Rachel leaned into the cot. 'Hello, little brother.' She read the blue crib label with his name and weight. 'Benjamin. Nice.'

'I like it. I thought he could be known as Ben. I didn't want a repetition of him wanting to change his name.'

'He'll like Ben. It's cool.' She turned back to me. 'I think he looks a bit like me.'

'I'm sure he does. Of course, I never saw you after being born but' – I reached for her hand – 'I reckon you must've looked just like him.'

Chapter Fifteen

Rachel

Phil cuddled up to me as we waited outside Peggy's porch.

Adam opened the door. 'Hello there, Rachel. Thanks for coming. Come in. Hi again, Phil. How you doing, mate?'

'Good thanks,' Phil answered as we stepped into the hallway where pink and white balloons hung from the banister.

'Where's the birthday girl?' I asked.

'In there. Come through.'

We followed Adam into the lounge. I glanced around the room at Kate, Sheila, Malc, Joe and Miranda, but there was no sign of Peggy.

'Happy Birthday.' I kissed Kate on the cheek. 'You look stunning.' She was wearing a 'V' necked peach frock in georgette fabric. 'Did you get your dress from Linda's boutique?'

'I did. And she gave me a twenty percent discount. By the way I've invited her and Stu.'

'Awesome.' I hadn't seen Linda for a couple of weeks what with the new baby being born and me being busy at work. In any spare time I'd seen Phil. I turned to Joe. 'How are you?'

'Good thanks, Rach.'

'Have you and Miranda found anywhere to live yet?'

'Nah. Her mam and dad says we can stay at theirs while we save up for a deposit.'

'Be tricky once the baby's born.'

'It'll be okay as they have plenty of room.'

'When did you say you were due, Miranda?'

'Sometime around Christmas.'

Kate put her arm around me. 'Won't it be exciting having a baby brother and a new nephew or niece?'

'Sure.' I was still convinced the pregnancy was a lie. 'Any of your friends coming this evening, Kate?'

'No. Just family apart from Linda and Stu. I wanted to keep it small with Mam only just out of hospital.'

Adam came into the room. 'Take a pew, Phil. Can I get you a beer?'

'Cheers, that would be nice.' Phil flopped into an empty armchair.

'Rachel?' Adam asked.

'Lager please. Where's Peggy?'

'Upstairs trying to settle Ben.'

'If it's all right,' I said, 'I'll whip up and see if I can be of any help.'

Adam patted my arm. 'She'll be glad of the company, I'm sure.'

'Will you be okay for a few minutes?' I asked Phil.

'Yeah, the beautiful Kate can keep me company,' he answered making Kate blush.

'Won't be long.' I brushed my lips across his. As I left the room I hesitated outside the door as I overheard Miranda say, 'Why does she always have to interfere?' I wanted to go back in and retaliate but decided against it as it was Kate's birthday. Instead, I hurried upstairs following the noise of the crying baby.

I knocked on the part opened door before pushing it wider. 'All right if I come in?'

Peggy looked up. Her eyes were glazed. 'I can't do anything with him. He never stops crying.'

'Here, let me take him for a bit.' I took the screaming infant from her arms. 'Do you think he's got colic? I've heard that a lot of new babies get that.'

'I don't know.' Peggy sobbed. 'I've given him gripe water but nothing seems to make any difference. I feed him but he never stops crying. The only time he stops is when he's on me. He's just so hungry.'

I perched on the bed, next to Peggy, rocking Ben to try and console him. 'This may sound daft but I heard someone saying the other day that a woman can have windy milk. Maybe you should try him on the bottle?'

'I suggested switching to the bottle to Adam but he thinks I should persevere for a bit longer as Ben's only ten days old.'

'Sod Adam. It's not him sitting here struggling.'

'My nipples are so sore. They even bled a bit this morning.'

I shook my head. 'It's not on. You need to do something.' I checked the time on my watch. 'Look, the chemist down the road should still be open. If I hurry, I'll catch it before closing.'

'What about Adam?' She blew her nose.

'Leave him to me. You get yourself freshened up so you can come and join the party. I'll take Ben downstairs.'

She squeezed my hand. 'Thanks, love.'

I took the stairs carefully with the screaming baby in my arms. Adam came out to the hallway. 'She can't settle him then?'

'No, so I'm going to the chemist for baby milk and bottles.'

'What?'

'Peggy's exhausted and Ben's hungry. Have you seen the state of her nipples?'

'No. She never said.'

I pushed Ben into his arms. 'I shan't be long.'

Linda snuggled Ben close to her chest while feeding him the bottle. She was a natural.

'Which formula is it?' she asked me.

'Cow & Gate. It's what they recommended.'

'Oh yep, that's what Mam fed me on. Nothing wrong with the bottle. I mean look at me.' She laughed. 'How about you, Miranda, are you planning to breastfeed?'

She screwed her nose up. 'Not on your life.'

'Want a cuddle once I've finished feeding him?'

'No thanks, you're all right. Can't abide new babies. They look like little old men and puke all over you. No thanks.'

Joe opened his mouth to say something but changed his mind. Linda held Ben upright and patted his back. He rewarded her with a loud burp and milk spill.

'See what I mean?' Miranda folded her arms.

Joe glared at her. 'Well, I hope you'll feel differently about our baby.'

She shrugged her shoulders. 'Maybe I'll continue to work and you can stay at home to do the feeding and changing.'

Joe's face reddened but he didn't say anything.

Linda stroked Ben's cheek. 'Wish it were me becoming a mam. I can't wait.'

Stu, the other side of Linda on the sofa, put his arm around her and said, 'Let's wait until after we're married though. Eh?'

Chapter Sixteen

Rachel

The jeweller's was crowded, but then it was a Saturday. A man and woman hovered close to the counter. He must've been close to fifty as his hair was partly grey. I wondered whether he was purchasing an engagement ring for the woman or maybe they'd been together for years and he was buying her an eternity ring. I strained to see but there were too many heads in front of me.

An assistant behind the counter rang a bell and two more sales people came out. Finally, we moved to the front of the queue.

'Can I help you?' the jeweller asked me and Linda.

'Yes please.' I took my purse out ready. 'I'd like a gold Saint Christopher for my baby brother's christening.'

The mature saleswoman spun ninety degrees, lifted a couple of jewellery trays from a shelf, and placed them on the counter. 'I'm sure that any of these will be a perfect choice.'

'What do you think?' I asked Linda.

She touched a tiny round one with a scalloped edge. 'How about this?'

'Yes, I like that. How much is it?' I asked the shopkeeper.

She checked the tag. 'Nineteen pounds ninety-nine.'

'I'll take it. Does it come in a special box?'

'Yes, it does.'

'I'm going to be his godmother.'

'I'm sure you'll make a very good one.' The jeweller placed the necklace in a dark blue box and popped it into a small bag and I handed over a twenty-pound note.

'That's you sorted,' Linda said, 'now I need something.' She peered around the shelves. 'Do you have any of those silver money boxes?'

The woman pulled out a drawer behind her and took out a selection. 'We have a teddy bear, train, or an old-fashioned car.'

'The train will be perfect. Thank you.' Linda passed her credit card.

※

'Two coffees,' Linda asked the girl in Elmo's.

I took the box from the jewellery bag. 'Do you think Peggy and Adam will like it?'

'Of course they will. It's perfect.' Linda grinned.

'You look like the cat who got the cream. Spill.'

She looked around the café before moving closer and whispering, 'You know at Kate's party Stu said about us waiting for a baby until we were married?'

'You're not, are you?'

'No.' She grinned wider. 'Better than that. We've set a date for the wedding. It's all hush hush and it'll be a quiet do. None of all that frilly stuff that Miranda and Joe had.'

'When?'

'Next month. September 22nd.'

'Gosh that's only' – I counted on my fingers – 'just under six weeks. And a Thursday?'

'Good afternoon, young ladies.' Elmo put two coffees down. 'Been shopping I see.' He leaned in to inspect the Saint Christopher. 'For the new baby?'

'Yes,' I said. 'It's his christening a week tomorrow. Did Joe tell you?'

'He did indeed. Talk about a proud brother. He showed me some piccies too. Gorgeous little guy. I hope it all goes well.'

'Thanks.'

Linda took the silver train from the bag. 'Stu and I have bought him this. It's a moneybox.'

'Aw he'll love saving up in that when he's older. Don't forget to put in a few coins to start him off.'

'Elmo,' one of the waitresses called across the café.

'I'd best go. You girls take care.' He patted me on the shoulder.

'Where were we?' I asked, packing the Saint Christopher necklace back in its box.

'I was about to say you'll need to get the day off work.'

'Have you booked the church?'

'Not a church. Register office. We don't want all that fuss. And we'll just have a few guests. I can't wait to become Mrs Pearson.'

'I'd better start looking for an outfit then.'

The family congregated in the first couple of pews on the left-hand side of the church. The godparents, including me, were next to Peggy and Adam. Phil was behind with Kate, Stu, Linda, Joe and Miranda. Miranda still showed no signs of pregnancy. Surely, she had to be close to five or six months so could anyone really still be that thin?

Two more families sat on the right-hand side while another family assembled behind us as three other babies were being christened. The vicar called up the godparents and parents to the font. I headed up with Aunty Sheila, Uncle Malc, Peggy and Adam. Peggy passed Ben to me. He looked cute in a little blue romper suit with matching hat. I held him up to my shoulder and he obliged by bringing up his feed on my cream jacket.

'Oops.' Peggy passed me a tissue.

'Now I know why you gave him to me,' I whispered.

The vicar instructed godparents and parents to answer his questions with, 'We will with God's help,' and afterwards he held the babies over the font in turn.

He poured water from the font over Ben's head three times as he said, 'Benjamin Adam, I baptise you in the name of the Father, and of the Son, and of the Holy Spirit.'

Everyone said, 'Amen.'

The vicar marked a cross on Ben's forehead. 'Benjamin Adam, I sign you with the sign of the cross to show that you are marked as Christ's own forever.'

Again, the congregation said, 'Amen.'

A curate passed candles to the godparents and parents, lighting them in turn. I shielded the bopping flame from a draught. The vicar said, 'God has brought you out of darkness into God's marvellous light. All shine as a light in the world to the glory of God the Father.'

The congregation clapped. A certificate was given to the godparents by the curate and he passed Peggy the baptism certificate. He leaned towards Ben. 'What a trouper this one is. Not even a teeny cry when his head was wetted. And look at those gorgeous sapphire eyes.'

We gathered in the function room of The Black Horse. Debs, the landlady, had put on a fabulous spread. Triangular sandwiches of egg and cress, cheese and tomato, and salmon and cucumber were set neatly on plates. Cheese and pineapple and sausages on sticks were stuck in cobs of bread to imitate hedgehog quills. We had the choice of strawberry or black forest gateaux for dessert, and in the centre of the trestle table stood an iced fruitcake on a stand inscribed with Ben's name and christening date 27th August 1977. Harry, the landlord, distributed glasses of sherry to us all.

Ben was passed from Peggy to each of the guests in turn and managed to remain asleep. When Linda held him, she called across to Miranda, 'I think you should go next. Get in some practice.'

Miranda sneered. 'No thanks. You're all right.'

Joe tutted at his wife, got up and took a seat at the side of Linda. 'I'll take my little brother.' He glared at Miranda.

She was no more having a baby than I was. I'd lay odds on it. It was clear she'd tricked Joe into marriage.

I slammed the front door shut and marched into the lounge muttering, 'Bloody woman.'

'I take it you didn't have a nice time?' Dad stubbed out a cigarette in the ashtray.

'No, I did. It was lovely. Wait until you see the photos once developed. And Ben was so good when the vicar did his stuff. He didn't cry at all and looked absolutely gorgeous.'

'If everything went so well, why are you in such a bad mood? Have you fallen out with Phil?'

'No. Everything's fine.' I leaned on the back of the couch.

'Who's in a bad mood?' Mum said wandering into the room with a tray of tea.

'No one.' I took a deep breath. 'Actually, if you must know, it's that bloody Miranda. She's still not showing and must be at least five or six months, and when Linda suggested she hold Ben she totally refused. Even Joe was cross. I could tell.'

Mum poured out three cups of tea. She passed one to Dad. 'One here for you too, Rachel.'

'No thanks.'

'It's chamomile. Might calm you down.'

'No, you're all right thanks. I think I'll head up to bed as I've an early start tomorrow.'

'Fair enough' – Mum sipped her drink – 'but remember, it's up to Joe to sort his life out. Not you. So, stop making it your business and concentrate on your own personal life.'

'I'll try. It just irritates me how she's making a fool of him. Apart from Linda and me, no one else seems to be able to see.'

Chapter Seventeen

Peggy

I peered up at the medical posters on the wall in the waiting area. Baby immunisations, what to do about cradle cap, and getting help for postnatal depression.

A health visitor came through. 'Mrs Davies.'

'Yes, that's me.' Holding Ben, I rose from the chair, glad to get away from the young mothers around me, and followed the nurse into the small room.

'How's Benjamin doing?'

'Good. So much better since I put him on the bottle.' I undressed Ben down to his nappy.

'My colleague mentioned you'd struggled. Such a shame. However, the main thing is that baby thrives. Shall I take him?' She took Ben from my arms and laid him onto the scales. 'Twelve pounds two. He's doing well.'

'Yes, he is now. He was losing weight.'

'They always do at first.'

'Yes, I understand that, but he kept losing, and he never stopped crying which is why my daughter suggested formula. He's been brilliant since then. Contented and a good sleeper. As you can see.'

The nurse checked Ben over. 'Oh, look at that. What a gorgeous smile. A real smile too, not wind, and what wonderful eyes this child has.' She passed him back to me.

'My hair colour but his father's eyes. Father's temperament too.'

'How are you doing, Mrs Davies? Do you have any other worries?'

'No, I'm fine, although there is something I wouldn't mind asking you, not related to me or Ben, if that would be okay?' I laid Ben on the examination table and changed his nappy, shoving the wet one in a plastic bag.

'Try me.'

'My daughter-in-law's expecting. She must be six months now but not showing any signs of being pregnant at all.'

'A loose dress can cover up a multitude of sins.'

'But she doesn't wear loose clothing.'

'What does her midwife say?'

'I don't know. She's rather evasive about her appointments. My daughter's convinced the girl's lying. What do you think?'

'I'm sorry, Mrs Davies, I couldn't possibly comment without seeing her but from what you say, something doesn't sound quite right. Maybe speak to your son.'

'Thanks.' I slid Ben's arms into his romper and placed a hat on his head, before positioning him against my shoulder, and picking up the baby rucksack.

'We'll see you next month then.'

'Yes, thanks. Bye.'

Potatoes simmered on the stove, along with boiled cabbage, and the aroma from the lamb chops in the oven made my stomach rumble.

The front door closed. 'I'm home.' Adam strode into the kitchen. 'How's my favourite girl?' He kissed me on the lips.

'Good thanks. We've been to the clinic and Ben's doing really well.' I took a seat at the table. 'Listen, before Kate comes in, I wanted to speak to you.'

Adam squinted. 'Oh?' He took a seat on a dining chair. 'What's up?'

'I've been thinking that Rachel could have a point about Miranda.'

'In what way?'

'About her not being pregnant.'

Adam tutted. 'Why?'

'She just doesn't seem pregnant. She's never been sick. Not complained about heartburn, and she doesn't wear loose clothes. I can't believe she could still look so good at six months. Anyway, I mentioned it to the health visitor…'

'Health visitor. What the hell's it got to do with her?'

'Nothing, I suppose I wanted her to put me at ease.'

'And what did she say?'

'She suggested I speak to Joe.'

A key turned in the lock. 'That'll be our Kate. Leave it for now. Let's see how things lie after Stu and Linda's wedding this Saturday.'

'Hi, Mam, Dad.' Kate went straight to the carrycot. 'Ah, he's asleep. I was hoping for a cuddle.'

'Plenty of time for cuddles after dinner.' I drained the water from the potatoes and cabbage in turn. 'You can bathe him tonight if you like, and give him his bottle. Pass the masher, will you?'

※

Kate cupped her hand as she leaned across the bath, pouring water over Ben's hair. She'd make a great little mam. 'It's difficult to do in here, isn't it?'

'Much harder but he's too big for the baby bath. He's got to go in the big cot next week too.'

'In your bedroom?' Kate lifted Ben onto the white fluffy towel and dabbed him dry.

'No, unfortunately. There's no room which means he'll have to go into the nursery. To be truthful, I'm dreading it.'

'He'll be fine, mam. He's such a good sleeper you won't notice the difference.' She shook Johnson's baby talc over his little body. 'Don't you just love the smell of babies?'

I laughed. 'Yes, I do. I wonder how your sister-in-law will cope with all this?'

'Probably fine once she has her own. A lot of women aren't that keen until it's theirs.'

'Not you though?'

'Nah, I love babies and especially my baby brother. And I can't wait to become an aunty.'

'How's work going?'

'Excellent. Dr Winter's really pleased with me. She's asked if I'll start a new support group for teenagers suffering from eating disorders.'

'How do you feel about that?'

She cuddled Ben. 'I'm happy to give it a go.'

Chapter Eighteen

Rachel

Half a dozen of us piled into The Three Horseshoes for Linda's hen party as the boys had bagged our favourite venue The Black Horse. Linda strutted around with a veil on her head and an 'L' plate on the front and back of her white blouse. Kate looked stunning in a light blue peasant dress and Debs the landlady from The Black Horse surprised us by wearing a sexy black halter neck. Quite different to the normal gear she wore behind the bar. Linda's mam passed for under thirty-five in white jeans and a purple T-shirt, while Peggy made a huge effort portraying elegance in a lurex shift dress. And then there was me. I chose a short tiered spotted skirt with matching top showing off my tiny figure.

Debs put a fiver on the table. 'Let's have a kitty.'

'Cool.' I added a note and the others did the same.

Debs picked up the cash. 'I'm going to surprise you all.'

I tugged at her arm. 'Don't you want a night off sorting out the booze?'

'Nah. I'm better off being busy.'

'What you thinking? A bottle of fizz? Let me go.'

'You'll see.'

'Okay. I'll come and help then.' I sauntered up to the bar with Debs.

'So, where's Miranda? I'd have thought she'd be here as Joe's at Stu's?'

'Well she's not really Linda's friend and, besides, you know she's pregnant?'

'What's that got to do with it? She could still join in the fun. You don't like her, do you?'

I shrugged.

'You or Linda. What have you got against the girl?'

'Nothing.'

'Six tequila shots please, Pete.' Debs handed over the cash.

'Tequila?' I said. 'I don't remember us asking for that.'

'Let your hair down. Time to have a bit of fun and loosen your tongue maybe.'

The barman lined up the small glasses and Debs and I carried them back to the table.

Peggy put a hand over her mouth. 'Tequila? Who's going to look after Ben if I get sozzled.'

'Adam.' I chuckled.

'You're joking, he'll be more intoxicated than me with that rowdy lot he's out with.'

'Perhaps you can persuade Sheila to stay over.' She'd come over to babysit Ben and hadn't taken much persuading.

'No. I don't think so. I'll just need to watch what I drink.'

The barman came over. 'You'll need these.' He left a dish of salt and a plate of lime wedges on the table. 'Let me know when you want the shots lined up again.'

'Okay girls, watch how you do it.' Debs sprinkled salt on the back of her hand, licked it, drank the shot down in one, and finished by sucking a wedge of lime. 'After three.'

Salt ready, on the count of her three we all licked, drank, and sucked roaring with laughter afterwards. Debs held her hand in the air, and the barman came over with refills.

'Cheers, Pete,' she said, 'and remember the landlord code – what happens in the bar, stays in the bar.'

'Mum's the word, Debs. I shan't be telling Harry a thing.' Pete moved nearer to Debs and positioned his face close. 'How about a kiss to keep me quiet?'

'On your bike, you randy dog. My Harry's enough for me.'

Pete playfully punched Debs on the arm. 'Only jesting, doll.' He chuckled, making his way back to the bar.

Debs turned to me. 'He's harmless. He'd act the same in front of Harry. They're best mates.'

'Oh right.'

As the evening progressed, we switched from shots to cocktails but Peggy insisted on sticking to lemonade.

'So' – Debs nudged me – 'are you girls going to tell me what you have against Miranda?'

Peggy glared at me.

'I've not said anything, honest.' I giggled.

'Will someone fill me in on the joke?' Peggy asked.

'No joke.' Debs spluttered. 'I was just wondering why the girl hadn't been invited.'

'She was feeling a little unwell,' Peggy lied, clearly wishing to avoid rumours.

'All I can say is' – I hugged Linda – 'with the state of you, it's a good job you have a couple of days to recover before the big day.'

We stood in the waiting area of the register office. The hem of Linda's strapless cheesecloth dress brushed her open shoes. She clutched a small posy of red roses and gypsophila. A matching single rose in her hair accentuated her flawless skin.

Stu and Joe's suits looked identical to the ones they'd worn to Joe's wedding, even the carnations.

'Doesn't she look stunning,' I whispered to Phil.

'She does but not as stunning as you.'

'Now now, you know I'm not allowed to upstage the bride.'

'I'm biased.' He kissed me lightly on the lips.

A woman in a dark two-piece peered out of the wedding room. 'May I have the bride and groom? The rest of you will be invited to come in shortly.'

'This is it.' Linda hugged me before going off proudly on Stu's arm.

Joe came over. 'Well, I don't know about you but there was a time I never thought they'd get here.'

'Yeah. I know what you mean. They've been through so much they deserve happiness.'

A steward strode over to us. 'You may all go through now.'

'You'd better get back to your wife,' Phil said to Joe.

Soft instrumental music played as the guests were seated. The groom's invitees were on the right-hand side of the room. I'd never seen Stu's parents before. With greyish hair, they appeared to be in their late fifties, like my Mum and Dad. A young-looking woman with a blonde pageboy hairstyle was next to them. That must've been his sister. His cousin, Ed, whom I'd met years ago in a pub, was with a larger woman who was trying to quieten three boisterous boys. Joe joined Stu's parents on the front row.

Unsure where to sit, Peggy looked from side to side, rocking Ben in her arms. Adam pulled her across to Stu's guests and Miranda followed. Phil and I took the front seat on the left with

Linda's mam and her new fellow, Keith. I signalled Kate to come and sit with us.

Chrysanthemum floral arrangements prettied up the desk along with bopping flames from the stubby scented candles. Linda and Stu were at the desk chatting to the registrar. She rose from her chair, they followed suit, and stood in front staring into each other's eyes like no one else was there.

'Are you ready to begin?' the registrar asked them.

They nodded and turned to her.

She coughed. The congregation went silent. 'My name is Louise Sharpe and I will conduct the ceremony, and Cyril Mansfield' – she signalled to the steward – 'will complete the schedule, which is the legal record of the marriage. This ceremony will be in accordance with the civil law of this country...'

So here we were. Joe married, Stu and Linda getting married, leaving me the only single one. Would I marry Phil? Not that he'd asked me but did I want to? I feared not. Maybe he felt the same. It wasn't like he'd ever said he loved me or anything like that.

Out of nowhere Ben gave a piercing cry. Embarrassed, Peggy tiptoed from the room, whispering, 'I'm sorry.'

In a clear voice to reach the back of the room, Stu said, 'I declare that I know of no legal reason why I Stuart John Pearson may not be joined in marriage to Linda Esme Smith. I call...'

They were actually doing it. My best friend was finally getting her happy ever after and if either of them had anything to do with it they wouldn't be hanging around in starting a family. When a tear dropped to my cheek I was surprised. I hadn't realised I was crying but maybe it was because things were going to change now that they were a married couple.

Phil squeezed my hand, reminding me he was there. 'Are you all right?' He passed me a clean white hankie.

'Cheers.'

Stu and Linda would be setting up home in their own little bedsit and I doubted they'd want me hanging around. I was so proud of her saying her vows. She'd come a long way from the insecure teenager she was when we first met.

'...that I Linda Esme Smith do take thee Stuart John Pearson to be my lawful wedded husband.'

At the end the registrar said, 'I now pronounce you husband and wife. You may kiss the bride.'

They didn't need telling twice and went into a full-on snog. Everyone clapped. Afterwards Joe and I were called forward to sign as witnesses and then Alan, the photographer from work, positioned us all to take some photos. He'd offered to do the shoot as a wedding present. He and Linda had become quite good friends since the article at the boutique. You couldn't help but like Alan, he was such a lovely guy, no sign of a girlfriend but then we wondered whether he may be more interested in his same sex.

Lemon and purple balloons hung on the inside of the village hall. Trestle tables along one side of the wall were crammed with a buffet wedding breakfast. Linda's mam and I circulated offering the guests a glass of fizz. As I was passing the open front door, I heard raised voices from outside. I looked out and spotted Joe and Miranda arguing but couldn't make out what they were saying. Joe threw his arms down, pushed past her and made his way back in.

'Champers?' I offered up the tray. 'Everything all right?'

'Cheers.' He took a glass. 'Everything's fine. Why shouldn't it be?' He made his way to the Gents.

Miranda followed Joe in, her face flushed, and darted to the Ladies. Had Joe finally discovered the truth about her lies. Oh well I couldn't worry about that now. Today was Linda and Stu's day and nothing was going to spoil it. I continued offering the drinks to the guests.

Dark Chaos set up their instruments on the stage. Linda and Stu glared at me. 'Is this your doing?' Linda asked.

'Mine and Phil's.' I smiled. 'I managed to negotiate a special deal with Paul to play this evening.' Although Stu and Linda hadn't wanted much fuss in their wedding, Joe and I had managed to convince them to have a small party later on.

Linda hugged me. 'You're such a great friend. Thank you.' She marched up to the stage and announced, 'Please help yourselves to food and there's plenty more fizz.'

The guests queued at the tables, lining their plates with sandwiches, crisps, peanuts, vol-au-vents, potato salad, lettuce, tomatoes and cucumber. I took a paper plate and loaded it with four ham and cheese triangle sandwiches, a couple of egg and cress vol-au-vents, a handful of crisps, and some salad for Peggy, as she had Ben on her lap.

'Here you go, Peg.' I placed it down on a small table in front of her. 'Let me take Ben while you get something to eat.'

'Thanks, Rachel. You're a good girl. I must admit I'm starving, what with getting him ready this morning I had to skip breakfast.'

'You eat. I'll get something later.' I lifted Ben and wandered over to Phil.

'You love looking after him, don't you?'

'I sure do. Don't get any ideas though as I'm not ready to have one of my own.' I chortled.

'Phew. Thank goodness for that as neither am I. In fact...'

'What is it?'

'Come and sit down, Rach.'

Oh my God, I hoped the wedding hadn't given him any ideas. Was he going to propose? I took a seat next to him and rocked Ben on my knee.

Phil leaned across to touch my hand. 'There's something I need to tell you but I've not been sure how.'

'Just spit it out is normally the best way.'

One of the kids skidded across the floor and almost hit us. I put my arm around Ben's head to protect him.

Phil frowned. 'Mind the baby.'

'Sorry.' The boy's face reddened.

Ed charged over to the child and clipped him across the ear. 'And so you bloody should be, carrying on like that with a young baby nearby.'

The boy shrieked. Ed pushed him. 'Outside.'

I was feeling sorry for the boy when Ed's wife came over. 'Really sorry about our Daniel. The lad's not had the chance to have a runabout today and because he's hyperactive, he kind of let loose. Trouble with these big halls is the kids see them like playgrounds.' She leaned across to Ben. 'Is he okay?'

'Fine, thanks.'

'He's a gorgeous little thing, isn't he? Is he your first?'

I laughed. 'He's not mine. He's my brother. Well, half-brother. Peggy' – I signalled across the room – 'that's his mum.'

As the woman turned to walk away, I said, 'There's a park across the road with swings and a slide if the boys needed somewhere to let off steam. It's stopped raining and you should have an hour or so before dark.'

'Thanks. Sorry I don't know your name.'

'Rachel. And this is my boyfriend Phil.'

'Pleased to meet you both. I'm June. I'd better find Ed and get those kids some playtime sorted.'

Once she left I said to Phil, 'And that's why I'm not ready for kids, thank you very much. Poor kid though getting a slap like that from his dad. How would Ed like it?'

'Quite.'

'Anyway, you wanted to tell me something.'

'I've been offered a job.'

'Congratulations. Where?'

'That's just it. It's in Paris.'

'Paris. That's amazing, Phil. You've always wanted to go there. Doing what?'

'Teaching. Jan too. Her old professor put us forward.'

'I'm so pleased for you.'

'You don't mind?'

'I'll miss you for sure but you've got to think of your career.'

'It's only for a year but obviously I can't expect you to wait for me that long. But there is another solution. You could come with me.'

I chewed my lip. 'Talk about dropping things on a girl at the least appropriate time. When do you leave?'

'Next week.'

'Bloody hell.'

Ben burst into a cry.

'Sorry, little man, didn't mean to give you a fright.' I rocked him on my lap again.

'I understand if you need time to think about it but as you can see, we don't have a lot.'

He wanted me to give up everything to go to another country and further his career. But what about mine? I couldn't believe what he was asking me. I'd worked hard to get where I was. 'No' – I shook my head – 'sorry, Phil, but I can't leave. I love my job, but you definitely should go.'

The hall gradually filled up. Mum, Dad and Jenny came through the door armed with gifts. Sandra, Linda's mam, greeted them. 'I'm so pleased you made it. Come in and get yourselves a drink.' She pointed to a makeshift bar in the corner of the room. 'We've got most things. And a buffet will be going out shortly.'

'You look tired,' Mum said.

'It's been hard work but' – she patted my arm – 'your Rachel's been a godsend. I don't know what I'd have done without her help.'

Mum and Dad beamed with pride.

I pulled Jenny towards the bar. 'You didn't think of bringing your young doctor then?'

She laughed. 'Which one?'

'You mean you've got more than one?'

'I might have.' She grinned.

'What do you fancy to drink?'

'I'll have a cider.'

'Two ciders please, Harry.' Harry and Debs had offered to do a bar on a sale or return basis and supplied the glasses.

'Sure, love.' He poured out the drinks.

I passed a glass to Jenny. 'I thought you were seeing a certain doctor?'

She licked her lips. 'Yep, that all fell through. Where's that handsome Phil?'

'Somewhere around. Let's sit.' I led her to a couple of plastic chairs at the side of the hall. 'He's off to Paris next week.'

'Not taking you?'

'Not for a holiday. He's got a job.'

'I'm sorry, Rach.' She put her arm around me as the band kicked in with their first number.

Stu and Linda took to the dance floor. The guests clapped, letting the newlyweds dance alone for a while before joining in.

'You know I'm not even that bothered about Phil going. So, what does that tell you about our relationship? Look at those two. Don't they look happy?'

She stroked the back of my hand. 'You'll get your happy ever after one day. We both will. Come on, let's dance.'

We got up on the floor and wrapped our arms around each other and swayed in a smooch. Phil interrupted. 'May I?'

'Go on, it's okay,' Jenny said, 'I'll get Dad to dance with me.'

Phil held me tight. His breath smelt of beer.

'How many have you had?'

'Not that many. I was drowning my sorrows.'

'Why? You're doing what you want.'

'Yes, I am, but I thought you might've at least put up a bit of a fight.' He kissed me on my lips.

I pulled my face back. 'We can't make something that isn't there. Yes, I like you a lot. You're wonderful company and a great kisser but if you mean, do I love you, then the answer has to be no. I'm sorry.'

He led me away from the dance floor. 'I think I'll head off home. I'm not in the mood for all this wedding stuff. You don't mind?'

'No. You go. Will you get a taxi?'

'Nah. Think I'll walk to clear my head.' He kissed me on the cheek.

'Take care, Phil.' I watched him head out of the door.

Joe came up to me. 'Where's he gone?'

'He's not feeling too good,' I lied. 'How about you? What was all that with you and Miranda earlier?'

'Nothing. All sorted now. So, are you and Phil okay?'

'There won't be any me and him soon. He's off to France. Got a new job for a year in Paris.'

Joe stared at me with those tender eyes.

I slapped him playfully on the arm. 'Don't worry about me. I'm fine. You should get Miranda up for a dance unless...'

'Unless what?'

'She's not up to it with the baby.'

'Oh.'

'Is there a baby?'

He took my hand and led me outside.

'Where are we going?'

'Somewhere we can talk without prying ears.' He made his way to a low wall with me in tow. 'Let's sit here for a while.'

I shivered.

Once we were seated, he took off his jacket and wrapped it around my shoulders.

'Cheers, but won't you be cold?'

'I'll be fine.'

'So, spill.'

'There is no baby.'

'Did she lose it?'

'No. There never was one.'

'I knew it.'

'Shh. It wasn't her fault. She thought she was when we got married, and then afterwards, once she realised, she was too nervous to tell me. I mean do I look like a monster?'

I squeezed his hand. 'You could never be a monster, Joe.'

'Anyway, she blurted it out today before we came in here. I wasn't cross for her not being pregnant but cross that she kept it to herself once she found out. Making me look like a fool.'

'You deserve better.'

'Yes, but I can't have better' – he stared into my eyes – 'can I?'

'You know you can't. What will you do now that you know?'

'Nothing. I mean nothing's changed. Only that we won't have the worry about a baby coming along. I need to tell Mam and Dad. How do you think they'll take it?'

'I think they may already have an inkling.'

'So, she has made a bloody fool of me. Oh well.'

Linda charged over to us. 'What are you two doing out here?'

'Just having a breath of fresh air,' I said, 'but we're coming back in now. Fancy a dance?'

'Sure. You all right, Joe?'

He blinked. 'Fine. I'll go and chat to my mate, Stu, if you two are up dancing.'

Chapter Nineteen

Rachel

I gripped the rail and trod carefully down the stone stairs to the basement flat. Before I had the chance to knock, Linda had opened the door. 'Hiya. Come in.'

'Those steps are a bit hairy. Must be awful in the dark.'

'No, they're okay. We just have to remember to turn the outside light on before we go out. And not come home too drunk.' She laughed. 'And at least there's a banister to hold on to.'

'I suppose so.' I followed her into the bedsitting room. 'How's married life?'

'Love it.'

'Is Stu out?'

'No, he's in the kitchen.'

'You have your own kitchen?'

'Yep. Come and see. This way.' She led me back through the hallway. 'The loo's in there. That's ours too, but if we want a bath, we have to share the bathroom upstairs with the landlord.' We continued down to the kitchen. Stu was pulling his overalls out of the spin dryer.

I winked at Linda. 'Trained him well.'

'Not really. I'd happily do them but he insisted. He's always washed them himself as his mam refused.'

'I don't blame her with all that grease and oil. Enjoying married life, Stu?'

'Sure. It's cool.' He hung the overalls over a wooden clothes horse.

I was drawn to the worktop display of red and white accessories. A rolltop breadbin, matching mugs on a pine wooden tree, and a four-slice toaster, all co-ordinating with the gingham café style curtains. 'Did you make these?' I signalled to the small window.

'I did. Do you like them?'

'Yes. You have hidden talents, Linda Pearson.'

Stu put his arm around Linda. 'We had a fab time in Devon for our honeymoon, didn't we, Lind? Even if it did piss it down most of the time. Have you told Rach the news?'

'News?' I asked.

'I'll make a pot of tea. Go and sit down and Lind can tell you.'

Surely, she couldn't be expecting already. I followed Linda back into the bedroom come lounge, taking a seat on the beige corduroy sofa. 'This is comfy.'

'Yeah, it is.' She curled up next to me. 'The downside, well one of the downsides about this place is... You saw those stairs as we passed?'

'Yes. What's up there?'

'The landlord.'

'You said the downside?'

'Up the top, there's no door between us, which means they can come down whenever they like, and they do.'

I shook my head. 'That doesn't seem right.'

'No, especially not on our wedding night. We'd not long got in when the old guy from upstairs walked in to congratulate us.'

'What?'

'I know. For eff's sake we were in bed. So embarrassing. It was a good job we weren't you know...?'

I roared with laughter as Stu came in carrying a tray of tea. He put it down on the teak, tiled coffee table. 'Budge up, Lind.'

She moved closer to me. I inched over further to give them more space.

'Have you just told her about...?' He leaned forward and passed me a mug.

'Cheers. If you mean about the guy upstairs coming in, then yes.'

He shook his head. 'Bloody geezer's mad. When we first came to look around the place, he made a big deal of saying that he and his missus weren't old age pensioners but senior citizens. Really embarrassing too as she had a massive bra hanging over the back of the sofa. I didn't know where to look.'

I took a sip of the tea. 'Not brilliant then?'

'Worse than that.' Linda said. 'When I got in from work the other day, I put the washing machine on. You saw the twin-tub in the kitchen?'

'Sure. Stu was taking out his overalls. Why? It's not broken, is it?'

'No.' She threw her head back in laughter. 'But you're not going to believe this. The old guy came down, hobbled into the kitchen, and said it shouldn't be making that noise. He came to the conclusion that I shouldn't have the *on* switch on. I mean how else is it going to bloody work?'

I squinted. The man sounded loopy.

'And then yesterday I was baking a cake with the food mixer you bought us for a wedding present and he came down to see if I had the washing machine on.' She nudged Stu. 'You didn't cut a slice for Rach.'

'Sorry, I'll have my tea first and then get it, but have you told her the news?'

'No, she hasn't and I'm getting impatient.'

'Let me get the cake first.' Linda got up and left the room.

I glared at Stu. 'I suppose you could tell me?'

'Nope. Has to come from Lind.'

'She's not?'

He shook his head. 'Nope, nothing like that. You'll never guess.'

'Here we go.' Linda passed me a plate with a slice of Victoria sponge. 'I made it myself. Taste it.'

I took a bite. 'Wow, it's yummy. Really light. But now please put me out of my misery.'

'Okay.' She flopped down on the sofa in the middle of Stu and I. 'As you can see this place isn't great.'

'But it's a start. At least it's your own place unlike Joe who's living with Miranda's parents. This must be better?'

'Yep, except it's damp. Our clothes are wet when we take them out of the wardrobe.'

'That's not good. You'll get ill.'

'Exactly.'

'But what's the news?' I'd forgotten how much she loved to drag a story out. 'Tell me.'

'Oh okay.' She slapped her hands on her lap. 'Me mam and Keith popped round earlier and you'll never guess what?'

I nudged her arm. 'No, I won't, so just bloody tell me. What?'

Stu laughed. 'Get on with it, Lind, or I'll have to tell her.'

Linda's green eyes sparkled. 'They've only gone and got hitched. Slipped off quietly, two strangers for witnesses, didn't want to spoil our limelight. Isn't it great?'

'Wow. Yes. I'm so pleased for her. She deserves some happiness. They didn't hang around though, did they?'

'Mam said at their age there was no point in waiting. Especially as Keith's ten years or more older than her. "Grab it while you can," Mam said.' Linda continued to stare at me with a smile on her face.

'Is there more?'

'Yep.' She leaned forward and took a swig of tea from her mug. 'Like you've noticed, this place really isn't suitable but...' She put her drink down, took my plate, placing it next to the mugs, got up off the sofa and pulled me up with her. The next thing she's dancing around with me like a school kid.

I chuckled. 'Come on. What else? And can you stop spinning me because I'm getting dizzy.'

'Sorry. I'm just so excited.' She took a deep breath and flopped back on the couch, taking me with her. 'Mam's moving in with Keith. He's bought a new gaff and they've said we can live at hers for the same rent as we're paying here.'

'Isn't your mam's place rented?'

'Nope.' Linda folded her arms. 'She owns it outright.'

I blinked. 'I'd always thought it was rented.'

'Nope, it was her grandparents' home, and once they both passed the house went to Mam.'

'Not to her parents?'

'No. It seems they were estranged and Linda's mam and dad didn't want anything from them. So, my mam took up residence when she was expecting me after her parents disowned her.'

'That's wonderful then that you'll have your own place.'

'I know. Mam reckons fate stepped in and everything's slotted together like a jigsaw.'

'That's fantastic.'

'I know.'

Sandra's grandparents must've really loved her to have left her the house. She deserved happiness. 'When do you move in?'

'The week after next. It's all been such a shock. You know, finding out about my mam getting married, and us taking over the house. On top of us being newlyweds too.'

'Yeah, I bet.'

'How about you? Any goss?'

I leaned back on the sofa. 'Well, yes, actually. We were right about Miranda. She never was pregnant.'

Stu shot up to his feet. 'How's Joe?'

I shrugged. 'I've not seen him since your wedding but he seemed okay then.'

'He knew then and didn't say anything to me?' Stu sighed.

'I imagine he didn't want to spoil your day but apparently, according to Joe, she really did think she was pregnant. At least that's what she told him.'

'Poor Joe.' Stu lit up a Woodbine. He offered the packet to me.

'No thanks. Joe was upset, but not because she wasn't pregnant, but because she kept it from him once she realised she wasn't.'

'Yeah, I would be too. Upset is putting it mildly, I'd be bloody fuming. I'll give him a ring.' Stu went out to the hallway.

'You're on the phone?' I asked.

'Yep. Shared with them upstairs,' Linda said. 'Did you not see the green trimphone in the hall on your way in?'

'No, I didn't. It's good to know though. You'll have to give me your number.'

'I will but don't forget it's only for a week but once we move into Mam's we'll get a phone sorted there.'

'Smashing.'

'So how are you coping without Phil?'

'Fine. I miss his company but I always knew he wouldn't be my happy ever after.'

Chapter Twenty

Peggy

The table was set with dinner plates, salad and cold meats. I was looking forward to seeing Joe and Miranda as I hadn't seen them since Stu and Linda's wedding. Rachel said she'd try to join us for tea too.

Kate came into the lounge rocking Ben in her arms. 'He's been fed and changed but still fighting sleep. What time are you expecting them?'

I looked up at the clock. 'Any minute now. Around five I told them. Do you want me to take him?'

'No, you're all right, Mam. Take a breather before they arrive.'

'You're a good girl.' I peered out of the back window. 'I hate these dark nights.'

'Me too,' Kate said as the key turned in the lock. 'That sounds like them now.'

Joe strode into the lounge. 'Hiya, Mam. Kate.' He kissed his sister on the cheek and took Ben from her arms. 'Hiya little bro. What's all this noise?' He stroked his brother's cheek and Ben immediately stopped crying. Joe grinned. 'And how are you, sis?'

'Good,' she answered. 'No Miranda?'

'She wasn't feeling great.'

'Oh.' I perched on the edge of the couch. 'Is it the pregnancy?'

'About that. Where's Dad?'

Adam walked into the room. 'Dad's here. What's up?'

'You might want to sit down.' Joe passed a sleeping Ben back to Kate.

'I'll just put him down now that big brother has settled him,' she said. 'He's obviously got the magic touch.'

'Thanks, love.' I was about to say Joe would make a great dad and then remembered he was about to make some kind of revelation, so I just smiled.

Kate moved slowly out into the hallway carrying Ben. 'Close the door behind me, Dad.'

'Sure.' Adam pushed the door. 'Cigarette?' He offered Joe the Player's packet.

'Ta.' Joe took one from the packet and lit up the ciggie.

'So, what gives?' Adam sat down next to me on the couch.

'Miranda's not pregnant.' Joe puffed on the cigarette.

'What do you mean?' I asked. 'Has she lost it?'

Joe shook his head. 'Nope. It seems there never was one.'

My stomach bubbled. So, Rachel had been right all along about Miranda lying to get him to marry her. I took a deep breath. 'Is that why she's not here? Too ashamed to show her face.'

'Calm down, Mam,' Joe said. 'She's actually not feeling well, for real.' He gave a small laugh.

'But why did she lie?' Adam inhaled the cigarette smoke.

'She didn't. Well not exactly.' Joe tapped ash into the ashtray. 'When we got married, she thought she was.'

'Surely it hasn't taken her until now to realise she couldn't be?' I said.

'No. She knew at least two months ago but was too scared to tell me.'

'Scared of you?' Adam said.

'I know. I mean what am I? An ogre? She didn't want me to think I'd been trapped into marrying her.' He shrugged. 'Which I don't, but I won't lie, I was bloody livid with her for not telling me. Making me look like a fool.'

'So, what now?' Adam stubbed out his ciggie.

'Nothing. I mean I'm quite glad there's no baby. So...'

'I'm sorry, son.' Adam patted Joe on the shoulder. 'She got you to marry her on false pretences. So where does that leave things?'

'Nothing's changed except no baby, and as I said, I'm kind of relieved about that.'

'But marriage is based on trust and if she lied to you about that then what else might she lie about?' Adam pressed.

'Makes no difference to me. I mean, it's not like I can marry the woman I really love.'

I shot up from the couch. 'For God's sake, Joe, please tell me you're not still holding a torch for Rachel. You know she can never be yours. She's your sister.'

Joe's face flushed. 'Don't you think I bloody know that. Why the hell do you think I married Miranda? I'm trying, Mam. I'm trying.'

I put my arms around him. 'I know you are love. We're here for you. And you're right, you should stay with Miranda and one day you'll find you're no longer pretending to be in love with her, you will be.'

'If you say so.'

'Let's have tea. Doesn't look like Rachel's coming.'

Chapter Twenty-One

Peggy

I finished feeding Ben his bottle and popped him in his beautiful pram to sleep. I'd longed for a Silver Cross when Joe and Kate were babies but we simply couldn't afford it. Apart from the gorgeous navy and white coach-built body, the suspension made it easy to push. Adam and I were older now so Ben had wanted for nothing.

'Are you ready?' I shouted to Adam.

'Just coming,' he answered as the doorbell rang, making it to the door before me.

'Who is it?' I called.

'You'd better come in,' I heard Adam say before entering the lounge with a policeman, and a woman around the same age as me.

'Oh my God. Has something happened to Kate? Or Joe?'

'No, they're fine.' Adam led me to the couch. 'Sit down, love. They want to ask you a few questions.' He turned to the officer and woman. 'Please, take a seat.'

'Thank you,' the policeman said. 'I'm Police Inspector Evans and this is Mrs Stepney, director of Woodhaerst Adoption Agency.'

I rushed up to the pram and lifted Ben out. What were they doing here? They couldn't have my baby. 'Who's sent you? You can't take my baby.'

Mrs Stepney rose from the chair and came over to me. 'We're not here to take your baby, Mrs Davies, but we do have some questions about an adoption situation you may know something about. Perhaps there's somewhere we can talk in private?'

'There's no need, I have no secrets from my husband. He knows all about the adoption and I'd like him to stay.'

'Very well. If you could sit back down, please, and I'll explain.' She stroked Ben's cheek and smiled. 'He's adorable. How old is he?'

'Three months.' I wandered back over to the sofa and sat closely to Adam, whilst cuddling Ben to my chest.

Mrs Stepney returned to the adjacent armchair. 'Firstly, may I ask you to confirm that you're Margaret Davies, nee Carter, who gave birth to a child at Woodhaerst Mother and Baby home on 19th June, 1953.'

I nodded. 'Yes, that's me.'

Adam took my hand. 'Why are you interested in a child my wife had adopted more than twenty-four years ago?'

The inspector coughed. 'If you don't mind answering some questions, Mrs Davies.' He took out a notebook and biro from his uniform pocket. 'A serious allegation has been made about a staff member at the home on the night you gave birth.'

'What's that got to do with my wife?' Adam squeezed my fingers.

The policeman ignored Adam again. 'May I just check your date of birth, Mrs Davies?'

'12th March 1936.' I squinted. 'What's this all about?'

'There was another young mother who gave birth to a daughter the same night as you,' the inspector continued. 'No other infants were born at the home on that date.'

'So?' I answered.

'An accusation has recently been made that on the night you gave birth to your daughter, a female attendant is said to have swapped your baby with another.'

'Swapped the babies?' Adam frowned. 'What are you saying?'

'We're not saying anything yet, Mr Davies.' Miss Stepney smiled. 'We're in the process of investigating the allegation.'

The inspector chewed on the end of his pen. 'This is rather delicate but, we have to ask, Mrs Davies, were you involved in this swap?'

'What? Involved in a baby swap. No, of course not.'

'So, you didn't suggest to the attendant at any point to switch the babies?'

Adam jumped up. 'What sort of bloody question is that? Why the hell would my wife do that?'

The inspector stared at me. 'Sit down please, Mr Davies, and let your wife answer the question.'

'Of course I didn't ask her to swap the babies. Like my husband says, why the hell would I?'

'We need to establish whether you had any part in it.'

'Look, Inspector Evans, there's no way I'd have asked for my baby to be swapped.'

'Our records show that the child was adopted?'

'That's right but that was my father's doing. I never wanted that. He dealt with everything. They wouldn't even let me see my baby.'

'Mrs Davies, do you remember who was present when you gave birth?' Mrs Stepney asked.

'Yes. A nurse, and the attendant who took my baby from the room.' I blinked my eyes to prevent tears. 'I begged her not to take my baby. To let me see her but the nurse ushered the attendant out.'

'It's all right, darling. Don't upset yourself.' Adam sat back down and put his arm around me. 'Look what you're doing to my wife. Now you've established she had nothing to do with a baby swap, can you bloody tell us what's going on?'

'What the inspector didn't mention,' Mrs Stepney said in a soft voice, 'is that the attendant who worked at the home, Ada James, also aunt to the other young teen who gave birth that night, admitted to her niece on her deathbed that she switched the babies.'

Adam shook his head. 'That doesn't make sense. Why would anyone do that? And why wait to reveal this until she's dying?'

'Apparently, she didn't want the secret to go to her grave. It seems the young mother's parents had promised Mrs James that she could bring up the infant as her own.' Mrs Stepney adjusted her spectacles. 'But things changed when the baby's father asked the young mother to marry him leaving Mrs James redundant regarding the child. Angry and distraught, she supposedly swapped the babies.'

'But I'm reunited with my adoptive daughter. Are you saying that she's not my child?'

'No, that's not what we're saying,' the inspector said. 'Nothing has been proven.' He flipped through the pages of his notebook. 'You and the other mother will need to have tests along with the two girls born at the home on 19th June 1953. Only then will we know whether there's any truth in what Ada James claimed.'

I squeezed my eyes shut. 'This is a nightmare. Should I phone Rachel?'

'No,' Mrs Stepney said, 'in fact we must ask you to please keep this information to yourselves until we have spoken to the adoptive parents. We have their address and shall be speaking to them and their daughter.'

'If you're in agreement we will need you to come into the station and have serological testing,' the inspector said.

'Serological testing,' Adam asked. 'What's that?'

'It will help us ascertain which of the girls is Mrs Davies' biological daughter?' Mrs Stepney smiled reassuringly.

'When?' I held Ben close to my chest.

'Someone from the station will be in touch with the time and venue.' The inspector rubbed the top of his lip. 'I must stress though, if it is found that there's no living criminal, there will be no crime to proceed with, therefore the police will have no further involvement.'

'That doesn't seem right,' Adam raised his voice, 'so if what you're saying is proven then surely someone must be accountable?'

'Yes, you're quite right, Mr Davies,' Mrs Stepney said, 'and if it's proven then I advise you to seek independent legal advice to take forward any civil claim you might want to make and to prepare any petition to a court for establishment of identity from a legal viewpoint.' She turned to me. 'And might I suggest counselling, Mrs Davies, again from an independent source.'

My stomach churned. What were they saying? That Rachel may not be mine. 'Counselling?'

'Yes. This is a lot to take in.' The woman from the adoption agency smiled.

'And who's going to pay for this counselling?' Adam frowned. 'If you hadn't noticed we're an ordinary working-class family. We don't have that sort of money.'

'Naturally, Mr Davies, the agency will pay,' Mrs Stepney said. 'I can arrange to send a list of independent counsellors and psychologists if you like.'

'Thank you,' Adam said, 'that would be very helpful.'

'I apologise for giving you both such a shock,' Mrs Stepney continued, 'but what with the seriousness of this allegation it has to be investigated.'

'Yes, yes of course.' I stood up. 'Thank you.'

Mrs Stepney looked towards the police officer. 'Inspector?'

The policeman popped the notebook and pen into his pocket. 'Yes, of course.' He rose from the armchair and joined the woman from the adoption agency.

I placed Ben in the pram before seeing them to the door.

Mrs Stepney touched my hand. 'We're very sorry to have to worry you like this. We'll be in touch shortly.'

After closing the door, overcome by nausea, I stumbled to the stairs. Adam was at my side. 'Come and sit down, love. I'll make you a cup of sweet tea.' He led me back to the lounge to the sofa as Ben cried.

'I'd best...' I flopped back down knowing that if I picked up Ben I was likely to drop him.

'He's fine for a minute. He may even go back to sleep. Now sit back while I get you that cuppa and then we'll try and digest this mess.'

Chapter Twenty-Two

Rachel

As I closed the front door, voices I didn't recognise travelled from the lounge. Standing at the doorway, I spotted a policeman and a woman on the couch drinking from Mum's best china.

'Is everything all right,' I asked.

'Yes.' Dad got up. 'Come on in. These people are here to ask us some questions about your adoption.'

'My adoption, why?'

'Sit yourself down, Rachel. I'll get you a cup of tea.' Mum poured a cup and passed it to me once I was settled in an armchair.

'Why are the police interested in my adoption?'

The woman adjusted her spectacles. 'Rachel, I'm Mrs Stepney, and I'm not from the police but the director of Woodhaerst Adoption Agency. Police Inspector Evans and I are investigating a serious claim of misconduct at the mother and baby home where you were born.'

'I don't understand.' I took a sip of the Earl Grey.

'All will become clear soon enough, Miss Webster,' the police inspector said, 'if you could just allow us to continue questioning your parents.'

'Right.' I slumped back in the chair.

'Now as I was saying, Mr and Mrs Webster,' the inspector continued, 'so you didn't witness any unusual behaviour from anyone in the home?'

'No,' Dad answered. 'I was only there a couple of times. Firstly, when they called me in just before the birth, and then a couple of days later to pick up the child.'

'How about you, Mrs Webster?'

'I never visited the home at all. My husband dealt with that side of things. Please can you tell us what this misconduct is you're investigating?'

The police inspector nodded to the woman from the adoption agency. She answered, 'An allegation has been made that on the night Rachel was born, two babies may have been switched.'

'Switched.' I put my hands to my face. 'You mean my mother, Peggy Davies, may not be my mother.'

'That is a possibility. But at this stage that's all...'

Dad interrupted the woman. 'Let me get this straight. You think that two babies may have been swapped, and our daughter may be one of those infants in question? May I ask where this allegation has come from? I mean it seems a little far-fetched and especially to surface now over twenty-four years after she was born.'

'It does seem rather absurd, I admit,' Mrs Stepney said, 'but this information has only recently come to light. There was an attendant at the home, Ada James. Did you meet her, Mr Webster?'

'Er, yes, I did. I remember her well. A kindly woman. Made a point of offering me tea and cake. Very chatty lady.'

The inspector took a notebook from his uniformed jacket. 'And did you by any chance ask Mrs James to exchange the child you were to adopt for another infant?'

'What sort of question is that to ask? Absolutely not. I mean, why would I? For what reason? My wife and I wanted a baby. We were delighted with the details we'd been given of the baby we were to adopt. Of course, I didn't suggest to this woman to swap the babies. And if I'm honest, I can't see Ada James having done such a thing. So why would you think she had?'

'I know this is a shock and these questions seem outrageous but it is an investigation so we do have to ask them,' the inspector said. 'However, the allegation has cropped up because Ada James confessed to her niece, who was the other young mother in question, on her deathbed, that she swapped the babies out of spite but didn't want to go to her grave without telling the truth.'

'What?' I spluttered.

'Let's just say,' Dad said, 'that Ada James did swap the children. Why would she do such a thing? You say out of spite but spite for what?'

Mrs Stepney coughed to clear her throat. 'Because the family had agreed that Mrs James could bring up the new baby as her own. Ada was widowed in the early days of her marriage, and had always longed for a child, so it was decided rather than the baby being adopted Ada would take her.'

'But,' interrupted the inspector, 'things didn't go to plan when the father of the infant stepped up and asked the mother to marry him in order to bring up the child together. So, Ada' – the inspector sipped his tea – 'supposedly swapped the infants as a form of revenge. Apparently, she felt guilty watching the girl grow up and said she couldn't die peacefully without telling her niece what she'd done.'

'However,' Mrs Stepney said, 'I must stress that at this stage this is just hearsay so nothing is proven. This is what we're investigating.'

'What happens next?' I couldn't believe what I was hearing. What did this mean? After waiting eighteen years to find Peggy, was she now to be lost to me? I'd be no further knowing my roots than I had been five years ago. This was an absolute nightmare. And what of Peggy. How was she taking this news?

'The other girl, her mother, the woman you know as your mother, and yourself,' Mrs Stepney said, 'will need to be tested to see whether there is any truth in these allegations.'

'However, no matter what the outcome,' interrupted the inspector, 'if it's found that there's no criminal alive then the police will take no further action.'

'What do you mean no further action?' Dad asked.

'Simply,' the inspector continued, 'that if there's no living criminal then there's no crime for the police to proceed with.'

Dad sat upright. 'No, I'm sorry, that can't be right. Someone must be liable for this mess-up, surely?'

'You're quite right, Mr Webster,' Mrs Stepney said, 'which is why I advise you to seek independent legal advice to take forward any civil claim you might want to make and to prepare any petition to a court for establishment of identity from a legal viewpoint. I also suggest counselling for Rachel and yourselves, from an independent source, to be paid for by the agency.'

'Thank you.' Dad relaxed back in his seat. 'Although, let's hope it doesn't come to that. Our daughter's been through enough trauma without her whole life falling apart again.'

Mrs Stepney smiled. 'I quite understand, Mr Webster.'

'Someone from the station will be in touch to advise Rachel where to go for testing and at what time.' The inspector closed his notebook and popped it into his pocket.

'Is there anything else?' Dad asked.

'No. I think that's all' – Mrs Stepney passed me her card – 'if you have any questions, please do not hesitate to contact me.'

'Thank you.' My hand shook as I took the card. What did all this mean?

Dad stood up. 'Then I'll see you out.'

I followed Dad and the visitors out to the hallway.

'Once again, I apologise for disturbing you and your family and thank you for your co-operation.' Mrs Stepney shook Dad's hand, and then mine.

Dad closed the door behind them and sighed. I gave him a hug.

'Hey, what's that for?'

'Oh Dad, what does all this mean? My life's falling to pieces again.' I wiped my eyes. 'Do you think there's any truth in it?'

He patted me on the back. 'Let's not worry too much at this stage, Rachel. The likelihood is that this Ada James wanted a last laugh with her niece and this was her revenge, and she never swapped the babies at birth at all.'

That sounded logical. I mean who in their right minds would swap two babies for no reason? But then what sane person would admit they'd done it if they hadn't? I had to see Peggy. My stomach churned.

Chapter Twenty-Three

Rachel

I tapped on the brass knocker and after a few moments Adam opened the front door. 'Rachel, come in. This is a nice surprise. Peg didn't mention you were coming.'

'She doesn't know. It's not a problem, is it?'

'No, no. Of course not. Peg,' he hollered upstairs. 'Rachel's here.'

I hovered at the entrance. 'Is she busy?'

'She's just feeding Ben and getting him ready for bed. You'd better come in.'

'Thanks.' I followed Adam into the lounge and took a seat on the sofa. 'Is Kate in?'

'No. She's out. To be honest, Rachel, Peg and I were hoping for an early night. It's been quite a day.' He sank into the armchair.

'I won't stay long.'

Peggy wandered into the lounge. 'We weren't expecting you. Is everything okay?'

'Yes. Well sort of. I wondered how you got on with the police.'

'Police?' Adam asked.

'Didn't you have a visit from the adoption agency and a policeman asking questions?'

'Oh, so you know.' Adam picked up a packet of Players from the coffee table. 'Want one?'

'No thanks. I gave up ages ago. And yes, I know.'

He lit up a cigarette and threw the packet back onto the table. 'Sorry, I wasn't being evasive but we were specifically told not to mention it to you. It's all been rather a shock.'

'For me too.' I glanced at Peggy. 'They said you may not be my mother.'

She bit her lip. 'There's a slight chance that may be the case but they need to complete the investigation. Adam thinks it's nonsense.'

I touched Peggy's hand. 'How do you feel if it's true?'

'Devastated, naturally. I'm sure you must feel the same.'

'Yes, yes of course. We've managed to build up a close relationship and I hope whatever happens, we can still be friends.'

'I suggest we don't think about it too much, Rachel,' Adam said, 'it could all be a false alarm.'

'But, Peggy, don't you think we should tell Joe.'

'No, not yet.'

'But if you're not my mother' – I fiddled with my fingers – 'that means he's not my brother. He has the right to know.'

'Now, Rachel' – Adam puffed on his cigarette – 'like I just said, the chances are that it will not be proven. No one is saying anything to Joe.'

'You can't stop me.'

Adam stubbed out his cigarette in the ashtray, got up and stood over me. 'I'm telling you now, Rachel, nothing is to be mentioned to Joe, or Kate for that matter, until the case has been concluded.'

'But it doesn't seem fair.'

'Joe's married anyway' – Adam rubbed his smooth chin – 'so I don't see how you think this will make any difference.'

'He's not happy though.'

'You don't know that. Just leave well alone.'

I turned to Peggy. 'Tell him.'

'Adam's right.'

I might've known she'd have agreed with him but I didn't want to leave things strained so I said, 'I wonder when the test appointments will come through.'

She blinked slowly. 'I've no idea.'

'Me neither. I wish they'd hurry up so we can find out.' I rose from the sofa. 'And I don't care what you say because once it's proven we're not related, Joe will come to me.'

'Look in there'– Adam turned me to the mirror – 'then look at Peggy. Then tell me you're not mother and daughter. You're the image of each other.'

'And what about Miranda? She looks like me so it doesn't mean a thing. Like Stu observed, it's the dark hair and oval face that do it.' I frowned at Peggy. 'Well, I hope you're not my mother and at least then I can have Joe.'

'Thanks, Rachel. After all this time I thought we'd come a long way.' She took a deep breath. 'But it seems I mean nothing to you. I've grown to love you as my daughter and if it is proven that you're not mine it will break my heart.'

'I'm sorry, I didn't mean to say that. I don't even know why I did. Of course, I don't hope you're not my mother, please, I'm sorry. I love you too, it's just... I don't know what came over me.'

'I think you should go' – Adam headed for the hallway – 'before one of us says something else we'll regret.'

'But, Peggy?'

She shook her head. 'Do as Adam says.' She followed him into the corridor.

'All right, I'll go' – I stepped out of the lounge – 'but first, Peggy, are we all right?'

'Just go, Rachel,' Adam said.

'But...'

'Go' – Adam opened the front door – 'my wife has had enough upset for one day. So, if you don't mind, I'd like you to leave.'

'Peggy?'

'Go, Rachel.' Peggy turned away from me.

'And remember,' Adam said, 'if any of this gets back to Joe, before Peg's ready, then you'll be banned from this house and from seeing any of the family. No matter how the case concludes.'

≺∻

I charged up to my bedroom and sobbed on the bed. Ashamed for the way I'd spoken to Peggy, I dabbed my eyes. I'd been so wrapped up with a happy ever after with Joe that I hadn't thought things through. If Peggy wasn't my mother, then I was no further forward knowing my roots than I'd been five years ago. And was I kidding myself that Joe would come running? Supposing he wanted to stay with Miranda. Where did that leave me? Adam was right. I should keep quiet as I didn't want to cut ties with Peggy and the family.

'Rachel?' Mum knocked on my door. 'Are you all right, dear?'

'Fine, thanks.' I blew my nose.

'May I come in.'

'Er, yes, all right.' I sat upright.

'Darling' – Mum took me into a hug – 'whatever is it?'

'Adam was horrid to me.'

Mum frowned. 'That doesn't sound like Adam. Why?'

'I wanted to tell Joe about this adoption mess up.' I sniffled. 'Adam said if I did, I wouldn't be allowed to see the family again.'

'I can understand they don't want Joe to know anything until we know the outcome but that seems a little strong to ban you from the household.'

'Mum' – I started sobbing again – 'I said some awful things to Peggy. I don't know what got into me. I said I hoped she wasn't my mother, but that's not what I hope at all.'

'There there, now.' Mum patted my back. 'Why don't you come downstairs and have a cup of tea?'

Mum thought a cup of Earl Grey would put everything right.

It seemed strange knocking on the door of 7 Springfield Road expecting Sandra to answer but now it was Linda and Stu's home.

Linda opened the door. 'Hello, you. What's up?'

I shrugged. 'Just need someone to talk to. Are you on your own?'

'Yeah. Stu's gone to his mam and dad's but he'll be back soon. Come and see what we've done with the place.'

I stepped into the hallway and admired the mirror tiles along one side of the wall, giving the impression the corridor was wider.

'What do you think?'

'Nice. But I wouldn't fancy cleaning all of those.'

'It'll be fine. Come into the kitchen.'

I glanced around. Tucked underneath a pine worktop was a Bendix automatic washing machine with white fitted cupboards either side and a larder fridge on the opposite side of the wall. Replacing the Formica table and chairs was a large octagonal smoked glass table with four wicker-seated chairs.

'This is nice.'

'Yes. We bought it from MFI in the sale.'

I'd heard of this furniture specialist but never been in the store. Linda and Stu were now set up in their new home while I was still living with my parents. In a way I'd gone backwards after returning from college. I should think of buying a flat. It was affordable now with my good wage. I made a mental note to book an appointment with the Building Society, where I had my savings, and see how much I could borrow. On the other hand, maybe I should wait and see the outcome of this investigation first, just in case Joe and I could set up house together.

Linda filled the kettle from the tap. 'Coffee?'

'Ta.'

'And then we'll go into the lounge and you can tell me what's troubling you.'

'Cheers.'

'Fancy a slice of cake? I made it myself.'

'Go on then. You're turning into a proper Stepford wife.'

'Oi.' She nudged me. 'I love baking and being married to the man I love. The only thing that will make things complete is once the kids come along. I want at least four.'

Linda had her life mapped out. I was happy for her but it just brought home how I had nothing apart from my career. 'Rather you than me.'

'Grab that tin, will you?'

I picked up the red and white patterned tin from next to the breadbin. 'This one?'

'Yeah.'

'Open it up and cut us each a slice.'

I removed the lid and took out a chocolate sandwich cake. 'This looks yummy. How big a slice would you like?'

'Sod the calories, give us a nice chunk each.' Linda poured water into the mugs and gave them a stir. 'I'll bring the coffees and you bring the cake.'

I cut two huge slices, put them on small porcelain plates with white serviettes, and followed Linda into the lounge. 'Wow. You didn't waste any time, did you?'

'You like?'

'It's gorgeous.' I put the plates down on a square smoked glass coffee table and took a seat on the chocolate brown velour sofa. The suite was the only thing that was the same. 'Wasn't this your mam's?'

'Yeah. She and Keith bought a new one so said we could have this.'

'That's good because it's so comfy.' I peered around the room. 'You've decorated? I didn't think it was that long ago that your mam had this place done?'

'We wanted to put our seal on it. Keith helped Stu with the wallpapering before they moved out and Mam and I did the paintwork.'

'But you kept to the same chocolate and cream décor?'

'Only because it went with the sofa.' She laughed. 'Anyway, never mind that, you wanted to talk. And we've not got long before Stu's back.'

I blew on the hot coffee to cool it down. 'What I tell you now has to be in utter confidence. You can't even tell Stu.'

'You can't expect me to keep things from my husband.'

'In this case I do. It's imperative that what I tell you doesn't get back to Joe. If it does then Peggy and Adam will be done with me.'

'This all sounds rather ominous. Just spit it out.'

'This is going to sound far-fetched.' I drummed my fingers on the arm of the sofa. 'I might not be Peggy's child.'

'What?' Linda spluttered. Using the serviette, she wiped cake crumbs from her mouth.

'Ludicrous, isn't it? But we've had the police and adoption agency around to ours, they've been to Peggy's too, and it seems that one of the staff at the mother and baby home where I was born may have swapped two babies. One of them being me.'

'That's awful.'

'Yes, I know. I'll be back to square one again not knowing where I came from.'

'But, Rach, imagine if Joe's not your brother. You can be together.'

'Joe's always been my one, you know that. I've tried to push it away but no fellow has ever come close to him. But I'm so mixed up because I love Peggy and if Joe isn't my brother, then she isn't my mother.' I sniffled.

'Look, Rach, it has to be nonsense. You're the image of Peggy. How can you not be her daughter?'

'But what about Miranda? She looks like me.'

'Not as much as you're like Peggy. And Joe. Like you said all those years ago after first finding out, you were pulled together because of your genes. What's changed?'

'A woman on her deathbed confessed to swapping the babies.'

'Sounds like a drama queen to me.' Linda picked up her cup and took a sip of coffee.

'But supposing she was telling the truth?'

'Supposing she was. What then?'

'I've got to go for blood tests. Will you come with me?'

'Sure, so long as you give me notice to get the time off work. I presume it'll be morning rather than evening?'

'I've no idea. I'm waiting for the police to get in touch. I'll let you know as soon as possible.'

She put down her mug and took my hand. 'What do you hope the tests will reveal?'

'I don't know. I don't want to be Joe's sister, but I do want to be Peggy's daughter.' I put my hands up to my eyes and sobbed. 'Supposing I can have Joe and find when it comes to it, we've outgrown each other and I'm just mixed up with this happy ever after.'

'I suppose you'll never know unless you try.'

'But people could get hurt for nothing. Like Miranda.'

'You'll just have to go with it.'

'And if I'm not Peggy's daughter then whose daughter am I?'

'Will you try and find out?'

'I'm not sure. I don't know whether I have the energy to go through more. Mind you if I find out Mike's not my father then that won't be any real loss. And just suppose I decide that I'd like to meet these real parents, then who's to say they want to meet me? And who's this other girl? What's she like? Will she look like Peggy too?' I cried some more.

'Hey.' Linda put her arm around me and let me cry into her chest. 'One thing at a time. First of all get the test and we'll go from there.'

Chapter Twenty-Four

Rachel

'Hello.' I smiled at the receptionist. 'Rachel Webster. I've an appointment for some blood tests.'

The woman leaned forward and checked the diary. 'Ah, yes.' She looked up. 'Take a seat. Miss Styles is running a little late but will be with you as soon as she can.'

'Oh, how late? Only I've had to nip out from work.'

'As soon as she can. Take a seat, please.' She pushed her large-framed specs up against the bridge of her nose.

'Right. Thanks.' Well, she was a lot of help. I slumped into a blue chair and slung my coat over another to reserve for Linda. Where the hell was she? She'd promised to be here with me. I laid my hands into my lap trying to stop them from shaking. What was I so nervous about? The actual test? The results? Or maybe both? This would define whether Joe and me could be more than siblings, but at the same time, potentially destroy my relationship with Peggy. Whichever way it went it was going to cause pain.

There was no sign of Peggy, or the other mother and daughter for that matter. I picked up a *Woman's Companion* from the pile of publications on the table and flicked through. This magazine had never really grabbed me. What did Peggy see in it? I peered up at the sound of high heels echoing across the room.

'Sorry.' Linda caught her breath. 'Have you been in yet?'

'No. The receptionist said they're running late. What happened?'

'You wouldn't believe it but the minute I was about to leave we had a flurry of customers. I couldn't leave Tasha on her own like that. Anyway' – she slapped my arm – 'I'm here now and that's the main thing.' She giggled. 'Maybe it'll be your turn to wait with me soon, only in the doctor's surgery instead, to see if I'm, you know?'

'Do you think you are?'

'Too early to know yet but if I'm not it won't be for the want of trying, if you know what I mean?' She laughed again.

'Rachel Webster.' A blonde woman with her hair up and wearing a white doctor's coat came out of a side room.

'I'll leave my coat and bag here,' I said to Linda. 'See you in a min.'

She squeezed my fingers. 'Good luck.'

'Thanks.' But what was she wishing me luck for? Luck that Peggy was my mother or luck that she wasn't. Even I didn't know which was the right kind of luck. I followed the woman into the room.

'Take a seat.'

'Thanks.' I took the chair next to her desk.

'Can I just check your full name and date of birth?'

'Rachel Julie Webster. 19th June 1953.'

'And you're here for serological testing.'

'Yep. Whatever that is.'

'I thought it was explained to you.'

'Well, I know it's to prove whether Peggy's my mother or not. I thought she'd be here. Has she been in?'

'I'm sorry but I'm not at liberty to discuss the case. Roll up your sleeve please.'

I slipped off my cardigan and unbuttoned the blouse cuff.

'Just a scratch.' She filled a syringe with my blood and divided it into three small vials.

'What about the other two? Have they been in yet?'

'Like I said, I'm not at liberty to discuss. You can roll your sleeve down now.'

'Thanks.' I fastened my blouse button. 'How long do you think it will take for the results?'

'Again, I'm afraid I can't give you an answer.' She smiled. 'Don't worry, Miss Webster, I'm sure someone from the adoption agency will be in touch with you as soon as the case has been concluded.'

'Right. Thanks then.' I strode back out to the waiting room.

'All done?' Linda asked.

I nodded. 'Got time for a quick coffee before going back?'

'Sure.'

'Has Peggy been for her test yet?' Linda took a sip of hot chocolate.

'I've no idea and that police nurse, doctor, whatever she is, wouldn't tell me anything, and I haven't seen Peggy since we heard about the case. That was over two weeks ago. She's not even contacted me.'

'Have you contacted her?'

'No. I was waiting for her to get in touch but she hasn't. Normally she'd suggest meeting up in my lunchtime and I'd get to push Ben around the park. His pram's gorgeous, Lind. I'll buy one for you when you're pregnant. That is, as long as you make me Godmother.'

'It's a deal. How about Joe? Seen him?'

I shook my head. 'No, I'm too nervous in case I let anything slip. And then…'

'But he'll be suspicious if you suddenly stop speaking to him. Won't he?'

'Maybe.' I stirred my coffee not really wanting it as I felt too sick. 'That technician wasn't exactly friendly. She wouldn't tell me anything.'

'She's probably not allowed. You ask your Jen. I bet they have some kind of privacy code for doctors and nurses.'

'I suppose so.'

'How's work?'

'Okay. I've got an article to type up when I get back. Oh by the way, I had a postcard from Phil this morning.'

'Your post must come early.'

'It does.'

'What did he say?'

'That everything's going well and if I fancy a visit to Paris, he and his sister can put me up.'

'Will you go?'

'Maybe, although I don't want to give him the wrong idea.'

Linda glanced at her watch. 'Really sorry, Rach, but I'd best be getting back. Tasha will be wanting to go for lunch.'

'It's all right. I need to get back anyway.'

Chapter Twenty-Five

Peggy

Adam pushed open the lounge door. 'Hey, what's up?' He perched on the sofa and put his arm around me.

'Nothing.' I sobbed.

'Well, there's something. And where's your Sheila?'

'She's taken Ben for a walk around the park as he wouldn't settle.'

'Did you get your test done?'

I shook my head.

'Why not? Was Sheila late?'

'Nope.' I sniffled. 'We went to the centre but when it came to it, I couldn't go through with it.'

Adam took a clean handkerchief from his pocket and wiped my eyes. 'Let's go and make some tea and you can tell me all about it.'

I followed him out of the lounge into the kitchen where he flicked the kettle switch and added a teabag into each of two mugs. He led me to a seat at the dining table and sat down next to me. 'So why couldn't you have the test? It's not like you're nervous of needles. What was the problem?'

'I couldn't face the idea of finding out Rachel wasn't mine.'

'We'll cope with that, if and when.' He got up to the boiling kettle and poured water into the mugs, gave them a stir, spooned the teabags on to a saucer, and brought over the drinks. 'Here. Drink this.'

'But, Adam, I waited over eighteen years to find Rachel and when she came into our lives, I know it wasn't always easy...'

'That's putting it mildly, but we coped. Didn't we?'

'Yes, but...'

'If Rachel's not yours, wouldn't you like to meet your real daughter?'

I nodded. 'But I can't put you through that again. It wouldn't be fair. It almost broke us last time.'

Adam took my hand. 'This time we'll do it properly. None of this where you go off on daytrips with Mike, none of the cloak and dagger with the kids. Right from the beginning we'll all meet her together.'

'Really?' I smiled sensing a glimmer of hope.

'Yes, really. But hey, the test could show that Rachel is indeed yours. And my odds are on that. After all, can you really imagine a woman swapping two newborn babies?'

'It does seem madness.'

'Can someone give me a hand?' Sheila called from the front door.

I hurried into the hallway and Adam followed me.

'Hi, Sheila' – he signalled to the pram –'just leave it there and I'll sort it.'

'Thanks.' She flicked the brake on with her foot and swapped places with Adam in the hallway. He stepped outside, released the brake on the pram and pulled it up the step into the corridor and closed the front door quietly.

I peeped into the pram. 'He's asleep.'

'Yes,' Sheila answered, 'took him ages. I think he must be picking up on your unease.'

'You're probably right,' Adam said. 'Kettle's just boiled if you fancy a cuppa. We'll leave Ben in the hallway to sleep.'

'You're looking a lot brighter,' Sheila said to me as we headed into the kitchen.

'Yes. Adam and I had a good chat. I'm going to book another appointment.'

'Why don't you give them a ring now?' Adam poured boiling water over a teabag. 'Milk and sugar, Sheila?'

'Just milk, thanks.'

'Okay, I will.' I went into the hallway and dialled the number. 'Thank you.' I put the receiver down and returned to the kitchen. 'I've managed to book for the day after tomorrow. Are you free, Sheila?'

'Sure. Anything to spend a bit more time with adorable Ben. You're so lucky, Peg. Although...'

'What? Are you?'

She crossed her fingers. 'Malc's over the moon. We've got an appointment next week.'

'That's brilliant news, Sheila.' Adam put a mug down on the table. 'Sit down and have your tea.'

Chapter Twenty-Six

Rachel

I peered through the passenger car window at the women lurking around Le Gare du Nord train station. 'Look at them in their short skirts, showing off stockings and suspenders like St Trinian's.' I chuckled. 'Is there a special event on today?'

Phil glanced in the rear-view mirror. 'I hate to break this to you, Rachel, but they're not dressed up as St Trinian's.'

'What do you mean?'

Jan laughed. 'They're prostitutes.'

'But it's mid-afternoon?'

'Welcome to Paris, Rachel.' Phil turned right.

Jan chortled. 'You'll get used to it.'

Embarrassed and wanting to change the subject, I asked, 'How do you find driving on the right-hand side of the road?'

Phil moved into a lower gear as he slowed the vehicle down. 'A bit weird at first but after a couple of weeks it was okay.'

'What make is this car? Must be awfully strange having the gear lever sticking out from there.' I pointed to the dashboard.

'I rather like it. It's a Citroën 2CV, sometimes known as an upside-down pram.' Phil turned left into a cobbled street and pulled up outside a large corner building with black wrought iron window boxes. 'We're here.'

'Cool. You live here? It looks expensive.'

'Comes as part of the job. We're up on the third floor with no lift I'm afraid. Hope you're okay with stairs,' he said as we got out of the car.

'Sure. So long as you carry my suitcase.' I laughed.

'Of course.' Phil lifted my heavy case from the boot, proceeded into the entrance of the building and climbed the stairs with Jan and me behind him. On the third floor, he took a right, walked for a few yards and stopped outside a mahogany door with a number '21' brass plate. He put the suitcase down and stretched out his arm. 'Bloody hell, Rachel, what have you got in there? Bricks?'

'Nope. Just a few bits and bods of clothing. Oh, and one or two books.'

'Hmm. How many books?' Phil took the key from his pocket, unlocked the apartment and opened the door. 'Welcome to twenty-one Rue de Feu.'

I stepped into a bright hallway that had light wooden flooring. 'It's stunning.'

'Through here is the lounge.' Phil folded back two double white doors; the wooden flooring continued into the lounge.

I peered up at the decorative cornices on the ceiling. 'Wow. This is superb.' Magnolia painted walls gave the room a spacious feel. The centrepiece of the room was a large saucer-shaped marble table positioned on a plain emerald rug with a black and white striped border. Cream shelves, filled with books, fitted in arched alcoves either side of the open fire. I warmed my hands on the glowing embers.

'Are you cold?' Phil asked. 'I'll stoke it up.' He added a few lumps of coal from the brass scuttle and gave the cinders a poke. 'It won't take long to catch.'

'I've never seen a coffee table like that before.'

'Neither had we. Very avant-garde. The apartment came fully furnished.'

The light fitting dangling from the ceiling reminded me of a nineteen-sixties clothes airer except it was much smaller and round-shaped. 'I'll be able to write an article about the décor of this interior, never mind anything else,' I said admiring the Picasso prints in large black frames on the walls.

'Glad you approve. I'll give you a tour throughout while Jan makes us tea.'

I followed Phil into what must've been the dining room with its long onyx rectangular table with eight sturdy plastic chairs. On the facing wall, cream drawer units stood under numerous mounted prints. Some landscaped, some still life, and one a large portrait of a woman. 'Are these yours and Jan's?' I asked.

'Yes. You like?'

'I do. Is that one of yours?' I pointed to the picture of an attractive young woman with auburn curls falling across her bare breasts.

'It is.'

'Who's the girl?'

'Just a model. You're not jealous, are you? I can paint you, if you like?'

'I don't think I'd make a very good model.'

Facing me, Phil put his hands on my shoulders. 'I think you'd be perfect.' He moved his face closer to mine and kissed me on the lips. 'It's good to see you again.'

'You too. But we're just friends, right?'

'Yes, but that doesn't mean we can't be close friends.'

Butterflies fluttered in my stomach. 'No strings?'

'No strings.'

I put my arms around his neck and kissed him back making me feel warm inside.

'Well, you two didn't waste any time,' Jan said. 'Tea's in the lounge.'

I sensed myself burning up. 'We were just saying hi.'

Phil took my hand as we strolled along the cobbles. The weather was mild for the third week in November. After ambling up a few roads we stopped outside le Duc d'Orange. Its grubby walls and dark wooden window frames did nothing to excite me.

Jan must've seen my face because she said, 'Don't worry, it's much nicer inside. The food's good too.'

'Pleased to hear it.' I followed Phil and Jan through the door.

'Monsieur et Mademoiselle Jordan.' The maître d' greeted us. 'Welcome. And who is this?'

'Bonjour, Louis,' Phil said, 'this is Rachel Webster. Rachel's our friend from back in North Wales, and she's a journalist.'

'How do you do?' The waiter smiled.

'I'm well, merci. You speak very good English.'

'Mais oui. Back in the sixties England was my home for a while.'

'Oh really?'

'Mon père married an English woman not long after ma mère died.'

I touched his hand. 'I'm so sorry.'

Louis shrugged. 'It was a while ago now but Paris was where my heart was so I returned and opened this place. I hope you enjoy. S'il vous plaît.' He gestured us to follow him.

I gazed around the restaurant walls at pictures of peacocks, and women dancers, set in alternate wooded panels. Stunning golden arched windows reached up to a glass roof. The interior was much bigger, and posher, than outside.

'S'il vous plaît.' The maître d' pulled a maroon velour chair out from a small round table.

'Merci,' I said sitting down finding the curvy back comfy.

Phil and Jan took a seat either side of me and Louis handed each of us a menu. 'Someone will come and take your order shortly.'

'What are you having?' I asked the others as the menu to me read gobbledygook.

Phil perused the choices. 'I suggest we have steak, frites and petits pois. How does that work for you, Rachel?'

'Sure. I think.' I looked at Jan.

'In case you hadn't realised,' she said, 'he's talking about horse steak.'

'Ugh. No thanks. I don't fancy that.'

'It's tasty.' Phil grinned.

'Is that what you're having, Jan?'

'No way. I'm having salmon en papillote.'

'That sounds better. I like salmon. I'll have that too.'

The waiter came to the table. Phil ordered our meal along with a bottle of house red. Once the waiter had turned to a party behind us, Phil said, 'Tomorrow we'll go to the art studio and you can learn about watercolours.'

'And we must take you to the Orangerie while you're here,' Jan said. 'They do the best pastries, croissants and baguettes. You'll simply love them.'

'Sounds good,' I said as Louis, our waiter, returned with the wine.

He poured a drop of red into Phil's glass. 'Monsieur?'

Phil sniffed it, took a sip and let it circle in his mouth. 'Mmm. Merci.'

The waiter filled mine and Jan's glasses before filling Phil's.

'Merci, Louis,' I said.

'Your meal will be here shortly,' he said before moving towards the door to greet more customers.

'He speaks good English too,' I said.

'Yes, all the staff in here do. One of the main reasons we chose here to eat this evening was because you don't speak French.' Phil sipped his drink. 'Normally I'd have suggested a Bordeaux for wine but the grapes have suffered due to the awful weather we've had.' He took another sip. 'But this is nice enough. Ah look, here comes our meal.'

'Mademoiselle.' A waitress placed a plate in front of me. It looked delicious. Once Phil and Jan had their meals too, I took a bite of the salmon. It was really tender and the asparagus was delectable. 'A good choice,' I said to Jan. 'And how's your horsemeat, Phil?'

'It's wonderful. You don't know what you're missing. Want to try a bit?'

'No thanks' – I screwed up my nose – 'I can't think of anything worse.'

'Suit yourself.'

⇜

Back in the apartment Jan had gone to bed and Phil put an LP on the music centre. 'I remembered you loved Fleetwood Mac.'

The track played 'Rumours'. I smiled. 'You remembered well.'

Phil snuggled up to me on the green draylon sofa. I moved my face closer to his until our lips touched. My heart pace quickened. I'd forgotten how he could make me feel, but was this right? I didn't want to give him the wrong idea. 'No strings?' I repeated.

'No strings.' He put his tongue into my mouth and I returned his kiss and when he brushed his hand against my breast, I let it stay. 'I've missed you,' he said.

'I've missed you too. But there's something I think I should mention.'

'Can it wait?'

'Actually, no.' I sat upright and distanced myself on the sofa. 'I need to tell you now.'

The album track burst into life with 'I don't want to know'. Phil laughed.

'But you do need to know.' I chuckled.

'Go on then, hit me with what's so important that you have to interrupt what we were doing.'

'Okay. Before I came away, I discovered Joe and I may not be siblings after all.' I picked up my glass from the table and took a sip of wine.

'How come?'

'Seems there could have been some kind of mix-up at the mother and baby home where I was born. I've had blood tests and by the time I return home the results should be in.'

'I see.' He frowned.

'It's the truth.'

'If you say so.'

'No, seriously. We had the police and adoption agency around. But you see what this means?'

'Go on, you're obviously itching to tell me.'

'Don't be like that. It means if Joe and I aren't siblings we can be together.'

'But Joe's married and his wife's having a baby so how can you possibly make it work?'

'She's not pregnant. Never was, it seems. Joe doesn't know anything about the possible mix-up yet as Peggy and Adam wouldn't let me tell him, but once the truth's out...'

'You must be devastated at the thought of Peggy not being your mother?'

'I was at first but then I started to think if she wasn't my mother then Joe wasn't my brother and we could be together.'

He frowned again.

'You think I'm a bitch, don't you?'

'I never said that.'

'No but your face did. And you're right, I think I am too but I can't help my heart.'

'And if it falls the other way?'

'What do you mean?' I asked as 'Dreams' kicked in on the record player.

'What happens if he is your brother? Do you think there could be a you and me? You could come here once every couple of months and I'd return to Woodhaerst for visits. It's doable and my year here would be up before we knew it.'

'Maybe, but I can't think about that now. I don't want to hurt you, Phil, so if this is too much, please say so now.'

Phil took my glass and placed it on the table alongside his. 'Like I said, no strings.' He moved closer and I let him kiss me fuller but when his kisses became deeper and more demanding I pushed him away. I wasn't ready to lose my virginity quite yet.

We stopped at a stone building with dark blue window frames and a psychedelic front entrance. 'This is it.' Phil beamed as he unlocked the heavy door and a woody aroma escaped.

'It certainly smells like an art studio.' I said, as Jan and I followed him in.

Unframed portraits, landscaped paintings, and still life pictures, in oils and acrylic, leaned against the walls. Shelves were stacked with jars, paintbrushes and paint. It appeared cluttered unlike the immaculate venue back in Woodhaerst.

'Quite a difference to your other place,' I said.

'Don't forget this is a teaching studio.' Jan took a couple of jars and brushes down from the shelf. 'The gallery was for exhibiting. We do have an exhibition room here too.'

'Right,' I answered feeling rather stupid.

'In here' – Jan opened a door – 'this is where we'll paint today.'

I followed her into a well-lit room with half a dozen trestle tables and chairs.

'And through here' – she walked through an arch – 'is where we teach acrylics, chalks and charcoal. We tend not to teach much in the way of oils.'

I peeped my head into a smaller room with wooden easels. An ashy odour of charcoal dust made me cough. 'So, we don't use an easel for watercolours?'

She smiled. 'No. That definitely wouldn't work for a beginner and you'll see why once we get started. What time does Alan land?' Alan was flying in to take photos for my article.

I glanced at my watch. 'Half past ten. He was getting a cab so should be with us soon.'

'Where did you say he's staying?'

'You may want to sit down. He's staying at Le Meurice. But he's coming here first.'

Phil strode in. 'Bloody hell. Is he made of dough?'

'Nope. He's billing the newspaper. Said he's only here overnight and needs to know he'll get a good sleep.'

There was a bang on the door. 'That's probably him now,' Phil said. 'I'll let him in.'

'Grab a couple of pieces of paper from over there' – Jan pointed – 'and bring the tape.'

I did as she instructed. 'What now?'

She passed me an old shirt. 'Here, put this on.'

I slipped the paint-stained top over my clothes.

'Now' – she tapped a table – 'you'll be working here and I'll be next to you.'

I perched on the tarnished wooden chair. Jan placed a piece of paper in front of me and another for herself. 'The first thing when painting with watercolours is to prep the paper. And we do that like this.' She dipped a paintbrush into the water and smeared it over the paper. 'This is called *stretching*.' Afterwards she taped it down using the masking tape. 'Now you have a go.'

'Bonjour.' Alan ambled into the room. He greeted me *la bise* like the French did.

'How was your flight?' I asked.

'Good but I'd love a cuppa though if someone's making one.'

'Jan's teaching so I'll sort you out, mate.' Phil patted Alan on the arm. 'You're just in time as Rachel's about to prep her paper. Anyone else want a cuppa?'

Jan and I shook our heads.

'Did you want to take shots from now?' Jan asked.

'Can do. Give me a minute to set the camera up.'

'Sure. Tell you what,' Jan said, 'why don't we take a breather before you start? Give you a chance to recover a bit.'

'A woman after my own heart.' Alan beamed. 'I don't suppose you've got any cake or cookies to go with that tea? Had to miss brekkie this morning to catch the flight.'

'Follow me. I'll see what I can dig up.' Jan led the way to a large kitchen where Phil was drawing water from the tap into a large aluminium kettle. 'We've decided to have a cuppa first. Poor Alan needs a bit of a break before starting work.' Jan rummaged through some cupboards, took out a biscuit tin and opened it up. 'Caramel or shortbread?'

'Shortbread, cheers.' Alan selected a seat by the small table.

'Good idea.' Phil lifted four brown mugs hanging on hooks from a shelf. 'Sure you don't want a cuppa, Rachel?'

'Go on then,' I said.

'Help yourself.' Jan placed a wooden salad bowl onto the table.

'Cheers.' Using the tongs, I served myself a couple of lettuce leaves, cherry tomatoes and a few slices of cucumber, setting them next to the large portion of quiche, potato salad and coleslaw on my plate. Did you make this?' I pointed to the cheese and onion flan.

'Nope. I did.' Phil grinned. 'You didn't know I was a good cook, did you?'

'I'd better taste it first before answering.' I chuckled.

'Shame Alan didn't fancy joining us for dinner.' Phil poured three glasses of white wine into goblets and passed one to each of us.

'Can you blame him when he could eat at Le Meurice?'

'Suppose not. You pleased with the way the shoot went?' Jan put a forkful of potato salad to her mouth.

'Yes, I think it went well. I loved doing the painting.'

'You did brilliantly,' she said. 'You weren't afraid to mix colours to create the shade you wanted, and I loved your stormy skies and dark muted greens.'

'Shame you're not teaching in Woodhaerst as I'd definitely join.'

'Don't forget we're only contracted here for a year. We'll be back home in less than ten months and I'll most likely continue to teach. The time will fly. You can take your painting back with you.'

'Thanks. What's happening tomorrow?'

'Well, I have a class but I believe Phil would like to take you for a tour around Paris and maybe a trip up the Eiffel Tower.'

'That sounds brilliant although maybe I'll just check the Eiffel Tower out from the ground as I don't like heights.'

Phil touched my hand. 'Well, I never. I had no idea. It seems, Miss Webster, that there's still a lot I have to learn about you.'

'Probably is.' I took a final bite of the quiche. 'That was delicious, Phil. Seems we don't know each other as well as we thought.

I'd just placed my knife and fork in the finished position when Jan said, 'You know what guys, I think I'll hit the hay. I've got a bit of a migraine.'

'Oh no, I'm sorry to hear that,' I said. 'Do you have anything for it?'

'Yeah. Don't worry. I'll get some painkillers and go to bed. I may be gone before you wake up so, I'll see you tomorrow night.'

'Night then. Hope you feel better soon.'

'Night, sis. Get a good night's rest.' Phil beamed at me once she'd gone. 'Fancy picking up our wine and sitting by the fire?'

'All right. But what about the dishes?'

'We'll leave them in the sink. I'll get up early and do them in the morning.'

'If, you're sure.'

'I am.'

I grabbed my glass of wine and headed for the lounge. The candlelit lighting, vibrant flames from the fire, and the vanilla fragrance incense sticks, were not only romantic but inviting. Moments later, Phil followed me in, took my glass and put it on the coffee table. 'Now, Miss Webster...' He put his arms around me, kissed my neck and moved his lips up to mine. 'I've been waiting to do that all day.'

'Nice.'

'Only nice?' He guided me over to the sofa and we flopped down laughing. 'It's great having you here. Did you enjoy your class today?'

'I did. Jan's an excellent teacher.'

'She was taught by the best. What about the singer from that group. Have you been tempted to go out with him again?'

'Steve. Gawd no. I've not been out with anyone since you left.'

'Now why is that? Could it be... Anyway, that's enough talk.' He held my face in his hands and kissed me.

The days whizzed by and in the morning I would be going home. My case packed for my flight, I sat down at the desk with a notebook and pen to jot down recollections to type up when back at work. Phil and Jan had been great tour guides. They'd taken me round The Musée de l' Orangerie where we stopped for refreshments. Jan loved the baguettes and pastries so much she bought half a dozen croissants for next day's breakfast. The Louvre was magnificent with its splendid baroque style palace and wonderful statues in the courtyard. After exploring the art collections we had a picnic by the Seine. Next to the river was Jardin des Tuileries where we grabbed a coffee in one of the cafés. Jan tried tempting me up Mont Martre but with the 130-metre climb, and my fear of heights, I knew I couldn't do it, even though a spectacular view of Paris from the Sacre Couer was being dangled as bait.

A couple of days ago we'd explored the Pompidou Centre which was not only a library but an impressive modern art gallery. The architecture of this futuristic building was amazing although I did think it looked a little like scaffolding with its rectangular frame made of steel and glass. Bold colours of blue, red, yellow and green brightened its facades and outlined the structure. Neither Phil or Jan could persuade me to go up the escalator, known as *the caterpillar*, that snaked up the outside of the building. The thought of it gave me shivers. Later at Le Clipper restaurant we'd enjoyed a big bowl of sliced braised onions in sherry gravy topped with a thick baguette slab smothered in melted gruyere.

The day before yesterday Phil had driven us to nearby Pigalle. Here we'd peeped in sex shop windows giggling, and strolled past glamorous bars, and yesterday I'd stood under the Eiffel Tower and thought how it resembled lace. Part of me longed to go up this iconic building but my racing heart had other ideas. It had been quite a fortnight. I'd miss walking past the Eiffel Tower and Arc de Triomphe on our daily outings. Now it was time to go home, yet part of me wanted to stay. And then there was earlier this evening. I put down my pen.

Phil and I had stood on the bridge overlooking the Seine, admiring the magical view in the moonlight. The sharp coniferous scent reminded me of a cool mountain stream. Phil took my hand as we trudged onto the Bateaux-Mouches cruise boat.

'Outside, or inside in the warmth?' he'd asked.

'Let's stay on deck. You can keep me warm.' I laughed, pulling my knitted scarf closer to my neck.

The boat cruised past the Eiffel Tower, and when we passed Notre Dame, I couldn't get over the stunning rose window. Phil had tightened his arms around my waist to protect me from the cold wind, and kissed me on the lips.

I closed my eyes. He was a fabulous kisser and it had been brilliant spending time with him, but while there was even the slightest hope that Joe could be mine, I wouldn't allow myself to contemplate anything other than Phil and I being just good friends.

I closed my notebook as Phil came up behind me. 'How you doing?' he asked.

'Just about there. Think that's enough work for tonight. I've got enough down to remind myself of everything we did. Hopefully Alan got shots of all the sights you briefed him on, and I'll be able to marry up his pictures with my article. Thank you, Phil, for everything.' I stood up and kissed him.

He kissed me back, holding me close. Twenty-four and still a virgin, I wondered whether I should give myself to him tonight. Who better for my first time than gentle Phil? But suppose I broke his heart; although he'd repeatedly said *no strings*, did he mean it? I kissed him hard with passion, our breathing becoming heavy, and I guided him into my bedroom.

'Are you sure?'

'Yes.'

After undressing we fell into bed. The warmth of lying next to him naked excited me. He kissed me all over. I was in Heaven until he jolted me when whispering, 'I love you so much.'

I pushed him away, and sat upright. 'Phil, you said no strings.'

He tried pulling me back down. 'I'm sorry, I didn't mean to say it. It just slipped out. What with you seducing me, I was overcome by it all.'

'But, darling, don't you see, we can't go any further. Not now that I know you feel this way. Maybe if it turns out that Joe is my brother then *yes* we can give it a go, but would you really want to be second best?'

'I love you, Rach, and I'll take whatever's on offer.'

'I'm sorry, Phil. I can't.' I slid off the bed and grabbed my clothes.

Chapter Twenty-Seven

Rachel

'Welcome back, my girl.' Betty hugged me when I entered the back office of The Echo. 'How did it go?'

'Never mind me. How are you? Are you feeling any better?'

She peered up at the clock. 'Ten minutes before we open. Let's grab a quick cuppa.'

'Sure.' I picked up the stainless-steel kettle. 'Ooh. About time we upgraded to an electric one.' After flicking the switch, I pulled Betty down to a chair and sat next to her. 'Tell me.'

'I'm good. The doc prescribed me HRT and now I feel right as rain.'

'That's brilliant news.' She did look well. Her eyes appeared bright and she even had a bit of pink in her cheeks. 'So, you won't be retiring?'

'Not on your nellie. Now, girlie, tell me about Paris and that hunk of yours.'

I chuckled. 'He's not mine. We're just friends. We broke up before he went out there, remember?' I stood up and took two mugs from the shelf and stuck a teabag in each of them.

'Send him over to me. I wouldn't say no.' She chuckled.

'Actually, he was lovely. Told me he loved me.'

Betty wiggled her finger. 'Do I hear wedding bells?'

'Alas, no. He excites me and I adore being in his company but I don't love him. My heart belongs to another.'

She frowned. 'Who? You've never mentioned anyone else.'

I poured the boiling water into the mugs and added a dash of milk. 'Hopefully I'll have something to tell you soon. I've got a phone call to make and then I'll know whether I can have this guy or not.'

'He's not married, is he? Don't go getting yourself mixed up in an affair, my girl. That will end in tears. Mark my words.'

'It's complicated, Betty, but I promise to reveal all once I know more, whether it goes my way or not.' I picked up my mug. 'Right now, I'd best get upstairs before John has my guts for garters. I've an article to get out.'

She squeezed my hand. 'Take care, pet, please.'

John came in with two white mugs as I put the phone receiver down.

'You finished?' He placed a coffee in front of me.

'Yep, you want to check it over?'

'Absolutely. I've got a good feeling about this one.'

I stacked the pieces of paper and passed them to him. 'And then there's the photos that Alan took. Have you seen them?'

'Yes. Alan has the piccies ready. You won't be disappointed.'

'Did you know that he booked himself into Le Meurice?'

'I did hear that, yes. He and the governor have a special arrangement, if you know what I mean, nudge nudge, wink wink, but you didn't hear that from me.'

'Really? Are you saying what I think you are?'

'Depends on what you think I'm saying?' He sipped his drink.

I wasn't going to say it out loud in case I was reading him incorrectly and it looked like John didn't want to commit to anything either. Better to leave it alone. Whoever they saw in their own time was none of my business. Seemed a bit unfair though that I didn't get offered any expenses. Just the two weeks paid leave on the condition that I provided a story. Still at least that meant my holiday allowance was still intact.

John scanned the papers, nodding his head as he read through my story. 'This is perfect, Rachel. The girl has done good.'

I smiled. 'Thank you.'

'Play your cards right and we may be able to send you over to other places in Europe.'

'Really?'

He shrugged. 'You never know. Let's see how many newspapers this sells. In fact' – he passed me back my article – 'I've been speaking to Mr Strange about you having a weekly column of your own where you can let our readers know what you've been up to.'

'Pardon?' I glared at him.

'I didn't mean in your private life but your day as a journalist. Shall we say a Tuesday feature? What do you think?'

'Sounds interesting.' I looked at my watch. 'Do you mind if I rush off now as I have an appointment?'

'Oh, I didn't see anything in the diary. Who's this with?'

'This one's personal. I'll have it as my lunch break but I might be a little late back. Will that be okay?' I held his gaze. 'It's important.'

'Go on, of course you can. You're a good worker, Rachel, and in every employment, there needs to be a bit of give and take. We'll see you once you get back. And in the meantime, I'll get your story off to Press.'

'Thanks, John.'

I hurried downstairs and was just going out of the door when Mel grabbed me.

'Hello, stranger. No time to say hi?'

'Sorry, Mel. I'll catch you once I get back. I'm running late.'

I got out of the car and hesitated before pushing open the glass entrance to the adoption agency. Once inside, there was a wooden door on the left, and straight ahead, a sign pointing to *Reception* via a flight of stairs. I plodded upstairs and pushed open another door.

'Good afternoon,' the curvy woman on the desk said.

'Hi. I'm here to see the director, Mrs Stepney. She's expecting me.'

'Name?'

'Rachel Webster.'

The receptionist picked up the receiver and dialled a number. 'Rachel Webster's here.' She returned the receiver to its cradle. 'Take a seat. Mrs Stepney will be with you in a few minutes.'

I dropped on to one of the red upholstered chairs opposite, hoping she wasn't going to be too long. My legs shook so I pressed my knees together to try to still them. A door slammed and I gazed up at the woman who'd visited our home.

'Miss Webster. Thank you for coming in.' She glanced around. 'Where are your parents?'

'It's just me. I was at work so came straight from there.'

'I'd prefer it if you had someone with you.'

'I'm twenty-four years of age and don't need anyone with me.'

'Very well, if you're sure. Come through.'

I followed her up another flight of stairs and through a door leading to a small office. Between the venetian blinds, I could make out the roofs of the buildings outside.

'Please, sit down.' Mrs Stepney took a seat on the opposite side of the desk and opened a file.

'Thanks. So do you have the results?'

'Yes, we do.' She bit her lip.

'May I know?'

'Would you like a cup of tea?'

'No thanks. I'm on my lunch break so I'd rather just hear the news and get back.'

'Of course.' She flicked some pages. 'I'm sorry to tell you...'

Oh my God, what was she going to tell me? Was she going to tell me that Peggy wasn't my mother? Is that what I wanted? I squeezed my eyes closed. 'Yes?'

Mrs Stepney stretched her arm out to touch my hand. 'Are you sure you wouldn't like to wait for your parents to be here with you?'

'No, please. Just tell me.'

'Very well.' She coughed to clear her throat. 'I'm sorry to inform you that the woman you know as your mother, Margaret Davies, isn't your birth mother.'

I breathed out. 'I see.' That meant Joe wasn't my brother and although I was gutted that Peggy wasn't my mother, she could become my mother-in-law. Yes, that would be a solution.

'Are you all right, dear?'

'Yes, yes, I'm fine.'

The director checked the paperwork. 'Your birth parents are Denise and Gordon Coles.' She wrote something down on a piece of paper and passed it to me. 'This is their address, if you decide you'd like to meet them.' Mrs Stepney smiled reassuringly. 'They'd very much like to meet you.'

I glared at the address. 29 Springfield Road. Bloody hell that was only a few houses away from Linda. Maybe Sandra knew them. Maybe they were even her friends. Talk about a small world. 'Thanks. I'll need to think about it. Does Peggy, I mean Margaret Davies, know? Have you told her?'

'Yes, Mrs Davies has been advised. I'm sure she'd like you to visit.'

'Is that it then?'

'Well, almost. We'll arrange for the necessary documentation about your birth identity to be sent to you. Did you take up the counselling that was offered?'

'Nope, I didn't need it.'

'I think you should reconsider. This is a lot to take in. Have a chat with your parents about it. I shall give them a call to advise on any complaint they may wish to take forward and the same applies to you, Rachel.'

'Okay. Thanks.'

'I'm sorry to have to break this sad news. Are you sure you're all right? Would you like me to call your parents?'

'I'm fine thanks. I have to get back to work.' I rose from the chair and shook her hand. 'Thanks for everything.'

'Mum, Dad.' I slammed the front door.

Mum hurried into the hallway. 'What is it? Has something happened?'

'Yes.' I nodded. 'I phoned that woman from the adoption agency and...'

'When's the appointment? Your father and I will come with you.'

'No need.' I grinned. 'I've been. I went today. And guess what?'

'What did they say?'

'Joe's not my brother.' I threw my coat over the banister. 'You know what this means, don't you?' I hugged my mum. 'Joe and I can be together again.'

'Come in and tell your father what you've just told me.'

I followed her into the lounge. 'Hi, Dad. I've been to the agency and they said Peggy isn't my mum, which means...' I felt my whole face beaming.

Dad stood with his mouth wide open.

'My God, Charles,' Mum said, 'you know what this means? We stole a child from its mother.' She grabbed the back of the couch to balance.

'Come and sit down, Rosalind.' Dad led her to an armchair. 'Rachel, get your mother a glass of water.'

I hurried into the kitchen, filled a glass from the tap and rushed back in. 'Here you are, Mum.' I passed her the water.

'Charles, what does this mean? Can we be liable?'

'No, darling. We've done nothing wrong. I'll contact Mrs Stepney to find out where we go from here. It's the other poor couple I feel sorry for. Unknowingly they lost their child and have brought up another one as their own.'

'But if that hadn't happened then you wouldn't have ended up with me.'

'That's true, Rachel,' Dad said, 'but you must see how this will have come as a shock to others. Not everyone will be celebrating right now. I wonder how Peggy's taking the news.'

I flopped in the armchair. 'I don't know. I haven't seen her yet as I wanted to tell you two first. But aren't you happy for me?'

'It's not the case of not being happy, it's about having empathy for others. And this is a shock for your mum and me too. Look at your mother, she's worried we've done something wrong. We adopted a child who wasn't ours to adopt.'

'But if you hadn't, you wouldn't have got me. At least now it means Joe and I can get married.'

Mum blinked. 'But, Rachel, Joe's already married.'

'He can get a divorce. I'm sure it's not that hard.'

She glared at me. 'So, you'd break up a marriage.'

'One that's not happy, yes, why not? Why shouldn't I have my happy ever after?' I got up from the chair. 'I thought you'd both be pleased for me but you're obviously not. I'm going back out.' I grabbed my coat and slammed the door behind me.

―――

Adam opened the front door. 'Come in, Rachel, we wondered when you'd show up.'

'Cheers.' I folded my arms. 'Bloody freezing out there. Do you think we're going to get a white Christmas?'

'We may well do. It's certainly cold enough for snow. Peg's in the kitchen sorting dinner. Go through.'

'Hi, Peggy.' I wandered over to the stove and kissed her on the cheek. 'What you cooking?'

'Just spag bol. We weren't expecting you. I'd ask you to stay but...'

'No, that's okay.'

'You're back from Paris then?'

'Yep. Got back late last night. I saw the woman from the adoption agency today and she filled me in. I was wondering if you'd told Joe yet.'

'No, not yet. I'm expecting him around shortly. Just Joe on his own, not Miranda.'

'Oh, great.' I grinned. 'We can tell him together.'

'No, Rachel, please. Let Adam and I do it alone.'

'But...'

'You heard what Peg said, Rachel.' I hadn't heard Adam come into the kitchen. 'I'll make you a coffee and you can tell us about Paris but you need to be gone before Joe arrives. If he's interested in taking things further then I'm sure he'll come and find you.'

'Okay. I suppose that's fair. I'm just excited.' I turned back to Peggy. 'I'm sorry you're not my mum though but wouldn't it be wonderful if you became my mother-in-law?'

'Don't get ahead of yourself.' She stirred the pan. 'We don't know yet what Joe will want to do. He may not want to break up his marriage.'

'He will. You'll see.' I took a seat at the table.

Adam poured boiling water into a mug and brought it over to me. 'How was Paris?'

'Good. A full-page article will be in this Friday's paper.'

'And how did you and Phil get on?' Adam sat down at the table next to me.

'All right. Their apartment is lovely.'

'No reconciliation then?'

'No. I wanted to see what happened with Joe.' I smiled. 'And now, well it looks like Joe and I may finally get our happy ever after. Start choosing a hat, Peggy.'

Peggy gave a slight smile.

'Does Kate know?' I asked.

'Yes'– Peggy lowered the gas under the pan – 'we told her as soon as we found out.'

'Does she know everything? I mean about Joe and me before?'

'Yes, she knows everything. She knows about you and Joe before we discovered you were supposed brother and sister, if that's what you mean.'

'How did she take it?'

'She was cross at first because we hadn't confided in her, but more concerned about how this latest news was affecting me.'

'Understandably. But happy for me and Joe?'

'I'm sure she is.' Peggy balanced the lid on the pan.

'Adam,' I said, 'you should take Peggy to Paris. Kate and I could manage looking after Ben between us for a weekend.' I picked up the mug and sipped the drink.

'Now there's a thought. What do you think, Peg? Fancy being swept away for a dirty' – Adam laughed – 'I mean romantic weekend?'

'Actually, I'd love to go to Paris. Maybe once it's a bit warmer though. You could take me in March for my birthday?'

'Sure.' Adam smiled. 'Me and the girls will get together and sort it out.'

'Peggy' – I warmed my hands on the hot mug – 'I hope you don't mind me asking but do you think you'll meet your real daughter?'

'If she comes looking then, yes.' Peggy took a deep breath. 'I'm not going to turn her away. Only this time' – she looked across at Adam – 'we're going to do it together as a family. How about you? Will you meet your birth parents?'

'I'm not sure. It seems they only live a few doors away from Linda. Can you believe that? The woman at the adoption agency said they'd like to meet me but I'll think about it once Christmas is over. Right now, all I can think about is Joe.' I put my mug down. 'Right, I'll leave you to get on then. I don't want to make things harder for you than they already are.' I got up and went across to Peggy and hugged her. 'I still love you and hope we can continue our close relationship, whether Joe wants to be with me or not.'

Peggy beamed. 'I'd like that, Rachel. Take care going home now with that ice.'

Chapter Twenty-Eight

Peggy

Kate set the table for four.

'Is Ben asleep?' I stirred the spaghetti.

'Yes. He was out the minute his head hit the pillow.'

'Thanks, love. Means we can eat in peace.'

'Was that Rachel I just heard leave?'

'It was.'

'Does she know then?'

'Apparently so. Found out today and wanted to be here when we told Joe. Thankfully she didn't make a scene.'

Kate came up behind me and put her arms around my waist. 'You okay, Mam?'

'I will be.' I took a handkerchief from my pinnie pocket and wiped my eyes. 'Rachel wants to stay in touch, no matter what happens between her and Joe so that's made me feel a lot better. What do you think about us getting to know your new sister if she comes looking?'

'I think it's a great idea.' Kate's eyes twinkled. 'I quite like the idea of another sister as long as there aren't any others lurking in the cupboards.'

'Definitely no more, darling.' I turned the gas off the stove and hugged my girl.

'That's him now,' Kate said, as a key turned in the lock and Joe entered the kitchen.

'Hi there, Mam, Kate. What's all the secrecy about? Miranda wasn't too happy that she wasn't allowed to come.'

'All in good time. Let's eat first. Spag bol. Your favourite. Give your dad a yell, will you, Kate?'

'Sure.'

Joe took off his leather jacket and hung it on the back of the chair as I dished up the spaghetti and Bolognese onto plates.

Joe glanced at the jug on the table. ''Woodpecker? What's the occasion?'

'Who said we need an occasion? I spotted it on offer in the off-licence window and I thought, how long has it been since the four of us sat down together for a meal? Too long. So I popped in the shop and bought a couple of bottles.'

'Well, I'll just have a small one as I'm on the bike.'

I put the plates of dinner onto the table. 'Your dad and I thought you might like to stay over, what with it being so icy out. Your room's all made up.'

'I'm not sure, Mam. We'll see. It could cause a row. As I said, Miranda's already put out by not getting an invite.'

'You don't have to make up your mind now.'

Adam strolled into the kitchen. 'Mmm, that smells good, Peg.'

'Hope so. Can you pour the cider? Just a half for Joe in case he decides to go home on the bike.' I'd never thought of Miranda's parents' house as Joe's home and I would've been happy if he did leave that wife of his. After discovering she'd deceived him about the baby, I hadn't been able to trust her. At least Rachel was lovely and like she said, I could be her mother-in-law. Still, it was better not to get ahead of myself just in case Joe's feelings towards Miranda had changed.

We sat around the table chatting. Kate told us how her new support group was going and how it was helping her too. Now and then we'd seen a sign that she might be slipping back to the anorexia but working closely with the doctor at the hospital always gave her a safe place to talk.

'That was yummy, Mam.' Joe put down his cutlery. 'Best spag bol I've had since leaving home. Is that rhubarb crumble I smell?'

'It certainly is. I'll just get it out of the oven and warm up the custard.'

'Nah, you're okay, Mam. Let me.' Joe got up and headed over to the stove, put the saucepan on the gas and took the crumble out of the oven. He served it into four dishes and poured the heated custard over it. 'Here we go,' he said as he passed each of us a bowl. 'Now are you going to tell me why you've got me here. Is it about someone's birthday?'

I looked at Adam. He nodded. I took a deep breath. 'Joe, we have some news but we couldn't tell you before.'

'Oh my God, you randy dog, Dad. You've never got Mam in the family way again.'

'No, I haven't and I'll thank you not to talk about your father in that way.' Adam grinned. 'Now listen to your mam.'

'A few weeks ago, we had some unexpected visitors. A woman from the adoption agency and a policeman.'

Joe squinted. 'Adoption agency. What was that about?'

Adam cut in. 'Basically, they were investigating whether there'd been a baby swap at the time Rachel was born.'

'I don't understand.'

'They were saying that Rachel may not have been my daughter,' I said. 'So, Rachel, me, and the other mother and daughter, had to have some tests.'

'Tests? Why am I only hearing about this now?'

'Because...'

'What?'

'We're telling you now because we've had the results.'

'And?' Joe glared at me.

'It seems,' Adam answered for me, 'it seems that Rachel isn't your sister after all.'

Joe put his spoon down. 'She's not my sister?'

'No,' I answered. 'She's not. How do you feel about that?'

Joe opened his mouth, shook his head. 'Tell me again.'

'She's not your sister.' I smiled.

'Oh my God. This is the best Christmas present I could have. Why isn't Rachel here?'

'She wanted to be here but we felt it was better to tell you without her. That way if you wished to stay with Miranda...'

'How the hell can you ask that, Mam? I want to be with Rachel. It's always been Rachel.'

'But what about Miranda?' Adam asked.

Joe shrugged. 'We'll get a divorce. I'll seek legal advice as I've no idea how to go about it.'

Adam patted Joe on his back. 'You have our support, Joe, no matter what you decide but please don't rush into things. Neither you or Rachel are the naïve teenagers you were back then. You've both changed. Grown up. Matured.'

'I hear what you're saying, Dad. Don't worry. And, Mam, how's this news affected you? Are you okay?'

'I will be, darling. The main thing is that you're happy.'

'You know what, Mam? If that offer to stay over is still on, I'd like to take it.'

'Of course.'

'And fill my glass, Dad. This is a celebration.' Joe looked across at Kate. 'And how are you about this, sis? Has Mam filled you in on everything?'

'She has. And I think it's sad about Miranda but then let's face it, she's not totally innocent in all this. She did trick you into marriage, no matter what she said. So...'

Joe got up, walked around the table and hugged his sister. 'Thanks, sis. And this means, I suppose, that we'll have another sister to meet.'

'If that's what she wants, yes.' Adam swigged a mouthful of cider. 'But this time we'll meet her as a family.'

Joe raised his glass. 'Let's have a toast. To the future.'

We clinked glasses.

I laid Ben back into his cot. He looked so angelic in his white Babygro. No one would've believed he'd been screaming half an hour ago. I turned on the bunny lamp and switched off the main light. After taking one last peep at him sleeping, I crept out of his room, and left the door ajar before heading into our bedroom.

I slid into bed next to Adam. 'He's asleep.'

'Let's hope he stays that way for a while so you can get some rest.' He snuggled up closer. 'I thought this evening went well.'

'Me too. How do you feel about it?' I kissed him on the cheek.

'I'm pleased for Joe and Rachel if that's what they want, but worried about you, and I can't help feeling sorry for Miranda in all this. She's the innocent party getting hurt.'

'I'll be all right, love. But is Miranda really that innocent? Joe would never have married her if he hadn't thought there was a baby.'

'We don't know that. She may really have thought she was pregnant like she said, and she obviously loves him.'

'I'm not convinced. Yes, I believe she loves him, but I also believe she's used to getting everything she wants. Her parents have spoilt her.'

'It's going to be a difficult ride ahead with a divorce as well as us possibly meeting our new daughter.'

'Yes, but whenever have we had anything run smoothly?' I hoped it would all work out for Rachel and Joe, it would somehow correct the wrong that I'd caused five years ago. Although, Adam was right, they had a long road ahead of them, but Adam, Kate, and I would be there to support them. I kissed Adam on the lips. 'Night, darling.' I curled up behind him and closed my eyes.

Chapter Twenty-Nine

Rachel

'Would you like a lift, Mel?'

'Um, that would've been nice, but' – she peered across the road – 'isn't that Joe?'

'Oh yes. Yes, it is.' My pulse pounded. 'I'd better see what he wants. Sorry.'

She patted my arm. 'No worries. The bus will be here in a few minutes. Thank goodness I get my car back at the end of the week. I'll see you tomorrow.'

'Have a good evening.' I headed over to Joe. 'Hello there, are you here for me?'

'Certainly am.' He smiled. 'Got a few minutes?'

'Sure. Where do you want to go?'

'Wimpy?'

'Okay. Have you spoken to your mam?'

His chocolate eyes twinkled. 'Yes, I have.'

'So, what did Peggy tell you?'

'That you're not my sister' – he grinned – 'which means we can be together.'

'Excellent.' I squeezed his fingers. He'd come running just as I'd hoped.

He slipped his hand in mine as we wandered across to the café.

'There's a free table there.' I pointed to the back of the eating area.

Once we'd sat down, Joe reached for my hands and clasped them in his. 'This is the best news ever.'

'It certainly is. Perfect timing too. I thought we could do something special on Christmas Eve. Maybe even book a room?'

He bit his lip. 'Sorry, but I can't.'

'Why not?'

'Because... Er...'

'What?'

'Because I don't intend telling Miranda or her parents about us until after the holiday. It wouldn't be fair.'

I pulled back my hands. 'Fair to who? Certainly not me. I thought you'd be as keen as I am.'

'I am, Rach, but I've got to let Miranda down gently. Surely you can understand that?'

'Hi, what can I get you guys,' asked the young lad.

'Nothing for me, thanks.' I shot up from my seat. 'I understand nothing, Joe. If you think I'm going to be the other woman then you're in for a shock. I don't intend sharing you with anybody.'

'That's not what I meant, please, sit back down.'

'Nope. My mum will be wondering where I am. Let me know when you're as serious about us as I am.'

'Rach.' He stood up. 'Please, wait.'

I hurried out of the Wimpy. To think I thought he loved me as much as I did him. Who was I kidding? How the hell could he wait until after Christmas to tell her? I squeezed my eyes shut refusing to cry.

Voices came from the lounge. 'Is that you, Rachel,' Mum called. 'There's someone here to see you.'

'Shan't be a minute.' I rushed upstairs to the bathroom, washed my face and changed into my starry night swing dress. Taking a deep breath, I strolled downstairs to see who the surprise visitor was. As I entered the room I was gobsmacked. How? 'Phil,' I finally managed to say, 'what are you doing here?'

He rose from the sofa, came over and kissed me on the cheek. 'My grandmother's not well. We had a call not long after you left so Jan and I took the first flight over. I've just come from the hospital and it's not looking good.'

'I'm sorry.' I put my arms around him. I wondered what it must be like to have grandparents as I couldn't remember mine. Both Mum and Dad's parents had died before I was three.

'I'll get some tea,' Mum said, 'and give you two some privacy.'

'Thanks, Mum.' I led Phil back to the couch. 'So, where's Jan now?'

'She's with our parents but I couldn't come all this way without seeing my favourite girl. Also, I wasn't sure how things had panned out with your, well you know, so here I am.'

'You're very kind worrying about me when your grandmother's so sick.'

'I'm not quite as selfless as you're making out. I wanted to know whether you'd had the results.'

'Yes, yes, I have.'

'And.' His ice-blue eyes sparkled.

'Joe's not my brother.' Right at this moment part of me was wishing he was and then I wouldn't have to be dealing with this rejection.

Phil hugged me. 'My loss then, but know I'll always be here for you. No matter what. By the way, you look stunning in that dress.'

'Thanks. I call it my happy dress as it cheers me up whenever I wear it. Does that sound daft?'

'Yep, but I know what you mean.'

A tap on the door made us look up. Mum entered the room with tea and biscuits. 'I'll just put this down here and then get out of your way.' She placed the tray down on the coffee table.

'Thank you, Mrs Webster.' Phil smiled.

Mum rested her hand on his shoulder. 'You're welcome,' she said before leaving.

I poured the tea into the Royal Doulton china. 'Sugar?'

'No, ta, I'm sweet enough. Haven't you noticed?'

'I have. In fact, you're the sweetest, kindest man I've ever met.'

'Kinder than Joe?'

'Right now, yes. To be honest, Phil, I'm so angry with him. Actually, more than that. I'm fuming.'

'Why?' Phil picked up his cup and drank some of the tea. 'Earl Grey?'

'Yep. Mum's favourite.' I sighed. 'Joe came to meet me from work today.'

'That's good, isn't it?'

'You'd have thought so except he told me he wasn't going to break the news to Miranda until after the festive period. That means he's spending Christmas with her and not me.' A tear fell to my cheek.

'Hey.' Phil took a handkerchief from his pocket and dabbed my face. 'Don't cry. You've still got me.'

'I know, and I love you but not in the same way, although I wish I did.'

'But who knows in time you could?' he said with pleading eyes.

'I don't want to lead you on. That would make me no better than Joe. So, until I know there's definitely no Joe and me, I can't commit myself to you.'

'But we could be good friends. You know, really good friends?' He snuggled up towards me. 'I could really do with that type of friend right now.'

I hugged him. 'Like I said in Paris, until I know what's what, there can't be a you and me.'

The door burst open. 'Hey, I heard you were here.' Jenny kissed Phil on the cheek. 'How's Paris?'

'Good thanks. You ever been?'

'No, but if you're inviting me, I'm sure I could wangle a bit of time off work.'

'Sure. Anytime. Jan and I have plenty of room.'

I glared at Jenny.

'Well, you have my number.' Jen fluttered her eyelashes at Phil before leaving the room.

'Your sister's nice.'

'She can be.'

'If there is no you and me, would you mind if I asked her out to dinner before I go back to France?'

My stomach churned. Why should it matter to me? I was angry with Joe for keeping me dangling while he stayed with Miranda yet if I stood in Phil and Jenny's way I was no better. 'No, go for it,' I said.

'Cheers.'

'What was all that about?' I asked Jen.

She shrugged. 'Well, if you don't want him.'

'What about your doctor boyfriend?'

'Fizzled out. Seriously though, Rach, what's your problem? Dog in a manger, springs to mind.'

'It's not that, I've…'

'What? You want to keep him dangling on a string? That's hardly fair. If you don't give me the green light then I'll leave well alone.'

'No. That's fine. Phil asked me the same question and I told him I don't have a problem.'

'He's interested in me?'

'Well, he asked if I minded him taking you out to dinner.'

She rubbed her hands. 'Cool, that's brilliant. I need something to perk up my confidence after being chucked by Doctor Gorgeous.'

'You should know though, that Phil's in love with me.'

'Well, there's a challenge.'

'Girls,' Mum hollered from downstairs. 'Dinner's ready.'

'Come on.' Why was I so put out by the thought? Jenny was right, I absolutely was a dog in a manger.

Chapter Thirty

Peggy

Joe bounced Ben on his knee. 'Hi, little bro. Aren't you getting big?'

'He crawled for the first time yesterday,' I said tickling his belly and making him giggle.

'Awesome. Are you going to crawl for me?' Joe put Ben on the carpet but he just turned over from his tummy to his back and started crying.

'He's not a performing seal, you know?' Kate picked him up. 'Anyway, he needs a sleep. Shall I pop him in the pram, Mam?'

'Thanks, darling.'

Kate carried Ben into the hallway.

'She'll make a wonderful mam,' I said. 'Now are we going to talk about the elephant in the room?'

Joe pinched the bridge of his nose. 'Sorry?'

'What's happening with you and Rachel?'

Joe sighed. 'She didn't understand.'

'Understand what, son?'

'When I said I wasn't going to tell Miranda and her family until after Christmas.'

I chewed my lip. 'Hmm, I can see where she's coming from. So, Miranda doesn't know yet?'

'Not yet. I can't do it until after the holidays. It wouldn't be fair to Miranda or her family.'

'Rachel was so excited about spending Christmas with you.'

'I know. And I'd love to spend my time with her too but I have to tackle the situation gently otherwise I'll never get a divorce.'

'Have you seen a solicitor?'

'Yeah. He reckons a five-year separation unless I can get Miranda to agree, then we may be able to get it sorted in two. For God's sake that seems like a lifetime. How the hell am I going to stay married to her for five years? I love Rachel but she didn't hang around to let me say how I feel. She said she wasn't going to be the other woman.'

'I see.' I was pleased to hear Rachel still had her morals. 'I'm sure she's calmed down now and will listen to reason.'

'I hope so. Will you talk to her for me?'

'I could try or you could speak to her yourself later.'

'No, I can't. I only popped in to bring the presents as Miranda's parents have booked us a hotel in Liverpool for Christmas and we're leaving this evening.'

'For just you and Miranda?'

'Nope, for the whole family. Apparently, it's an annual event.'

'Then I'll try and speak to Rachel for you, but' – I took a deep breath – 'it isn't going to be easy, and I hope you don't blow your chance. That Phil she was seeing is over from Paris for a couple of weeks. Watch you don't lose her.'

'Come in.' Adam ushered Rachel through the door. 'I see you've brought the snow.'

'I hope it doesn't come to much as I hate driving in it.' She slipped off her boots and slid off her green-striped blanket coat.

'Here,' I said, 'I'll hang it up to dry.'

'Cheers, Peggy.' She handed me the coat and gave Adam a Santa sack. 'Christmas pressies for under the tree, and I'm afraid I've rather spoilt Ben. I know he's not my brother but I still feel like he is. Is that okay?'

'Of course, it is,' I said, 'and don't forget you're still his godmother so you'll always have a special place in his life.'

'Thanks, Peggy.' Rachel followed me into the kitchen and I hung her coat over the clothes horse.

'Where is everyone?' she asked.

Kate's upstairs getting ready and Ben's asleep. 'There's just the five of us this evening.'

'So, Joe's coming without Miranda?'

'No, I'm afraid he isn't coming. The fifth person is Kate's doctor friend. Between you and me I think it may be getting serious.'

'Cool. Can't wait to meet him. But no Joe. Why?'

I pulled a seat out from the table to sit down. 'Take a seat for a minute.'

She sat down next to me. 'So where is he?'

'He was here earlier to bring presents but he'll be on his way to Liverpool now. I do hope he'll be okay in this weather.'

'Is he driving? Was he called out on a breakdown?'

'No, nothing like that. It seems Miranda's parents booked a hotel for the whole family to stay over the festive period. He couldn't get out of it.'

'You mean he didn't want to. Why doesn't he just tell me straight instead of keeping me waiting in the wings?'

'He says he loves you.'

'Sure. He loves me but wants his cake as well as eating it. Well, I've told him I won't be the other woman. I don't intend sharing a man with anyone. I deserve more.'

I stroked the back of her hand. 'Yes, you do, but I don't think he's leading you on. From what I can gather he's trying to keep Miranda sweet so she'll agree to a divorce.'

'Likely story. You're not going to tell me he won't sleep with her while he's away. He disgusts me. I put off Phil. At least he knows how to treat a woman.'

'Have you seen him again?'

'Not alone, if that's what you mean. I wouldn't lead him on but if Joe has made his choice, then yes, maybe I will, although...'

'What?'

'I've kind of given him and Jenny the green light to see each other.'

Rachel took the tray of drinks and I followed in with a plate of hot mince pies. Kate got up as we entered the lounge.

'David, this is my mam, and Rachel my sort of sister. Rachel and Mam, this is my boyfriend. David's a doctor at the hospital.' Kate's hazel eyes sparkled.

'How do you do, David?'

David rose from the sofa. 'Very well thank you, Mrs Davies.' He looked older than Kate. When he smiled his large green eyes twinkled. He brushed a few strands of sandy hair from his brow. 'Thank you for inviting me.'

Kate returned to her seat, pulling David down with her, and snuggled up close to him.

'It's a pleasure,' I said.

Rachel passed David a glass of mulled wine. 'Pleased to meet you.' She turned to me and winked.

Adam strode into the room and I wondered what he'd make of this young man. David stood up from the couch again, his head almost touching the ceiling.

'Ah, you must be the David we've been hearing about.' Adam put his hand out to shake.

'Yes, how do you do, Mr Davies. I've brought a little gift for you and Mrs Davies.'

'I've already put it under the tree.' Kate beamed.

'Why thank you, David, but there was no need, and please, do sit back down.' Adam stretched across to pick up a glass of mulled wine from the coffee table. He sniffed it before tasting. 'Mulled wine always puts me in the Christmas mood, how about you, David?'

'Yes, Mr Davies.'

'Adam, please. We don't stand on ceremony in this house. Have they given you much time off work?'

'Not a lot. Unfortunately, I'm on shift tomorrow but thankfully not until the afternoon.'

'The penalties of being a doctor, I suppose,' Adam continued. 'My job has small similarities in so much as I'm often on call for vehicle breakdowns but Christmas Day and Boxing Day we close down completely.'

'Hopefully it won't be too busy tomorrow but it's normally a nice atmosphere as we decorate the wards and have Christmas carols coming through the speakers. We doctors and nurses add a bit of tinsel to our uniforms to cheer up the patients. And one of the volunteers comes in as Santa and gives presents not only to the children but the older patients too.'

'That sounds lovely, David,' I said.

'Yes, of course nothing makes up for them being away from their families, but Matron relaxes the visiting hours a little and lets them stay longer than normal.'

'Coffee anyone?' I asked once we'd finished charades. 'Rachel, fancy helping me?'

'Sure.' Rachel followed me into the kitchen and filled the kettle.

'Remind me to buy some bone china crockery,' I said taking five mugs down from the shelf. 'I'm totally embarrassed giving the doctor a mug like this.'

'Don't be daft, Peg. He won't care. I bet he drinks out of all sorts of mugs at the hospital. He's here for Kate not to see how you live.'

'They seem smitten, don't they?'

'Very.' She added a spoon of Nescafé into each mug. 'Do you like him?'

'Yes. Do you? Do you think Adam does? I mean he's a few years older than Kate, nearer your age.'

'Age doesn't matter. Kate's not a schoolgirl now.'

'No, I suppose not.' I pulled out a box of After Eight Dinner mints from the cupboard and put them on the tray with the drinks.

'I'll carry the tray,' Rachel said, 'you get the door.'

'Finally.' I packed up the Monopoly and as usual Adam had won. He always managed to buy Park Lane and Mayfair and strip everyone of their properties and cash.

'One of these days, Dad,' Kate said, 'I'm going to beat you.' She laughed. 'David's got to go shortly but before he does, we have something to tell you.'

'What?' I glared at my smiling daughter. 'Out with it.'

'Well, I hope you don't mind Mr and Mrs Davies' – David rose from the sofa – 'I mean Adam and Peggy, but I've asked Kate to marry me and she said yes.'

Kate stood up next to David and he put an arm around her.

I gulped and glanced at Adam waiting for him to say something. Instead, he surprised me by getting up from the armchair, heading over to Kate and hugging her. Afterwards he shook David's hand. 'Why, congratulations.'

'Yes, congratulations,' Rachel said.

'Congratulations,' I echoed. I hadn't been expecting that. 'So, when did all this happen?'

'Yesterday.' Kate grinned. 'I do have a ring, but' – she bent down, dug into her handbag and slipped a platinum band with a large emerald surrounded by small diamonds onto her finger and held it out – 'we wanted to tell you before I wore it.'

'It's gorgeous.' Rachel hugged Kate.

Gorgeous indeed. My little girl was all grown up. 'Have you set a date?'

'We're thinking July next year, around my birthday.' Kate stared into David's eyes.

'If that works for you folks?' David said.

'That sounds perfect. Come here you.' Adam cuddled Kate. 'I'll be the proudest father on earth when I walk my little girl down the aisle.'

'Will it be a church wedding?' I asked.

'Definitely.' Kate smiled. 'And Rachel, I'd like you to be my bridesmaid.'

'I'd love to.'

'This calls for a toast.' Adam rushed out of the room and returned with a jug of cider and five glasses. 'I know David and Rachel are driving but they can have a mouthful.' He poured the alcoholic beverage into the glasses. 'To my wonderful daughter, Kate, and her fiancé.' He clinked his glass with mine.

I breathed a sigh of relief as I'd half expected Adam to object about his little girl getting married. He'd obviously taken a shine to her doctor boyfriend, but then David was rather handsome, and had the personality to go with it. Rachel was smiling but I sensed she was hurting. I hoped she and Joe would get their happy ever after soon, although from what Joe was saying, they might have to wait five years before making it official.

Chapter Thirty-One

Rachel

Dad carved the huge turkey while Mum, Jenny and I set the table with sprouts, carrots, peas, roast parsnips and potatoes all in matching Royal Doulton serving dishes.

'It's good you were able to get today off from work,' I said to Jenny. 'Kate's boyfriend, I mean fiancé, had to work.'

'Yes, I was lucky. In tomorrow though. Kate's engaged?'

I smiled. 'Yes. She announced it last night while I was around there. You should see the ring. It's gorgeous,' I said as we sat down at the table. 'An emerald that matches her fiancé's eyes, surrounded by little diamonds. He's a doctor. I wonder if you know him.'

'What's his name?' Jenny spooned cranberry jelly on to her plate.

'David. That's all I know, apart from he has the most stunning green eyes.'

She laughed. 'That's not a lot of help. See if you can find out. This is a fabulous feast, Mum.'

'Yes, it is,' I agreed. Mum always made the perfect Christmas dinner.

'Thank you, girls. Jennifer, how did your date go last night with Phillip?'

I poured gravy on to my dinner. 'Yes, how did it go?'

'It wasn't exactly a date. Anyway, Jan joined us as I don't think either of us are ready for a new relationship. What with Phil still hung up about you and me hurting after Ian ditched me.'

'Did you go anywhere nice?' Dad put a forkful of food to his mouth.

'Lime's Bistro. We had a lovely meal. And they're both so nice. I'm going over to Paris next month for a couple of weeks and...'

Lime's Bistro. I had such wonderful memories of that place with Joe. My gentle Joe. Stop it. I didn't want to think about him.

'Will you be able to get the time off from work?' Mum asked.

'Should be able to. But...'

'What?' I glared at Jenny.

She put her knife and fork down. 'I've been thinking. I'm not really cut out for this nursing lark and I'm planning to hand in my notice.'

Dad frowned. 'And do what?'

'I'm not sure yet but Phil and Jan said I can help out in their studio if I like while deciding what I want to do. Jan said she'd teach me to paint, and you know I've always loved art.'

Dad slammed his cutlery down. 'You want to be an artist?'

'That's not what I'm saying but if it is, so what? Rachel's doing what she wants with her writing so why can't I follow my dream?'

'You've worked so hard,' Dad said. 'You're already a staff nurse and I'm sure you'll make it to Sister before too long.'

'Exactly, Dad. That's all I've ever done. Worked hard. I never got a break from college before going straight into nursing. I'm tired, and I'm not cut out for it. I get too attached and when we lose a patient...'

'Hey,' I said. 'It's all right, Jen. If that's not what you want to do.'

Mum shook her head. 'Jennifer, I don't think you've thought this through.'

'Maybe not' – she sniffled – 'but that's why I'm only going out to Paris for a couple of weeks at first. If I like it then I'll go back over and see where it takes me. It offers lots of possibilities, not just as an artist but a curator, an actress, musician, or basically anything I decide I'd like to do. Please try to understand.' She dabbed her wet eyes.

'Good for you.' I squeezed her hand.

Dad pushed his dinner plate away and threw down his napkin. 'I thought we'd finished with this kind of stuff. That our girls had matured to sensible young ladies. You're acting like a teenager.'

'You won't even try to understand.' Jenny sobbed again.

'Leave her alone, Dad. Can't you see she's upset.'

'Well, I'm bloody upset. That's our Christmas spoilt. Your mother's gone to all this trouble to cook a special dinner and now...' He got up from the table. 'Rosalind, fancy a stroll?'

'Erm.' Mum blinked. 'Yes, okay but what about all this?' She pointed to the table.

'Rachel and Jennifer can clear it up. It's the least they can do after spoiling Christmas dinner.'

Mum rose from her seat. 'I'll see you girls in a bit.' She followed Dad into the hallway and within a couple of minutes the door slammed.

Jenny broke down in tears.

'Hey, it's all right.' I put my arms around her and she sobbed into my chest. 'It will be okay. Just stick to your guns and don't let Dad try to change your mind.'

'Thanks, sis.'

I patted her back. 'This is because nursing isn't right for you though and not because of Ian?'

'No. It's not because of him. I've been feeling like this for a while now and watching you do so well in your job has heightened how unhappy I feel about mine.'

Mum and Dad sat either side of the sofa reading. Dad had a J R R Tolkien book and Mum was stuck into *The Thorn Birds*; presents they'd bought each other for Christmas. Jenny and I played Scrabble. This was the first Christmas Day we hadn't taken part in family games with the obligatory after dinner charades. Dad hadn't spoken a word since he came back in from their walk. I'd just put down a seven-letter word with 'picture' when there was a knock on the door.

Dad rose from the sofa. 'I'll get this.' He went into the hallway.

I stood up and watched from the lounge entrance as he opened the door.

'Good God, lad. What's happened to you? You'd better come in.'

'Thanks, Mr Webster.' Joe stepped inside.

I hurried to his side. 'Bloody hell, Joe. Your face.'

He put his hand up to his cheek. 'Reckon I'm going to have a right shiner in the morning.'

'It's okay, Dad,' I said. 'I'll take over.' I guided Joe into the kitchen and closed the door behind us. 'What the hell happened?'

'I told Miranda last night. I had to, because she couldn't understand why I wouldn't make love to her. Anyway, I explained I wouldn't leave her until after Christmas. She seemed to accept it but...'

'She didn't do this to you, surely?'

'Nope, not her. Her dad and his cronies. She must've gone straight to him with the news because when I popped outside for a smoke after dinner today, the next thing I knew a gang of blokes set on me. After being punched to the ground I peered up at Miranda's dad glaring down at me. "No one messes with my daughter." He kicked me where it hurt and said, "Now piss off," before marching away and leaving me howling. Once I could breathe again, I managed to hobble back into the hotel and got the receptionist to call Stu.'

Dad came into the kitchen and passed Joe a glass of whisky. 'Here, lad, get this down you. It'll help. Rachel, put something on that.' He signalled to Joe's face. 'I'll leave you to it.'

'Thanks, Dad,' I said as he left the room. I pulled a bag of Bird's Eye peas out of the chest freezer. 'Here.'

Joe put the frozen bag to his face.

'Where's Stu now?' I sat down at the table next to him.

'He's gone to Sandra's to collect Linda. I'm sorry to turn up so late but I had to see you.'

'I'm glad you did.' I leaned forward to kiss him but he quickly moved away.

'Sorry. My mouth.' He put a hand to his cut lips.

'They've proper beaten you up. Have they hurt you anywhere else?'

He held his ribs. 'They gave me a good going over. The bastards.'

'You should call the police.'

'Nah. Let's face it, I deserved it. I shouldn't have told her on Christmas Eve but she kept badgering me and I kept thinking of you, what you said about being the other woman.'

'Oh Joe, I'm sorry, darling. It's my fault.'

'No, it isn't. It would've happened anytime I told them and it always had to be said.' He took my hand. 'And if it takes a beating to mean we can be together then I'd happily have it happen again.'

'Well, I won't. If there's a repetition then I'll go to the police. So, does this mean we can be together?'

He nodded. 'Yeah, but I'm not likely to be free to marry you for at least five years.'

'We don't need a piece of paper, Joe.'

There was a tap on the door and Mum peeped in. 'I've made up a bed for Joe in the guest room. I presume tomorrow you'll go home to your mother's?'

'Yes, I will. Thank you, Mrs Webster.'

'And in the new year,' I said once Mum had gone, 'you and I will start flat hunting.'

'But what about you wanting to wait until you're married?'

'I've waited long enough. Twenty-four and still a virgin is a bit much for anyone.'

'Oh darling.' He hugged me close.

Chapter Thirty-Two

Rachel

Hand in hand we meandered up to the reception desk manned by a woman in a navy-blue uniform.

'We've a room booked for tonight in the name of Davies.' Joe beamed. 'We're just married.'

I twiddled the gold band on my finger bought from Woolies.

'Congratulations.' The receptionist scanned the diary. 'Ah, yes. Here you are, Mr and Mrs Davies.' She lifted a key from a hook behind her. 'Room 111 on the first floor. Do you need a porter for your luggage?' She glanced down at our small cases.

'No, thanks,' I said, 'we're travelling light. We've booked a table in the restaurant too. Can you tell us where to go?'

'Straight ahead for the restaurant. By the way, I've upgraded your room.' Her blue eyes sparkled behind the round-rimmed glasses. 'Have a lovely evening.'

'Cheers,' Joe said, 'that's really kind.'

I clung to his hand as we headed upstairs and around the corridor to our room. 'What do you think of this carpet?'

'Interesting.'

'Hmm, that's what I thought. The burnt orange shades are cool but the hexagon pattern is making me a bit giddy.'

'I know what you mean. This is it.' Joe unlocked the door.

'Awesome.' I said on stepping inside. 'It's fantastic.' An enormous four-poster with red-brocade curtains dominated the floor space. I bounced on the bed. 'Do you think she believed us?'

'Yeah. The ring did the trick. Once we're married though, you're going to have the most expensive wedding ring to make up for this.'

'I'll just be happy to finally be your wife.' I put my small suitcase on the luggage holder. 'Shall we go straight down to dinner? I'm starving.' Butterflies flapped in my stomach. I was finally going to be with Joe. We'd waited so long for this.

Joe's chocolate eyes twinkled in the candlelight. My heart beat so fast I reckoned it must've been going twice its normal rate. I was excited yet scared. What would it be like? Would I be disappointed? Would Joe be? I spooned into the prawn cocktail.

'You enjoying it?' Joe asked. 'You seem miles away.'

'Yes, thanks. Just thinking about later.' I smiled.

'We don't have to, you know?'

'I want to.'

Joe's eyes sparkled. 'If anyone had told me this would be happening, even three months ago, I'd have said, no way. I thought I was trapped in marriage with Miranda forever.'

'Why did you marry her?'

Joe shrugged. 'I thought she was pregnant, but then you know that, but...' He took a deep breath. 'It seemed like an answer to where to go next as I couldn't have you. I hoped being married to Miranda would help me get over you. Not that it did.'

'I never got over you either. I've had a few boyfriends, some really lovely, like Phil, but it's always been you. To think for the first time since nineteen seventy-one, we're going into a new year full of hope and dreams. I'm not sure how my folks will take us living together but they'll have to accept it.'

A waiter came to the table. 'Have you finished?'

I looked up. 'Yes, thank you.'

He cleared our dishes onto the undershelf of his trolley and gave us each a plate of steak, chips and peas. 'Enjoy your meal.'

'Thank you.' Joe smiled.

Once the waiter had left, Joe said, 'Mam and Dad should be okay about it. I mean it would be a bit hypocritical of Mam if she judged us, wouldn't it?'

'Yep.' I cut into the well-done steak. 'I don't know how you can eat the meat with blood coming out of it like that.'

'It's nice. Want to try?'

'No thanks. How do you feel about meeting your new sister if she comes looking?'

Joe tucked into his dinner. 'Okay I suppose. If it makes Mam happy…'

'It's been tough for Peggy. Mum and Dad made me think how my real parents must be feeling. It's not like they wanted to give up their child. They think I should get in touch. What do you think?'

'It's up to you, Rach, but if it was me, I'd be curious. Aren't you?'

'I suppose so, it's just' – I sighed – 'I'm not sure I can go through all that again. I'll think about it in the new year but if I do decide to go ahead, will you come with me?'

'You know I will.' Joe reached across the table and took my hand. 'I'd go to the moon and back for you. Have I told you lately that I love you?'

I smiled. 'Yes.' I put my knife and fork in position. 'I'm not really hungry. How about you?'

'No, me neither. Shall we go upstairs?'

I nodded. 'Yes, let's.'

Joe popped the cork and champagne bubbled over the bottle making us chuckle. I held the glass goblets as he poured the sparkling wine. 'It was really nice of the hotel to leave us this, and the chocolates.' I picked up the card.

> *Congratulations Mr and Mrs Davies*
> *on your wedding day*
> *from The George Hotel*

'Look.' I held up the tag. 'I feel guilty now.' I dropped the card back on the cabinet.

'Don't feel guilty.' Joe sipped his drink. 'Imagine this is our wedding night.'

'Okay. I'll try.' Butterflies partied inside my stomach. 'Here, try this.' I dipped a truffle into the fizz and fed it to Joe.

'Yum.' He did the same to me.

'Nice.' I giggled. 'Want another one?' I took a swig of the champagne.

'Later.' He took my glass and set it down on the tray next to his. 'Come here.' He moved closer, put his arms around me, and brushed hair behind my ear. 'I've been waiting so long for this.'

'Me too.' The champagne made me dreamy and when Joe unbuttoned my blouse, I let it slip from my shoulders, following his lead. He guided me to the four-poster bed, and we continued to undress each other, our kisses more urgent.

'Are you sure?' he asked.

'I'm sure.' I brought my lips to his and stroked his cheek. 'I love you.'

'I love you too. I can't believe we can finally be together,' he mumbled in-between kisses. He moved from my lips to my throat, cupped my breasts and kissed my nipples. I arched my back as he continued to kiss me all the way down. He paused, looked into my eyes and asked again. 'Are you sure?'

'Yes.' The moment came and clenching my fingers I gave a small cry.

'Are you okay?'

'Yes.' I smiled, letting him guide me with rhythm. He was experienced while all this was new to me. As far as I was concerned this was my wedding night. Who needed a piece of paper? We loved each other and that was all that mattered.

Afterwards Joe brushed his lips against mine. 'I hope I didn't hurt you?' He stroked my bare shoulder.

'Only at first. It was definitely worth waiting for. How about you with your bruised ribs? I didn't hurt you, did I?'

'I'm fine. You've made me the happiest man alive and if I had to take a hundred beatings to be with you it would be worth it.'

'Well, I wouldn't let that happen.' I snuggled closer to his naked body.

'I think I'll be walking around with this smile on my face forever.'

'I know what you mean. Just think, once we get our own place, we can lie together like this every night.'

'Are you serious about moving in with me? I mean before we're married?'

'Absolutely. There's no way I'm waiting five years until you're free. I'll book us an appointment with the building society next week to see how much we can borrow. In the meantime, we can find a flat to rent.'

'Sounds like a cool plan. I reckon that's enough talking. Now come here you sexy thing.' Joe kissed me passionately.

Chapter Thirty-Three

Rachel

I closed the front door behind me.

'Rachel, is that you?'

'Yes.' I strolled into the kitchen. 'Mmm, is that coffee I can smell?'

'Where've you been? You didn't come home last night.'

'I told you I wouldn't be home.' I poured a cup of coffee from the percolator. 'I really need this. It's freezing out there.'

'Did you? I must've forgotten. Who were you with?'

'Mum, I'm twenty-four. I really shouldn't have to tell you where I am but if you must know I was with Joe.'

'All night.' Mum frowned. 'Charles,' she called, 'can you come in here?'

'What is it, Rosalind? Good morning, Rachel.' Dad grabbed a coffee and took a seat at the table.

'Have you heard this? She spent the night with Joe.'

'Can you blame her?'

'You mean you approve?'

'No, I don't approve but let's face it, Rosalind, if it wasn't for the mix-up at her birth then she and Joe would've been married by now. And while I don't normally agree to couples being together before marriage, I think this is an exception.'

I smiled. 'Thanks, Dad. So, you will understand when I tell you Joe and I are moving in together as soon as we can get a place.'

'I do, love. Yes.'

'Charles, you can't be serious. What will the vicar say?'

'If anyone deserves happiness, Rosalind, it's these two. They've been through so much. Are you intending to buy a place, Rachel?'

'That's the plan although we'll rent while we're waiting for everything to go through.' I perched on a chair next to Dad. 'We've got savings so we shouldn't have any worries about a deposit, and both of us earn a good wage. We should be all right.'

'Anything we can do to help, love.' He rested his hand on mine. 'But will you do something for me?'

'What?'

'Get in touch with your birth parents.'

'Really? How come? You were so against it when I wanted to get to know Peggy.'

'This is different. This couple didn't put you up for adoption. Through no fault of their own, the chance of bringing up their child was stolen from them. They deserve the opportunity to meet you.'

Mum frowned. 'Where's my husband gone?'

'It's only fair, Rosalind. Imagine if Jennifer was swapped when she was born and it came out all these years later. Wouldn't you want to meet the child you gave birth to?'

'Yes. I see that but... What are your thoughts on it, Rachel?'

'I'm not sure, but I promise to think about it.' In my heart I knew they were right. My birth parents hadn't rejected me. In fact, they'd got married to ensure they could bring me up together. Mrs Stepney had said they were keen to meet, and Joe said he'd go with me. We'd get our flat first and then look into it. I wondered what the girl they'd brought up as their own daughter was like. Would she look like Peggy? Or maybe she was more like Mike? Would I look like my real parents? Dad was right, I should get in touch. I could have siblings, aunties, uncles, and maybe even grandparents.

'Rachel?'

I glanced up. 'Sorry, what did you say, Mum?'

'Would you like some breakfast?'

'Just a slice of toast will do me, thanks.'

I parked outside Linda's house and knocked on the door.

'Hello, stranger.' Linda almost dragged me inside.

'On your own?'

'Yes. Stu's gone to his Mum's.'

'Don't you ever go with him?'

'Sometimes, but like today, I make an excuse that it's a good time for me to clean the house. Great to see you. What gives?'

'Put the kettle on and I'll tell you.' I sensed myself beaming.

Linda's grin widened. 'Something's happened.' She flicked the kettle switch and stuck teabags into the mugs.

'Oh, sod the tea. Let's sit down.' I headed to the lounge, sank into the sofa and Linda curled up next to me.

'Go on, then. Is this something to do with Joe?'

'Yep. Did Stu tell you what happened in Liverpool?'

'Oh God, yeah, about Miranda's dad getting Joe beat up. Is he okay?'

'He's getting there. Anyway, last night we... I shrugged. 'Let's put it this way, I'm no longer a virgin.'

'Wow. About bloody time, Webster.' She pulled me close to her chest. 'I'm so pleased for you, but...'

'What?'

'You don't think Miranda's dad will set someone on you too?'

'Let him try. I shan't be afraid to report him to the police, that's for sure. Oh, Lind, last night was wonderful. Better than I could ever have hoped. And guess what?'

'What?'

'We're going to get a place together. Rent at first while we're looking to buy and get a mortgage.'

'Rachel Webster's going to live in sin? My God, it's a good job I'm sitting down.'

'Shut-up.' I chuckled. 'Anyway, these days people don't call it that. I'm certainly not going to waste five more years not being together until he's free.'

'How are your folks going to take that?'

I grinned. 'Strangely enough, Dad's fine with it. Mum, well that's another matter. She's more interested in what the vicar's going to say. Anyway, when I do get married, I'd like you to be my matron of honour.'

'I should think so too. Well as you're here...'

'Yep?'

'I have some news of my own.'

'You have?'

Her grin widened. 'Early days but hopefully we're looking at a September baby.'

'Congratulations. I hope I'm not too old by the time Joe and I can have a kid. I don't really want to start a family until we're married. Mind you, never say never. Wouldn't it be great if we were both pregnant at the same time, and our kids could go to school together and be best friends like us lot.'

'I love you, Webster.' Linda hugged me.

Chapter Thirty-Four

Rachel

Betty squeezed my hand. 'I'm pleased for you, pet, of course I am, but he's still a married man.'

'But he was mine before hers. If there hadn't been a mix-up we'd have been married by now. Even my dad can see that. Surely you can too?'

She shrugged. 'I'm just worried about this other poor girl.'

I blinked. 'Miranda always knew Joe didn't love her. That's why she tricked him into marrying her.'

'Well, I hope you know what you're doing.' She closed the filing drawer.

'Don't worry, I do. Joe's meeting me at lunchtime and we're off to the building society to see if we can get a mortgage.'

'I see. You're serious then?'

'Of course.' I glared at her. 'We love each other.'

'Then good luck to you both.' Betty squeezed my hand. 'Take care, please.'

After grabbing my handbag from under the desk, I put my coat on. 'Bye then, Betty.' I hurried outside to the pouring rain and spotted Joe by the window under a large umbrella. 'Hi darling, hope you've not been waiting long?'

'No, you're okay. Only just got here.' He lifted the brolly and kissed me on the lips.

I linked my arm in his, snuggling close to stay dry from the rain. 'You managed to get out of work, okay?'

'Yeah. No probs. Said I'd be back as quick as I could.'

'Shouldn't be too long as we've already filled out all the forms. How are you liking it at the Ford garage?'

He took my hand as we wandered across the road to the building society. 'The guys are nice enough. I preferred working on British Leyland cars but didn't really like having Dad as my boss. The foreman here is due to retire in a year or so and he reckons the position will be mine to take.'

'Cool.' I stopped outside the building society. 'You ready?'

He nodded. 'As I'll ever be.'

I pushed the glass door open and wandered up to one of the cashiers. 'We've an appointment with the manager.'

'What name shall I say?' the girl asked.

I rested my handbag on the nearby shelf. 'Rachel Webster and Joe Davies.' I couldn't help but grin.

'If you'd like to take a seat, Mr Dobson will be with you in a minute.' She signalled to the chairs by the entrance.

'Thanks.' Joe took my hand as we headed near the doorway. 'You nervous?' he asked.

'A little but it will be all right.' I perched on the chair. 'Dad reckons we shouldn't have a problem as we've both got good jobs and prospects so we're not a risk.'

Firm footsteps approached and I peered up at a man in a striped navy suit. Reckoned he must have been at least in his fifties with his greying hair. 'Mr Davies and Miss Webster?'

'Yes, that's us.' I got up from the seat.

'How do you do?' Mr Dobson shook our hands in turn. 'If you'd like to come this way.' He pushed open an office door. 'Please, sit down. Can I get you a cup of tea?'

'No thank you,' I said.

He scanned an open file. 'I see you're both first time buyers?'

'Yes,' I said. 'And we both have our savings with you. If you check our accounts, you'll see we have healthy balances.'

'Yes, I noticed that and both in full-time employment with decent salaries too. However, Mr Davies, there is something in your file that does alarm me a little.'

I frowned.

'What's that?' Joe asked.

'I see you're married.'

'Yes, but we're no longer together. We're getting a divorce.'

'That's as maybe but my concern is how that may affect your disposable income. What's happening about spousal maintenance?'

'I'm not paying her anything.'

'We will need written proof. However, there may be another way around things which would make the building society happier.'

'Yes?' I asked.

'Miss Webster could take the mortgage out in her name only. At such time Mr Davies becomes free then a transfer of mortgage could be arranged to add him to the deeds.'

'How will that impact on the amount we can borrow?' I asked.

The bank manager took out his calculator and inputted some figures 'As you are the major wage earner, anyway, on your salary alone, based on your income we can loan up to £12,500, subject to at least ten per cent deposit.'

I glanced at Joe. 'That sounds all right, doesn't it?'

'How much if you took my salary into consideration as well?' Joe asked.

'Using both salaries the maximum amount you could borrow would go up a small amount to £14,750.'

'It's not that much difference,' I said, 'but if we decide to go down the route with both of us on the mortgage, how complicated will it make things?'

'It would have to go to Head Office for approval, and that's on the basis we get written confirmation from Mrs Davies stating she has no intention of applying for spousal maintenance. There would be no guarantee of acceptance. Whereas'– he played with the paperwork – 'with your income and employment record, it should be an open and shut case.'

'Joe, shall we go with just me?' I held his hand. 'Are you all right with that?'

'Sure. If it makes it easier, and by the time my divorce comes through we can buy a bigger and better place in both our names.'

'Then we'll take that option, please, Mr Dobson.'

'A wise move. Do you have a property in mind?'

'Not yet,' I said, 'we wanted to know how much we could borrow before looking.'

'A good plan.' He jotted down something on the form. 'Have you brought in your last three months payslips?'

'Yes.' I passed over my documents. 'Oh, and here's my driving licence.'

'There's no need to worry about identification as you're an existing saver with us.'

'Okay.' I popped my driving licence back into my handbag.

'So, just to confirm, providing the background checks and references come back okay we should be able to loan you up to £12,500 subject to at least a ten-percent deposit on the property.' The manager shuffled the paperwork into the file. 'If you don't mind waiting a few minutes, I'll get a cashier to photocopy your documents.'

'Thank you.' Joe clasped my hand as the manager left the room.

'We should be able to buy something nice with that.'

'That's what I was thinking. Can't believe we're going to be homeowners.' Joe's dark eyes twinkled back at me. 'Well, you are, anyway.'

'Are you sure that's all right with you?'

'Of course. The main thing is we're able to get somewhere together.' He squeezed my fingers.

Mr Dobson returned. 'There you go.' He passed me back my payslips. 'Leave the rest with me. I'll arrange for an offer letter to be sent in the post once I've had the go ahead.' His eyes twinkled behind the metal framed glasses. 'And then you can start looking for your new home.'

Peggy served fishfingers and chips onto our plates. 'So how did you get on?'

'Good,' Joe said. 'We can borrow £12,500 with a ten percent deposit. We're going to see a two-bedroom house a couple of roads up from here.'

'Excellent. My son a homeowner.' Adam sprinkled salt and vinegar on his chips.

'Um, actually not quite.' Joe cut into his fishfinger. 'Seems because I'm married it may cause problems. So, we're going to do it in Rachel's name only.'

'And you're all right with that, son?' Adam asked.

'Yes. The main thing is we can set up home together, and it's silly for us to rent when we can buy. I'll still help with the deposit and mortgage payments.'

'I see. I hope you'll get something legal drawn up in the event something happens to you, Rachel?'

'We can do, yes.'

'Also, in the event you break up, if Joe's been helping with the mortgage payments he shouldn't come out with nothing.' Adam looked at me.

'That's not going to happen but I'm happy to have any paperwork drawn up that's necessary.'

'It isn't necessary, Rach.' Joe glared at Adam.

'No good looking at me like that, Joe, these things happen.' Adam rubbed his upper lip. 'No one knows what the future holds. It's better to be prepared.'

I nodded to Joe. 'It's all right.'

'Did the interview take long?' Peggy asked.

'Not at all. We were almost in and out.' Joe dipped a chip into ketchup. 'Only because we'd already given them details over the phone so it was just the case of us confirming a few things and showing proof of earnings.'

'It'll probably take at least a couple of weeks I imagine,' I said, 'for them to get my references and do the background checks, but we've made an appointment to check out a house up the road which is under eleven thousand.'

Adam blew his nose and looked at me. 'How do you think your parents will feel about you buying around here?'

'They'll be fine, I'm sure. It's not like it's a rough area. There's probably something close to my folks but we don't want to use all our savings as we'll need funds to buy furniture, carpets etc.' I grinned. 'It's so exciting.'

'We're very pleased for you, aren't we, Adam?' Peggy sipped water from a glass.

'Yes, of course. If there's anything we can do to help, just yell.'

'We will, don't worry.' Joe winked at me from the opposite side of the table. 'We've got a flat to rent too.'

'Already? Where's that?' Adam put his knife and fork down.

'It's over a shop next to the newspaper offices,' I said. 'The tenant's gone abroad for four months. Mr Strange knows the landlord, and he said the place is ours if we want. We'll have to put a deposit down plus Mr Strange has vouched for me. I've got the keys and we're going to take a look around after dinner.'

Adam frowned. 'How does the existing tenant feel about that? Does he even know?'

'Oh yes, the landlord checked with him before offering it to us and it means the tenant doesn't have to worry about paying his rent while he's away because we'll be paying. So – I shrugged – 'it works for us all. Keep your fingers crossed. Joe and I could be moved in together by the weekend.'

Peggy frowned. 'You don't think you're moving too quickly?'

'Absolutely not, Mam. We've wasted too much time already. We don't intend to waste a single moment. You're not happy for us?'

I glared at Peggy. 'What is it?'

'Call me stupid. It's just that... It's just over the last few years I've known and loved you as my daughter and now with all this...'

'It doesn't change anything.' I reached out to touch her hand. 'I told you. And you'll still be my mum in a sense.'

'Yes, yes of course. It's just me as a mam worrying. You'll understand once you have your own.'

Chapter Thirty-Five

Rachel

Smiling, I breezed down the metal flight of stairs from our new flat, down to the street, and ambled around to the newspaper office. How cool was this? Leaving home at quarter-to-nine to get to work. I pushed open the glass door and found Betty on the reception desk.

'Morning, Betty.'

'Morning, Rachel. Is it true you've moved up there?'

'Yep. We moved in last week. Sorry, I didn't get a chance to tell you.' I popped the door key into my handbag. 'Two minutes to get to work. I'm being spoilt. Do you fancy a tour when you finish today?'

She fingered her wedding ring. 'I really should...'

'It's okay, I understand.'

'No, it's not that I don't want to. I've got a man from the electricity board coming around at two. Tell you what, I'll knock off a few minutes earlier and you can show me then. If that works for you?'

'John's out of the office this week so that'll be fine. Mr Strange isn't going to complain as long as the work gets done. I'll meet you here at ten-to-one.'

'Great. Want a cuppa to take upstairs with you?'

'Go on then, you've twisted my arm. What are you doing on reception, anyway?'

'I'm not. I was just collecting a file. Lizzie will be here in a minute.' Betty waddled into the back office and flicked the kettle switch. 'Fancy a cup of tea, Mel?'

'Yes, please.' Mel turned to me. 'I'm so excited about this evening.'

Betty added teabags to the mugs. 'What's happening this evening?'

'I'm having a small dinner party.' I smiled. 'Our first one.'

'Who else is coming?' Mel asked.

'Linda, Stu and Jenny.'

Betty poured water over the teabags. 'I'm sure you'll all have a grand time. Right, young ladies, your tea is ready and you'd both better get to work. It's almost nine o'clock.'

'Thanks, Betty.' I grabbed the mug. 'See you later.'

'Are you okay with these stairs?'

'I'm not that decrepit, young lady. Of course, I'm okay.' Betty followed me up the metal stairway to the front door and I put the key in the lock.

'Come in.' I sensed myself beaming.

'Goodness. It's like a tardis, isn't it? I've never been in one of these flats.'

'Wait until you see the lounge. It's enormous.' I headed down the wide hallway.

'You're not kidding,' Betty said on entering, 'must be at least twenty-one-foot by eighteen. Be difficult to heat though.'

'The gas fire helps. And hopefully only a few more weeks of this cold weather left and we'll have our own place by next winter. Betty, aren't you happy for us?'

'Of course, I am. Why wouldn't I be?'

'I don't know, you just seem a little sharp. I know we're not married but it's almost the eighties and people think differently these days.'

She patted my arm. 'Aw, sorry, love, it's not you. It's me. I'm still getting these mood swings. Think I need to be on the HRT for a little longer before they disappear.'

'Maybe you're trying to do too much. Is there something else going on at home?'

'You're very perceptive for a young soul. There is, love. My mam's deteriorating quickly. She has dementia, and yesterday when I visited the care home, she didn't even know who I was.' Betty dabbed her eyes.

'I'm sorry. That must be hard.' I put my arms around her. 'Here's me all jolly while you're going through that.'

'Don't apologise, love. Now come on, show me the rest of this place.'

'Okay. This way for the kitchen.' I took her into a large area with fitted cupboards along both sides of the wall.

She investigated the stainless-steel sink, the large fridge on the opposite side of the room, and the electric cooker. 'I've got a Creda cooker too,' she said. 'I love it. And you have a nice space for your dinner party this evening with the pine table. You'll easily fit eight around this and anytime you need extra chairs, I'm sure Mr Strange won't mind you borrowing a couple from the staffroom.'

'Thanks, Betty. We're okay this evening as there's just the six of us.'

'Right, show me your bedroom and then I must rush off.'

'Just next door.' I took her in and made my way to the bay window. 'We get a good view of the village centre from here but I hate these sash windows.'

'I've never liked them either. Just make sure you don't put your head under.' She laughed. 'I'm really pleased for you and Joe, and I'm sorry if you thought I was being a sourpuss.'

I hugged her. 'No need to apologise. I understand now. It's a difficult time for you.'

'Thanks, pet.'

※

After flicking the sides of my hair back with the curling brush, I stared at my reflection in the mirror. The orange satin trouser suit brought out the brown in my eyes and the white T-shirt was a snug fit. My hair now almost reached my shoulders after I'd decided to grow it again. Linda had grown her short style out too. It meant less trips to the hairdresser.

Joe came out of the bathroom freshly showered wearing a striped dressing gown. 'You look divine.' He took me into his arms and kissed me on the lips.

'You don't look so bad yourself, Mr Davies, and you smell gorgeous.' I sniffed his wet hair. 'Mmm, this is nice. Coconut?'

'Glad you like it. Close your eyes, I've got a present for you.'

'A present. Why?'

'Just do it.'

I did as he instructed and only opened my eyes after he'd placed a package in my palms. 'What have I done to deserve this?'

'Just being you. Go on, open it.'

I ripped off the gold paper wrapping. 'Estée Lauder. Cool.' I opened the box and squirted a bit behind my ears and on my wrists. 'Awesome. It smells all flowery. Have a whiff.'

He lifted my hand to his nose. 'Oh yeah, I like that.' He took me into his arms again and kissed me fully on the lips. 'What time did you say they were arriving?'

'Soon.' I pulled away. 'Definitely not time for that.' I laughed. 'Right, I'd better get on with the preparations.'

'Need some help?'

'You'd best get some clothes on first.' I made my way into the kitchen and threw a pinafore apron over my head to protect my new clothes. The aromas from the oven were inviting. I grabbed the oven gloves from a hook, took out the casserole dish and gave it a stir. Taking a teaspoon, I dipped it into the stew and tasted. 'Yum. Not bad for my first effort.' The kettle had boiled so I added the water to a large pan of dried rice and put it on the electric ring.

While the rice was cooking, I threw a white linen tablecloth over the pine table, set out the blue-handled cutlery and lit a matching candle as a centrepiece. I was really excited about our first dinner party. I'd just finished stirring the rice when the doorbell rang.

'I'll get it,' Joe called.

Suddenly I was nervous, but why? I removed my apron and tossed it into a drawer. Although it was only my sister and friends we were entertaining I wanted to make a good impression. I took the chilled grapefruit portions from the fridge and put one in front of each place setting.

'Hiya.' Linda hugged me on entering. 'This looks nice.'

'Thanks.'

'Wow. That trouser suit was made for you.'

'Cheers. You're a good saleswoman. Does the table look okay?'

'It looks amazing. A proper little Stepford wife.'
'Oi.'
'Just getting my own back.'
'How are you?'
'Good. I'm one of those lucky women who doesn't suffer from much nausea. Just a bit in the morning and then I'm good.'
'Cool. I hope I'll be like that when it's my turn.'
The doorbell went again. 'I'll get it,' Joe said.
Voices travelled to the room before Jenny and Mel came in. I kissed them both in turn.
'This is a fab pad,' Mel said.
'Thanks.'
'It is nice.' Jenny kissed my cheek. 'The table looks good, sis. You been taking tips from Mum?'
'Yep.' I laughed. 'Just hope my cooking is as good as hers.'
'No worries if it's not,' Joe said as he came through with Stu. My pulse quickened at the sight of Joe in the black jeans hugging his slight hips and the cream silk shirt showing off his slightly hairy chest.
Stu glanced at the table. 'Wine glasses? No beer?'
'You can have beer if you prefer, mate.' Joe went to the fridge and took out a couple of cans of lager.
'Take a seat at the table,' I said. 'Asti Spumante okay for you girls?'
'Just juice or water for me,' Linda said as she sat down.
'Sorry, I should've thought. Joe, can you get the orange juice from the fridge for Lind.'
'Sure.'
Jenny and Mel nodded. 'This is all very pleasant,' Mel said.
Once everyone was seated and had a glass of sparkling wine, lager or orange juice, we dipped into the grapefruit servings.

'I reckon we should have a toast.' Linda raised her glass. 'To Joe and Rach. Took them a while to get here but I'm so glad they did.'

※

'That was a great dinner, Rach,' Jenny said as I showed her around the flat.

'Thanks. What's happening about your job?'

'I quit. My last shift is next week.' She sank down on the bed. 'This is comfy.'

'Not bad, is it? And what happens then?'

'I'm off to Paris for a few months. Just until Phil and Jan's contracts finish. They've said I can help them in the studio. Hopefully during that time I'll decide what I want to do when we return home.'

'You could always do something like Kate. She's a secretary/PA to a doctor at the hospital.'

'Nope. I don't fancy that.'

'How about a job with figures. Something in accounts?'

'Definitely don't fancy that. I don't know what I want but hopefully it will all click into place.'

'How are Mum and Dad now about you giving up nursing?'

'Still moaning. Remember when it used to be you they moaned about all the time? Now you're the golden child.' She chuckled. 'There was something I wanted to ask you.'

'Anything.'

'It's about Phil.'

'What about him?'

'I know I said before that we were just friends. Well...'

'You want more.'

She nodded. 'We both do but we don't want to upset you.'

I flopped down on the bed next to Jenny. 'Go for it, sis. I hope you and Phil can find the happiness that Joe and I have. I love you both and nothing would make me happier than if it worked out for you. You deserve it.'

'Thanks, Rach.' She hugged me.

'Right' – I slid off the bed – 'let's get back to making the coffee. The others will wonder where we've got to.'

Mel was filling the kettle when we entered the kitchen. 'I thought I'd start. Hope I'm not treading on your toes?'

'No, of course you're not. Thanks. Lind, are you drinking coffee?'

'I don't suppose you've got any hot chocolate or Cocoa?'

'Yep. I've got a tub of Cadbury's.' I poured milk into a saucepan and placed it on the cooker ring.

'So, what's the gossip?' Mel added a spoonful of Nescafé into five mugs.

'Did I tell you Kate's engaged?'

'No? When?'

'At Christmas. She's marrying a doctor.'

'Lucky cow.'

'And Jen's off to Paris. She's quit nursing, and –' I glanced at Jenny – 'is it okay if I say?'

'Yes.' She smiled.

'Jen and Phil have got together.'

Mel slumped into a chair. 'It's not fair. Everyone's moving forward with their lives. You and Joe, Jen and Phil, Kate and her doctor, Linda and Stu having a baby, and I'm still stuck going nowhere.'

Jenny put her arm around Mel. 'Aren't you seeing anyone?'

Mel shrugged. 'Nope.'

'When did you last have a date?' Linda asked.

'Hmm, I don't know. I've been out with a few blokes since Sam but they either two-time me or it just fizzles out. It's like

I'm sending an unconscious message of don't come near me, because I'm worried they'll turn out to be like him.'

'That's understandable,' I said, 'but not all men are abusive like Sam. Look at Joe, Phil, and Stu. And Kate's new man, David, seems kind, I can't see him ever hurting her.' I rushed over to the cooker and caught the pan of milk just in time before it boiled over. I poured it into a mug, added a couple of heaped spoonfuls of chocolate powder from the tub and stirred. Afterwards I poured boiling water into each of the coffee mugs, and a dash of milk into three of them. 'I've an idea.'

'What's that then?' Linda asked.

'For Mel, I'll see if Kate's fiancé has a friend to set her up with on a blind date. What do you think, Mel?'

'A blind date. I'm not sure. I'll have to think about that.'

'Blind date for who?' Joe asked as he and Stu wandered into the kitchen. 'We thought we'd better come and find you all as you've been so long.' Joe kissed me briefly on the lips. 'I thought it was supposed to be the men who always hang around in the kitchen at parties.'

I laughed. 'We're trying to fix Mel up with a date. Don't suppose you've got any mechanics who are single at your garage, have you? And how about you, Stu?'

Joe went to the fridge and took out a couple of cans of lager and passed one to Stu. 'Here you go, mate.' He glanced at Mel. 'Actually, we had a new guy start last week. Maybe we should have another dinner party and invite him. What do you think?'

Mel twiddled her diamante pendant. 'I suppose that would be okay as I wouldn't be on my own with him.'

'It'll be nice for Darren too, as he's new to the area and looking to make friends. What about Jen though? We can't have an odd number.'

'Don't worry about me, Joe, as I'm off to Paris shortly. Me and Phil are official now that Rachel's given us her blessing.'

'I'm sure you'll love Paris.' He tilted his glass and slowly poured in the lager. 'You loved it, didn't you, Rach?'

'I did. And Phil and Jan's flat is fabulous.'

Jen sipped her coffee. 'You two should come over and stay while I'm there.'

Linda peered up at the clock. 'It's getting late, Stu. Do you mind if we leave as I'm feeling tired and have to drive as you've been drinking.'

Stu took his hands out of his pockets. 'Sure, babe.'

'I'll come now too.' Jen picked up her handbag.

'And me.' Mel finished her coffee and put the mug on the draining board. 'We'll let you two wind down before going to bed.'

Joe collected the coats from the bedroom, and we kissed everyone on the cheek as they left. Once they were all safely in their cars, I closed the front door and switched off the outside light. 'Well, I think that went well.'

'It did.' Joe took me into his arms. 'Sod the washing up. I've been waiting all evening for this.' He kissed me hard, picked me up and carried me to the bedroom.

Chapter Thirty-Six

Peggy

Kate popped her breakfast plate in the sink, and kissed her brother who was in his high chair. 'See you later little bro. Oops.' She wiped Ben's breadcrumbs from her lips. 'Your big sis can't go to work looking like that. Have a good day, Mam.'

'Oh, before you go, Kate. Are you about this evening to babysit? Rachel and Joe have asked us over to see the flat but I don't fancy taking Ben with all those steps. They sound dangerous.'

'I'll be here, Mam, although the steps aren't that bad, but yep, I'm happy to look after Ben. David plans to pop round after his shift.' Kate kissed me on the cheek. 'Catch you later.'

'Just you and me now.' I wiped Ben's face with a warm flannel before taking him out of the high chair. 'Let's get you changed ready for when Aunty Sheila comes around.' She'd asked to visit so I hoped it wasn't bad news. And that reminded me, I must ask Rachel this evening if she'd managed to contact Mike to let him know she wasn't his daughter. Someone had to tell him.

The doorbell went, breaking my thoughts. I looked up at the clock. It was only just gone nine. Maybe it was the postman. I put Ben in the playpen. 'Mam'll be back in a minute.' He screamed as I left the room.

I opened the front door to a young woman. 'Can I help you?'

'I hope so. You don't know me but…'

'Can I help you?' I asked again. 'Only as you can hear the baby's screaming.'

'I…'

'Yes?'

She unbuttoned and re-buttoned her coat. 'I don't know how to say this.'

'Well, if you could hurry up and decide so I can get back in there.'

She blinked. 'I think you're my mother.'

'Oh' – I touched my brow – 'Yes. Sorry, you must be Teresa.' But she didn't look anything like me.

'I thought you might be expecting me.'

'Well, yes, and no… not like this.'

'The adoption agency gave me your details.'

'I see. I'm sorry for my reaction. You surprised me. You'd better come in. I thought you'd write or phone first.'

'It was a spur of the moment thing.' She stepped over the threshold and wiped her feet on the mat. 'Would you like me to take my boots off?'

'If you wouldn't mind. I'm sorry you've kind of caught me on the hop. I don't know anything about you other than your name.'

She followed me into the lounge and headed over to the playpen. 'Hello, little man. What's all that noise?'

I picked him up and he immediately stopped crying.

'Does he always do that?'

'What?'

'Stop when you pick him up?'

'Usually. Yes.'

'Is he your grandson?'

'No. He's mine. His name's Ben.'

'How old is he?'

'Six months and he's a little pickle.'

'He's my brother then?'

'Yes, I suppose he is. Sit down please, and maybe you could tell me about yourself.'

She slipped off her herringbone coat and black beret, folded them carefully and placed them on the back of the couch. This girl with short spikey blonde hair didn't look anything like me or Mike. There had to have been some kind of mistake. I chewed my lip. 'Look, Teresa, I think they must've got the tests mixed up. I mean, you don't look like me at all.'

'I don't look like my mam and dad either.' She perched on the edge of the cushion. 'This is a shock for me too, you know? To find out after twenty-four years that the people I've grown up with as Mam and Dad aren't my real parents.' Her faced reddened. 'You think I want this?'

'No, sorry, that's not what I meant. It's just that Rachel...'

'Rachel? Is she the girl you thought you put up for adoption?'

'Yes. Well, if you could see her, she's the spitting image of me which is why I'm wondering if they've got the tests wrong.'

'No, they haven't. I'm definitely your daughter.' She touched her hair. 'This is dyed. I'm really a brunette. Maybe if it was dark I'd look more like you.'

'Maybe.'

'Aren't you pleased to see me? The adoption agency gave me the impression it was what you wanted.'

'It's just a shock. It is what I want. I just hadn't realised it would be like this.'

'Sorry. I can be impulsive at times. I wasn't sure what to do and rather than keep going over and over it in my head I thought *go for it*. So here I am.'

'Can I get you a cup of tea? Coffee?'

'That would be nice. Would you like me to hold Ben while you make it?'

Could I hand my baby over to a stranger? She may be my daughter but I didn't know anything about her. Supposing she ran off with him? But then why would she? I was being paranoid. 'Thank you. Why not come through too? Otherwise he'll only scream if I'm out of sight. He's at that age.'

'Okay.' She followed me into the kitchen.

'If you sit there.'

Once she was seated at the table I passed her Ben, and I moved over to the sink to fill the kettle from the tap. 'Coffee or tea?'

'Coffee thanks.' She bounced Ben on her lap.

'Don't bounce him too much as he's only just had his breakfast.'

'Sorry.'

'So, tell me more about yourself.' I added instant coffee to a mug.

'Well, you know my birthday.' Teresa smiled showing off her crooked shiny teeth. 'What do you want to know?'

'Anything. All of it. What do you like? Hobbies?'

'I write poetry, and I like painting. The art kind not decorating.' She tittered.

'Do you still live at home?'

'At the moment, although I'm getting married later this year.'

'Oh really? My daughter Kate's getting married in July.'

'Kate. That's a nice name.'

'Thank you. What type of job do you have?'

'I'm a dance teacher.'

'What sort?'

'Tap, ballet, ballroom, Latin and American. You name it I can probably teach it.'

'Have you always liked to dance?'

'Yes. Been going to classes since I was three.'

'Sorry if this sounds impertinent, but are your parents well off?'

'No. Not at all. But they worked hard to make sure that me and my brother could do other stuff. Bobby, that's my brother, he did dancing and football.'

'How old is he?'

'Twenty-one this year. Although...' her smile dropped. 'I suppose now he's not my brother.' She sighed. 'I had a brother.'

'I'm sure Bobby will never stop being your brother just because of a piece of paper.' I poured boiling water into the mug. 'Sugar? Milk?'

'No, as it comes, please.'

'I like mine that way too. You know you have two more brothers. Ben, who you now know' – I smiled, softening to this girl – 'and Joe, he's a year younger than you. His real name was Neil but he changed it to Joe.'

Ben gave a little cry. Teresa lifted him to a standing position on her lap making him giggle. 'He likes being on his feet. Is he walking around the furniture yet?'

'No, not yet.'

'How old is Kate?'

'Twenty-one so a little older than your Bobby. Why don't I take Ben so you can drink your coffee?'

'Cool. Thanks.' Teresa passed Ben to me. 'What's my father like?' She picked up the cup. 'Will he be home later?'

'Mike Millar, that's his name, lives in the States. I'll give you his address if you like. We were never married.'

'Oh?'

'It's a long story, and I will tell you about it, but maybe not right now as my sister's due shortly.'

'I have an aunty? How about grandparents?'

'Just an aunty. You wouldn't have liked your grandfather. It's his fault I didn't keep you.'

'Oh?'

'Again, a story for another time.'

'I'm kind of glad I'm not related to my wicked great aunty. I mean how could a woman do something like that?' She shook her head. 'How could any woman swap two babies?'

'I don't know. Look, I'd better get Ben dressed before Sheila arrives. Do you mind?'

'No, of course not.'

'I'll be back in a minute,' I said, but changed my mind. 'Unless you want to come up too? You can see his nursery.'

Her face lit up. 'Yes, I'd like that, thanks.' She put the cup down on the table.

When we got to Ben's room, she headed straight for the baby changer unit. 'May I?'

'I'm not sure.'

'I know what to do. Please.'

'All right.' I passed her Ben.

She removed his Babygro with confidence. 'Are these his clothes for today?' She signalled to the Marks and Spencer navy blue romper outfit Sheila had bought him.

'Yes.'

'Teresa folded a napkin underneath him and pinned it firmly in place.

'Where did you learn to do that?'

'My cousin's got a little boy of similar age. I've been babysitting for him since he was born. I can't wait to have one of my own.' Teresa beamed. I liked her. She was different to Rachel, and to Kate, but there was something about her. A gentleness that drew you in. 'There he is.' She passed me Ben. 'All set for his Aunty Sheila. I'd best be getting off.'

'Thank you. I'll put him in his pram ready for when she comes. She'll be here in a minute. Have you got time to hang on as I'm sure she'd love to meet you?'

'All right, but then I'd better shoot off as I have a class at eleven. I'd love to come again though and meet the rest of the family.'

'I'd like that too,' I said as the doorbell rang. 'That'll be our Sheila now.' I hurried downstairs with Ben, and Teresa followed. I laid Ben in the pram before opening the door. 'Hi Sheila, come in quickly so we don't let the heat out. I've got a surprise.'

'Oh?' She stepped into the hallway and gazed at Teresa. 'This is...'

Before I got any further Sheila said, 'Your daughter.'

'How do you know?'

'She's the image of our mam at that age.'

'I am?' Teresa smiled.

'Really? I don't think I've seen the photos. This is Teresa.'

'Pleased to meet you, Teresa. I'm your Aunty Sheila. Me and Malc, he's my hubby, were browsing through a box of old photos only the other night and I'm not kidding you, it's like looking at me mam.'

'I'd love to see them,' Teresa said, 'but unfortunately, I must rush off now. Maybe...?'

'Tell you what love, get my details off Peg, and give us a ring when you fancy popping round. We're only five miles or so down the road.'

'Thanks. Nice to meet you, Aunty Sheila.' She turned to me. 'And you, Peggy. I look forward to seeing you again and meeting the rest of the family.'

'Me too.' I scribbled my phone number down on a piece of paper. 'This is my number. Give me a ring when you're free so I can make sure the others are here. You can come for tea one Sunday.'

'Cool.' Teresa put on her coat and hat hiding her spikey hair. 'Bye then. Till next time.' She opened the door and Sheila and I watched her go down the footpath.

Sheila pushed the pram out of the door with Ben bundled up for the bitter January day although at least the sun was shining. 'I reckon a brisk walk and back in for a cuppa,' she said. 'What do you say?'

'I agree. What did you think of her?'

'She seems nice. Uncanny the likeness to Mam though. Surprised you didn't see it.'

'No, I didn't. Actually, I thought a mistake must've been made because she was so unlike me. Hey, look at those snowdrops.' I pointed to a neighbour's garden.

'Gorgeous, aren't they. Sign of spring not too far away, thank goodness.'

'Anyway, I presume you've some news of your own.' I smiled.

'Aye. I have.' Her eyes sparkled. 'Remember I told you...?'

'I do. And are you?'

'I kind of didn't correct you last time but no, I'm not pregnant, but we are getting a baby.'

I shook my head. 'I don't understand.'

'We're adopting.'

'Oh.'

'We gave up trying to have one of our own. It was soul destroying, having our hopes raised only to lose them, so a couple of years ago we spoke to an adoption agency. It's taken ages but...'

Ben gave a little cry.

'Shh, it's okay little man.' Sheila rocked the pram as she pushed. 'We've got a little boy. He's three months so a little younger than Ben.'

'That's wonderful. I'm so pleased for you.'

'Yeah, us too. The poor little love has been in foster care since his birth. We've been allowed to visit him a couple of times and next week we get to bring him home. Wait until you meet him. He's adorable.'

'That's really good news, Sheila. Congratulations.' I wondered whether this was how Rachel's adopted parents felt when they'd collected her. A little boy. A playmate for Ben.

Rachel showed us into their bedroom. 'And finally, this is the master bedroom' – Rachel's eyes twinkled – 'of course it's the only bedroom.' She chuckled.

'It's lovely,' I said. 'I love the purple colour scheme.'

'Thanks, we do too. Only curtains and accessories as obviously we can't redecorate. The curtains and bedding came from Mackays in Brixham Road.' Rachel picked up a plastic plant pot. 'And these and the artificial violas we got from the new Homebase. Have you been in there yet?'

'No, we haven't,' I said. 'Is it any good?'

'Brilliant. Lots of bargains.' She sighed. 'I don't know what's happened to Joe.'

Adam gazed out of the window. 'Maybe he was sent on a breakdown.'

'Possibly,' Rachel said, 'but I don't know why he hasn't rung. I hope nothing's happened to him.'

'I'm sure he's fine,' I said but my stomach tightened. Supposing something had happened to him?

The phone rang. Rachel's eyes sparkled. 'Ha, that'll be him now.' She headed into the hallway and picked up the phone. 'Kate, hello. Yep, your mum and dad are here. Your dad? Hang on.'

I hurried out to Rachel. 'Is Ben all right?'

'I think so but she's asking for Adam.'

Adam was by my side. Rachel passed him the phone.

'Hello, love. Everything all right?'

'What's she saying?' I asked.

Adam waved his hand. 'Oh my God. Are you all right, Kate?'

'What's happening?' I asked again.

'Good. Yes, and you're okay to carry on looking after Ben? Yep. We'll let you know when we get there. All right, love.' Adam handed Rachel back the receiver and turned to me. 'It's Joe.'

'Joe.' I held my stomach. 'Please, please tell me he's all right.'

Rachel's face was almost white. 'What's happened?'

'Joe's been stabbed.' Adam rubbed his brow. 'No more details except he was rushed to casualty. I'll drive us.'

Chapter Thirty-Seven

Rachel

Adam charged to the reception desk. 'Our son, Joe Davies, was brought in by ambulance after a stabbing.'

The receptionist studied the ledger in front of her. 'Mr Davies' injuries are being assessed so you can't see him yet. However, I'll get a porter to show you to the relatives' room. His wife's already in there as she arrived with him.'

I clenched my fists. What the hell was she doing there?

'Here's a porter now,' the receptionist said. 'Can you take Mr Davies' family to the relatives' room?'

'Certainly. Come this way.'

We followed the porter through the double doors and down a corridor. He stopped at a door marked *Relatives' Room* and pushed the door open. 'You can wait in here. The doctor will be with you as soon as possible. There's a vending machine so you can help yourselves to a hot drink.'

'Thank you,' Adam said, holding the door open to allow Peggy and me to go inside first.

Miranda had her head down but I knew it was her because the receptionist had said she was here.

Raising my voice, I asked, 'Why the hell are you here?'

She looked up, rubbing her bloodshot eyes. 'They called me. I am his wife after all.'

'In name only,' Adam said, 'and after what your thug father and his mates did to Joe, he wants nothing to do with you. None of us do. So, clear off. We don't need the likes of you here.'

'But they didn't call her, Adam,' I said, 'they can't have. She's not down as next of kin. Joe and I made sure of that. You and Peggy are. And the receptionist said she came in with him.' I glared at Miranda. 'This has something to do with your lot, doesn't it?' I moved closer.

'No' – she pushed me away – 'the hospital called me. I didn't know anything about the accident until I got the phone call.' She sobbed.

I grabbed her arm. 'You're a liar. Accident? This was deliberate. Was it your father's doing?'

Her face flushed.

'You know something, don't you?' I pressed my fingers into her arm. 'Tell us what you know.'

'I didn't mean to.' She sobbed again.

'Didn't mean to what?' Adam asked.

'I didn't mean to. I just had the knife to threaten him.'

'My God. It was you.' I was about to give her a slap when Adam pulled me away. 'Don't, Rachel. She'll get her comeuppance.'

Miranda aimed for the door.

'Oh no, lady. I don't think so.' I grabbed her by the hair. 'You're not going anywhere except to the police station and you'd better pray to God that Joe's all right otherwise you'll be going down for murder. You wicked bitch.' I punched her arm. 'How could you do that?'

Peggy dragged me away. 'He'll be okay, Rachel. I can feel it,' she said as a nurse came through the door.

'Mr and Mrs Davies?'

'Yes,' Adam said. 'What's happening?'

'Joe's been taken down to theatre. He has a punctured lung.'

'Is he going to be okay?' I asked.

'It's too early to say, I'm afraid. He's lost a lot more blood than we'd have liked. Unfortunately, there was a delay in the ambulance being called.'

I took a deep breath. 'Are the police here?' I pointed to Miranda. 'She...'s the one who did it.' I clenched my jaw. 'And she didn't even call for help straight away. What a cow.'

Peggy held me back.

'The police are in reception. I'll send them through.'

Miranda tried to follow the nurse through the door but Adam stood in front of her. 'You're not going anywhere, young lady. You're going to pay for what you've done to our son.'

Peggy gripped my hand as we entered the ward. We stopped at the nurses' station. 'We're here to see Joe Davies,' I said.

'Mr Davies' bed is at the end. You can only stay for a few moments though as it's gone visiting time.'

'Thanks.' The three of us made our way down the ward. I wasn't sure who was the most nervous. What state would Joe be in?

We stopped at his bed where he was hooked up to a heart monitor, and a bag hung from a stand transfusing blood into his arm as he slept.

'Joe?' I whispered.

He opened his eyes. 'Rach.'

'I'm here. So are your mam and dad.' I took his hand. 'Do you remember what happened?'

'Think so.'

'Don't try and talk, lad,' Adam said. 'Plenty of time for that.'

'Miranda turned up at work.' Joe took a deep breath.

'It's all right, love.' Peggy patted his arm. 'You're safe now.'

'The police are questioning her,' I said.

'We had a row. She begged me not to leave her.' Joe blinked. 'She got hysterical.' He took another breath. 'Said no one else was to have me.' He rubbed his temple. 'The foreman saw her off.'

'It's all right, lad.' Adam patted Joe's shoulder. 'Take your time.'

'After work I was jumped. Too dark. Must've been one of her father's thugs.'

A nurse came to Joe's bed. 'Mr Davies needs to rest now as do all of you. Come back tomorrow at visiting times and bring some of his personal stuff, pyjamas, toiletries etcetera.'

Joe already had his eyes closed when we kissed him in turn before we tiptoed out of the ward so as not to disturb the other patients.

Joe was slightly propped up in bed when I arrived and smiled as I approached. I kissed him on the cheek. 'Don't ever do that to me again.' I sniffled. 'Thank God you're okay. I'm going to church this Sunday to thank him properly.'

'Sorry.'

'It wasn't your fault. I thought I'd lost you.'

'You don't get rid of me that easily.' He squeezed my hand.

'They've taken Miranda in for questioning.'

'Have they found out who did this to me?'

'It was Miranda.'

'That can't be right. You mean her dad?'

'No. She admitted to doing it to me and your folks.'

He squinted. 'She must be covering for her dad. I know she threatened me but I'm sure that's all it was. A threat. She wouldn't want to hurt me.'

'She did it, Joe' – I held his hand – 'I'm sorry. And what's more she delayed getting you help.'

He ran his tongue across his lips. 'I can't believe it.'

'Your mouth looks dry.' I poured a glass of water. 'Here drink this.'

He took a sip from the tumbler before pushing it away. I returned it to the cabinet and held up a rucksack. 'I've brought you some stuff. PJs, toothbrush and that type of thing. Your mam and dad will be here shortly. They're just waiting for Sheila to come around to watch Ben.'

Joe closed his eyes. 'I'm not feeling that good. Rach, I feel dizzy and...' He held his ribs and winced. His faced paled and the monitor bleeped.

'Nurse,' I shouted.

A nurse hurried over. 'Out of the way, please.' She rang the bell and pulled across the curtain.

I stood back as a doctor and another nurse rushed to Joe. The curtain was drawn back and the next thing they wheeled him out.

'Where are you taking him?' I moved close to Joe's side.

'Back to theatre,' the doctor answered. 'Go to the relatives' room and I'll send someone to fill you in with what's going on. In the meantime, it's imperative we get him down to surgery now.'

Adam tapped his foot. Peggy rubbed her hands. I clenched my fingers. What if he didn't come through? It wasn't fair. We'd waited years to be together and now when I thought we had our happy ever after everything was going wrong. I sobbed. 'I can't lose him.'

Peggy put her arm around me. 'None of us can, love. We have to pray he'll be okay.'

'It's the waiting. It's too hard. They said someone would come and tell me what's going on. Where are they?'

'They'll be here. It's more important that they take care of Joe.' Adam went over to the vending machine in the corner of the room. 'Cup of tea, Rachel, while we wait?'

'No thanks. I think if I drink anything I'll be sick.'

'Peg?'

'No thanks, Adam. I'm with Rachel. It'll just come back up again.'

When the door opened Adam sat back down. The same nurse who hurried me away in the ward entered the room and took a seat next to Adam. 'I'm afraid there's been a further development and your son's condition is life threatening. Unfortunately, there were complications from the second wound. It's looking like peritonitis. If his spleen's ruptured, they'll need to remove it. All you can do is hope and pray.'

I screamed. 'Oh my God. I don't want to lose him.'

The nurse came across to me and took my hand. 'He's in the best hands. The surgeon's one of the best in his field. If anyone can pull Joe through, he can. Try and stay positive.'

'Thank you.' *Please God, please let Joe be okay. I'll try to be a better person just let him be okay.* I couldn't believe Miranda had stabbed him twice. The evil bitch should be locked up for life even if Joe managed to come through this. *Please, God, let him come through this.*

'We should let Kate know what's happening.' Adam went to stand up but Peggy pressed him back down.

'No, not yet,' Peggy said. 'Let's wait until we know more. No point upsetting her while she's working. Wait until they tell us he's going to be all right. And they will. I know they will.' She rested a hand on the left-hand side of her chest. 'I can feel it in here.'

'I hope so, darling.' Adam pulled Peggy closer.

'We should let our Sheila know though,' she said. 'I told her we'd be back in a couple of hours. Will you phone her?'

'Yes. I'll go and do that now.' He squeezed Peggy's hand. 'I'll be back in a few minutes.'

It was almost seven o'clock and Joe had been in surgery for over four hours. Peggy was sleeping on Adam's shoulder and he was staring into space. There was no way I could sleep. What was happening? Why was it taking so long? Kate would be home now and Sheila would have filled her in. I wondered if David was with her. I hoped so. Footsteps reached the door. I jogged Peggy. 'Someone's coming.'

She straightened up, tossing her hair out of the way as the doctor entered.

'Good news, Mr and Mrs Davies. The operation went well. Joe's going to be all right. He's still in recovery so I'm afraid you can't see him but suggest you go home and get a good night's rest. Come back at visiting time tomorrow.'

I stood up. 'Please can I see him now? Just for a couple of minutes. I really need to see him.'

'I'm afraid that isn't possible. Go home and get a good night's rest.' He touched my shoulder. 'I promise someone will call you if there's any change. Right now, he needs rest and so do all of you.'

Adam rose from the chair. 'Thank you, doctor. Thank you so much.'

'You're welcome.' The doctor yawned. 'Try and get some rest. I'm knocking off now myself.' He yawned again. 'It's been one hell of a night,' he said on leaving.

'Let's go home,' Adam said. He turned to me. 'And you, young lady, had better stay with us tonight. We don't want you on your own.'

Joe was asleep when I arrived. I kissed him on the cheek and sank into the green chair next to him.

He opened his eyes. 'Rach, is that you?' He stretched out his hand.

I rose and leaned over him. 'It's okay darling. I'm here. How are you feeling?'

'Like I've... I don't know. Bloody awful.'

'I'm not surprised. They had to do a second operation.'

'Another one? Why?'

'It seems she stabbed you twice and the second wound caused complications.'

'Are you still saying it was Miranda that did this to me?'

'Yes. They've charged her.'

'Surely, there must be some mistake. Miranda loves me. There's no way she'd...'

'She admitted it, Joe. I thought I'd lost you.'

'Sorry to have worried you.'

'It wasn't your fault.'

'Anyway' – he squeezed my hand – 'you don't get rid of me that easily.' He frowned. 'I still can't believe Miranda would do such a thing. Are you sure you've got it right?'

'Yep. And it can't have been an accident because, like I said, she stabbed you twice. Not once. I mean how could she do that?'

He shook his head. 'It's my fault for breaking her heart. She probably didn't know what she was doing.'

'Don't make excuses for her. They need to lock her up and throw away the key.' I glanced up the ward. 'Here comes your mam and dad.'

Peggy's eyes lit up as she approached Joe. 'Thank God.'

Adam rested a hand on his son's arm. 'You gave us a bit of a fright, lad.'

'Sorry, Dad.'

A domestic stopped her tea trolley at Joe's bed. 'Cup of tea? Coffee?'

He shook his head. 'No, ta.'

Peggy moved to the other side of the bed and stroked Joe's cheek. 'You should at least try.'

'Listen to your mam,' the tea lady said. 'What can I get you?'

'All right.' Joe smiled. 'I'll have a tea no sugar.'

'Your mam looks like she could do with one too.'

'I'm fine thanks. Just pour one for Joe.'

'Here, I tell you what, I'll pour one out for you too and it's up to you what you do with it.' She winked.

'Okay, thanks,' Peggy said.

'Milk?'

Peggy nodded. 'Thank you.'

The woman placed the drinks on the locker. 'They never stop being a worry, do they?' She squeezed Peggy's fingers.

Peggy shook her head. 'No, they don't. Thank you.'

'You probably don't remember' – I held up Joe's rucksack – 'I brought this in yesterday. I went back to ours to get your PJs, toothbrush, that sort of thing. They reckon you could be in here for a week.'

'A week? Bloody hell, I'll go mad in here. Can't you stay too. I'm sure I can make room for you in here.' He grinned.

'Well, you must be feeling better,' Adam said. 'Listen, lad, once you're out, I think you should come back home while you recover. They reckon it could take four to six weeks.'

'But I want to be with Rach.'

I glared at Adam. 'I'm quite capable of looking after him.'

'I don't doubt that for one moment but I can't see him managing those stairs of yours, can you? It's only while he recovers. We don't want him having an accident now, do we?'

'No, of course not.' I suddenly remembered the news I'd received before the stabbing. 'Guess what, Joe?'

'What?'

'You know that house we went to look around?'

'Yeah. Have they accepted our offer?'

'Yep. And I got in touch with the building society and they're getting a survey done as soon as poss. We could be in there by April.'

'Thank heavens for some good news. Rach, get me a glass of water, will you? My mouth's really dry and a cup of tea won't cut it.'

'Sure.' I poured water from the jug into the plastic tumbler. 'Here you are, darling.' I held it to his lips and let him sip. Afterwards I returned the glass to the locker.

'Are my motorcycle magazines in that bag?'

'Absolutely.' I pulled out a couple. 'Knew you'd want them.'

'Cheers. See, Mam and Dad, look how well she knows me? How's our Kate?'

'Relieved like the rest of us,' Peggy answered. 'If you're up to it, she'd like to pop in after work.'

'I'd like that. Who's looking after Ben?'

'Aunty Sheila.' Peggy lifted the cup of tea to her mouth.

'Great. Does she have any goss?'

'She does actually, if you're sure you're up to chatting.' She returned the cup to its saucer. 'I don't want to tire you out.'

'No, go on. As long as it's not bad news.'

Peggy grinned. 'Sheila and Malc are adopting a little boy. He's three months old.'

'That's great news,' Adam said, 'when did all this happen?'

'Sorry, love, I didn't get a chance to tell you. I was going to bring it up at Joe and Rachel's when we were around there but then...'

'It's okay.' Adam put his arm around her. 'Totally understandable.'

Joe's eyelids fluttered.

'You're looking tired,' I said. 'I think we should let you have some rest. I'll come back tonight.'

'Thanks, darling. I'm exhausted.'

'Not surprisingly.' Adam patted Joe on the shoulder. 'Get some rest, son. Your mam and I will be back tomorrow.'

Joe was asleep before we'd even moved from the bed.

Chapter Thirty-Eight

Rachel

A nurse hovered over Joe's bed as I headed down the ward. I hoped nothing was wrong but when he beamed at me I knew all was well.

'Hello, gorgeous.' I brushed my lips against his. 'How are you today?'

The blonde-haired nurse smiled. 'Are you going to tell her?'

Joe grinned. 'The doctor said I can hopefully go home tomorrow.'

'That's brilliant news.' I picked up *The Echo* from the bottom of his bed. A photo of Miranda and a headline WIFE STABS HUSBAND stared back at me. 'You've seen it then?' I threw it back down. 'Evil bitch.'

'Yep. The tea lady brought it in.'

'Joe said you're a journalist,' the nurse said. 'Did you write the article?'

'I am, but no, I didn't write it. My boss did. Better The Echo got the story than some other rag that would've told a pack of lies.' I took Joe's hand. 'I'm sorry you had to see this, darling. Are you all right?'

'I'm cool. You can't protect me from everything, Rach.'

'Okay. It's just...' I found involuntary tears falling. 'Oh God.'

The nurse passed me a tissue. 'It's understandable. You've been through a lot too. I was just saying to Joe he needs to get some counselling after this. I'm sure the doctor will refer him... But it looks like you could benefit too. You should contact your GP.'

'Thanks.' I blew my nose. 'I may well do that.'

The nurse rested her hand on Joe's arm. 'I'll leave you and your fiancée to have some time alone. By the way,' she said to me, 'Joe's been telling me about your story. You poor things. I reckon you both deserve some happiness after everything you've been through. Maybe you should write a book?'

What had Joe told her? Surely not about us thinking we were brother and sister. After deep thought I answered, 'I'm not sure about that, living through it once has been enough without doing it again, but thanks.'

'See you later, Joe. Nice to meet you, Rachel.' The nurse moved to the bed opposite.

'She seems nice,' I said.

'You're not jealous, are you?'

'Um, maybe a bit. After all she is hanging over my fiancé while he's in bed.' I laughed. 'No, of course I'm not.' I picked up the newspaper again and glared at the picture. 'Look at those evil eyes. I can't believe I thought she looked like me.'

He pushed the paper away. 'I'd rather not if you don't mind.'

'Sorry. Shall I put it in the bin where it belongs?'

'Yeah. I can't believe I fell for her charms. Stupid me. At least you saw through her when no one else did.'

'Well, Linda did too. There was something about her. I couldn't quite make out what, a slyness maybe, and then when she said she was pregnant I guessed she was lying. She obviously sensed you didn't love her so trapped you into marriage the only way she knew.'

'Can we not talk about her anymore?'

'Sorry.' I placed a carrier bag on the locker. 'I brought you some clean PJs and picked up a couple more mags. Motor ones this time. Hope that's okay. I don't think you've read them.'

'Cheers, Rach. Are you still at Mam's?'

'No, I've been staying at the flat with Jenny but she's flying out to Paris the day after tomorrow.'

'But if I've got to go to Mam's you'll come and stay too?'

'I don't know. Your dad's planning to bring a bed downstairs and put it in the living room so I don't think it would be appropriate. Anyway, they've not asked me.'

'But...'

'What?'

'I need to hold you next to me.'

'I know. I feel the same.' I peered up at the sound of footsteps. 'Look, here's your mam now.'

'Hello, Joe.' Peggy made for the other side of the bed and kissed Joe on the cheek before settling down in the soft chair. 'You're looking better.'

'I was just telling Rach, the doctor said I should be able to go home tomorrow.'

Peggy glanced at me. 'That's amazing?'

'Isn't it? Anyway, darling, I'll leave you to have some time with your mam as I must pop back to work for a couple of hours. Mr Strange has been really accommodating.'

'All right, babe. Will you come back tonight?'

'Try and keep me away.' I brushed my lips against his before turning to Peggy and kissing her cheek. 'I'll see you later, Peg.'

Mel filled the kettle. 'How's he doing?'

'Really good.' I perched on the edge of a desk. 'He's looking more like his old self, and hopefully they'll discharge him tomorrow.'

'Why the long face?'

'Because he's got to go back to his mam's. As Adam pointed out there's no way Joe can manage the stairs up to the flat. He's right of course.'

'Will you go there too?'

'That's what Joe asked but I haven't been invited. I don't think Peggy and Adam will be up for it. Mind you, I'm not sure I'd want to be there like that with Joe either. It seems a bit weird.'

'I can stay with you in the flat, if you like?'

'That's awfully kind. Our Jen's staying with me at the moment but maybe once she's moved out. Is it okay if I let you know?'

'Sure. Just shout.'

'The sooner our house is ready the better.'

'Do you have a moving date?'

'Not yet but the building society have the survey booked. I'm not sure how long these things take but we're hoping for completion in no more than three months, fingers crossed. But it's not just up to our building society, it's the solicitors, our sellers and all sorts of things.' I slid off the desk and poured boiling water into the mugs. 'I'd better get upstairs, I don't want Mr Strange thinking I'm taking advantage.'

'Betty said she'll try and pop in to check on you later.'

'She did?' Betty and I had regained our close relationship since she'd opened up about her mother. What a remarkable woman thinking of me while going through her own darkness.

Mel and I stepped outside in the dark cold air leaving Mr Strange alone in the building.

'Roll on the light nights,' she said.

'Yep. I can't wait. Fancy a quick coffee before I leave for the hospital?'

'I can't. I'm really sorry but I've promised to meet an old friend in The Red Lion.'

'Never mind. Have a nice time. See you tomorrow.'

'Ta-ra.' She headed across the road to the pub.

I was making my way around the back of the offices towards the flat when someone yanked my arm and pushed me against the wall. 'What the hell?' I glared into savage eyes.

'So, you're the dirty tart that stole my sister's husband.'

'What?'

I tried to work my way free but he pulled out a knife and held it to my throat. 'Move one inch and you get this.'

'No, please.'

'Shut your gob.'

'What do you want?'

'Justice.'

'What are you talking about?'

'Shut up, tart. Make one sound and I'll fuckin slit your throat.'

'Please.' My stomach churned. My heart banged. *Oh, please, God, don't let this happen.* 'Please, no.'

'Please, no,' he imitated in a squeaky voice. 'It's your fault our Miranda's been charged with attempted murder, but now you and that bastard boyfriend of yours are going to put an end to it.'

'How, when she's guilty?'

'By getting that Joe Davies to drop the charges or else.' He held the knife closer to my throat. 'Understand?' He jabbed my arm with his other hand.

I nodded.

'This is what we're going to do. Without a sound make your way up to the flat and once we're in there you and I can have a bit of fun.' He sniggered. 'If you know what I mean? Bastard Davies won't want you then.'

'No, you can't. You won't get away with this.'

'What did I tell you?' He held me in a half nelson holding the knife under my throat. 'Now move.'

Slowly, my pulse vibrating, I climbed the steps with him right behind me. I tried to look around for help but it was dark and quiet with no one about. When we reached the top, he nudged me. 'Get the key and don't try any funny business.'

Trembling, I managed to take the key from my coat pocket and insert it into the lock. He pushed the door open, pulled me inside and slammed the door behind us. I clenched my fists trying to work out a way to distract him.

He kicked the bedroom door open and dragged me through and hauled me on the bed. 'Time for you to find out what it's like to have a real man.' He unzipped his trousers. This was my chance. I picked up the bedside lamp, hit him across the head and ran out into the hallway making for the front door but I was too late. He was behind me and holding the knife under my throat. 'Bitch. You'll be sorry for that. Move one more fuckin inch.' He glided the blade across my cheek. 'Maybe I'll leave you with a souvenir. Fancy a nice scar? You won't look so pretty then, will you?'

'Please don't.'

'I'm gonna make sure that Joe Davies won't want to go near you again.' He ripped my blouse and stuck his hand up my skirt.

I kicked his shins but he held me firm. Heavy footsteps rattled the metal stairway. 'Help,' I screamed as loud as I could. My attacker pressed his left hand against my mouth and dragged me back towards the bedroom wall.

Someone kicked the door several times. It finally bashed open and two policemen stood inside the hallway by the bedroom door but held back from entering. 'If you know what's good for you, lad,' the older policeman said, 'you'll put the knife down. There's no escape.'

'Come any closer and I'll slit her throat.' His hand shook as he held the knife closer.

'If you do that you'll be in prison for life,' the same policeman continued. 'Is that really what you want? Is that what your mother would want? It's highly likely that your father, sister and uncles are going to prison. Who's going to look after your mam?'

His eyes darted from the policemen to me and back again.

'I remember you,' the younger policeman said. 'Jamie, isn't it? We were at school together.'

'Don't know what you're talking about.'

'Yeah, you do. I came to tea at your house one day. I remember your mam. A nice lady. How's she going to feel if you're locked up?'

'This bitch stole my sister's husband.' The knife shook in his hand.

'I'm sorry,' I stuttered.

Come on, lad,' the older policeman said. 'Put the knife down now. Give yourself up and the court will go easy on you.'

His hand was still shaking as he held the knife under me but I sensed he was weakening.

'I met your mam, Jamie,' I said, 'at the wedding. From what I know of her she wouldn't want to think her son was capable of this.'

'Shut your gob.' The blade touched my neck.

'Back-up is on the way, lad,' the older policeman said, 'and you won't stand a chance. Give yourself up now and you'll get an easier sentence. Like my colleague just said, think of your mam. What's she going to think when she finds out what you've done?'

'I...'

'Think about it,' the policeman continued. 'Do you think she'll be proud? Or ashamed?'

'I...' He dropped the knife, and held his hands up. The policemen grabbed him either side and the younger one snapped a pair of handcuffs on the bastard.

Relieved I was out of his hold, I sobbed.

Strong arms were around me. 'It's all right now, Miss Webster.'

'Mr Strange.' My heart banged like a drum. Taking deep breaths, I asked, 'How?'

'I was suspicious after spotting him lurking outside the office so called the police. Thank heavens you're okay.'

'We'll need statements,' the older policeman said as they dragged Miranda's brother away.

Mr Strange pushed the flat door closed. 'I'll get someone around to secure the lock. The police will want a statement from you later and one from me as a witness. There'll be no wriggling out of the charges for that one.'

'Sorry.' I darted to the bathroom and threw up. It wasn't fair. How much more could Joe and I take? It wasn't fair. I screamed.

'Miss Webster,' Mr Strange called, 'are you okay in there?'

I swilled lukewarm water over my face, washed my hands and made my way into the lounge. 'Sorry, I...'

'No apologies necessary. Sit yourself down, take some deep breaths, and I'll make you a cup of tea.'

'Thank you.'

When there was a rap on the door my knees trembled.

'It's all right, Miss Webster' – Mr Strange patted my hand – 'you're safe now.' He went over to the door and opened it. 'Yes, she's in here. Thanks for coming.'

Betty hurried to my side. 'Oh my God, thank goodness Mr Strange realised something wasn't right.'

'Betty.' I cried into her chest. 'I thought he was going to kill me. He was like a mad man holding a knife at my throat.' I sobbed some more.

'And Mr Strange was your knight in shining armour.'

'He certainly was.'

Mr Strange put a mug of tea in front of each of us. 'Yours is sweet and weak, Miss Webster. The best thing for shock.' He took a seat next to Betty. 'Look, I've had an idea. Say no if you want, Miss Webster, but you'd be wise to say yes.'

What was he talking about? 'Yes?'

'I have a holiday bungalow just outside Southport, and I propose you and Mr Davies stay there during his recovery period. Everything you need is there. Village shop with groceries, a pub and café. It's on the seafront and equipped with a television, fridge and washing machine.'

'But what about work?'

'Take a month off or six weeks if Joe's recovery takes longer. There's a doctor's surgery around the corner where you can both register as temporary patients. The property's sitting empty so it may as well get the use and you'll be out of the way from those gangsters.'

'That's really kind, Mr Strange.' Betty picked up her cup. 'Isn't it, Rachel?'

'Really kind. I don't know how we can repay you.' I sighed. 'But how much is the rent?'

'No rent required. It's yours for as long as you and your fiancé need it. Your time off work will be fully paid too. You've both been through so much. And obviously Mr Davies can't come back here with those steep stairs, and after today's events I'm not sure either of you should until these people have been tried, found guilty and locked up.'

I hugged Mr Strange. He didn't push me away but gently patted me on the back.

Chapter Thirty-Nine

Peggy

I had just finished bathing Ben when the key turned in the lock.

'Is that you, Adam?' I called. 'You're just in time for a cuddle.'

Adam hurried upstairs and took Ben from me. 'How was Joe today?'

'Good. He's coming home tomorrow.'

'I'd better get the bed downstairs in the lounge then. I wonder if Stu will come around this evening and help me. I'll give him a ring after tea. What's for nosh?'

'Chicken chasseur. Kate's favourite. Surprised you didn't smell it cooking. Kate should be home in a minute. How was your day?'

'All right but I'll feel better once that bitch has been sentenced.'

'I know what you mean. Was that a knock?'

'Here, you take Ben and I'll see who it is. Are you expecting anyone?'

I shook my head. 'No.' I hoped nothing had happened to Kate. All this Joe business had been too much for us all. You didn't expect things like that to happen to your loved ones.

Adam rushed downstairs and opened the door. 'Rachel, come in,' I heard him say.

Once I'd finished dressing Ben in his Babygro, I made my way down. 'Rachel, you look dreadful,' I said. 'Joe's not had a turn for the worse has he?'

She shook her head. 'No.' Her eyes filled up.

I passed Ben to Adam. 'What is it?'

She fell into my arms and sobbed. 'Miranda's brother attacked me.'

'What?' Adam put Ben down in the pram. 'Come through to the lounge and tell us what happened.'

'I was walking back to the flat when...' She sobbed again.

'Get her a cup of tea, Peg. She's not making any sense.'

I hurried out to the kitchen, poured a cup from the brew I'd made earlier for Adam, and rushed back into the lounge. 'Here, drink this.'

Rachel gave a nervous laugh. 'I've had that many cups of tea.' She sniffled, blew her nose, and took a deep breath. 'I was lucky as my boss was suspicious when he saw a bloke lurking around the newspaper office so called the police. I thought this mad man, Miranda's brother, was going to kill me when he held a knife to my throat. The whole bloody family are insane. They all need locking up and the key thrown away. And the police said Joe must press charges for the battering he got at Christmas. It's the only way we'll get them all behind bars.'

'Yes, I can see that' – Adam rubbed my arm – 'you've had an awful ordeal. You should stay here tonight.'

'No, I'll be all right as Jen's still with me and then tomorrow...' – she bit her lip – 'I'm taking Joe to Southport to recover so I thought I'd better let you know before you start getting the bed down ready.'

'What are you talking about?' I asked.

'My boss has given us his holiday bungalow to stay in while Joe recovers.'

'It's going to take more than a week or two,' Adam said.

'I realise that, Adam. I'm not flamin stupid.' She started crying again. 'Mr Strange said we can have the place for as long as it takes. Four weeks. Six weeks. Whatever it takes. And he's given me the time off work to look after Joe.'

'That's very generous of him,' Adam said.

'Yes, we thought so too.'

Adam chewed his lip. 'Did you still manage to see Joe this evening?'

'Only briefly. I promised I'd be there so couldn't not turn up. Jenny wanted me to telephone the hospital but I knew Joe would be worried if he couldn't see for himself that I was all right. We only had around fifteen minutes but enough time for me to tell him about the plans.'

I frowned. 'And Joe was in agreement with this?'

'Absolutely. He agreed it was a great idea. It means we can be together.'

'But Joe needs his mam,' I said.

'Peg,' Adam said, 'Joe needs Rachel. He wants Rachel not us.'

Adam was right of course. Rachel and Joe had been through so much. I was being selfish. So much had happened these last few months. Discovering Rachel wasn't mine, Joe breaking up with Miranda, getting beaten up, the stabbing and now this with Rachel. It must've been so frightening for her. Teresa. Oh, my goodness, I'd forgotten all about her phone call. I nudged Adam. 'Are you awake?'

He rolled over. 'What is it, Peg? Can't you sleep? Joe's going to be fine.'

'It's not that.'

He stroked my cheek. 'What is it?'

'Remember we talked about Teresa coming over for tea to meet everyone.'

'Sure. And that still goes.'

I propped up my pillows, turned on the lamp, and sat upright. 'I think you'll like her. Did I tell you she doesn't look anything like me or Mike? And when she took her hat off, well, she looked a proper hard nut with bleached spikey hair, but...'

'You did.'

'But once I got to know her a little, she seemed nice. Quiet. Gentle. Knowledgeable about babies too. Even changed Ben's nappy and got him dressed like she was an expert.'

Adam plumped up his pillows and pulled himself up. 'A bit like our Kate.'

'Yes, except Teresa writes poetry and loves painting, oh and she's a dance teacher. Maybe she could teach us.'

'I don't know about that, Peg.' He sighed. 'Shall we try and get some kip now?'

'I can't.'

Adam leaned across to the cabinet, grabbed a packet of Players, took one out and lit it up. 'I really should give these up,' he said coughing.

'You're right. You should. Maybe then you'd get rid of that awful hack. Anyway, lying here thinking about our family made me think about Teresa and the plan to invite her over to tea. But as Joe's not going to be around, do you think we should go to the hospital in the morning and tell him about her?'

'No. Joe and Rachel have enough on, and if Rachel's not made up her mind yet whether she wants to meet her birth parents this could add extra pressure on her and they don't need that right now.'

'You're right as always.'

'We can still go to the hospital if you like? What time's he being discharged?'

'He reckons sometime in the afternoon.'

'Okay, I'll pop home at lunchtime to pick you up. What about Ben?'

'I'll ask Sheila to have him. She reckons Teresa's the image of my mam.'

'But you didn't see that?'

'No, but Sheila has photos of Mam in her twenties, and she and Malc had been looking at them the other day.'

'Right. Well, I look forward to meeting the girl.' Adam stubbed out his cigarette in the tin ashtray on the bedside cabinet and slid back down. 'But, Peg, if we go to the hospital tomorrow, remember don't mention Teresa. They don't need it. And we'll only stay for a few minutes to see how he is and what's happening about all this police business.'

'All right. Thanks, darling.'

'Should we try and get some rest now?'

'Yes, sorry.'

Adam turned over to sleep.

I switched the bedside lamp off and cuddled up close to him but after a couple of minutes I turned the lamp back on. 'Adam.'

'Yes.' He sighed, rolling back over. 'What now, Peg?'

'How could I not have seen it?'

'What?'

'Miranda. I thought she was good for our son but...'

'No one could've known.'

'But Rachel did. She said from the start something wasn't right. And then when Miranda said she was pregnant, Rachel knew. I'm Joe's mam. I should've known.'

'You couldn't have known, love. She blinded us all. I thought she was a good catch too. Now, shall we try and sleep?'

'Yes. Sorry.'

He nestled under the covers wrapping his arm around me. 'Night, Peg.'

'Night, Adam.'

'Peg, the light?'

'Sorry.' I leaned across and flicked the switch leaving the room in almost darkness. 'Adam.'

'What now?'

'I love you.'

He kissed me on the lips. 'I love you too, darling. Sorry for being an old grump.' He sighed. 'I'm wide awake now. Are you?'

'Yes.'

He pulled at my nightie. 'Why don't you get rid of this?'

'What did you have in mind, Mr Davies?' I slipped the satin nightwear over my head.

'Come here, wifey, and I'll show you.' He kissed me hard on the lips, cupped my breasts, and after teasing me with kisses, made love to me like he hadn't done for a long time. 'I love you, Peg. Everything's going to be okay.'

Afterwards I snuggled close to him just listening to the rhythm of his gentle snore. I was lucky. Adam was a wonderful husband and father. He was always there for me no matter what. Joe would be like that for Rachel. Reliable, loving and faithful.

So much had changed over the last year. Kate getting married in a few months, Rachel not being my daughter, she and Joe living together as husband and wife. Ben growing up quickly. Crawling and soon he'd be walking. Then there was Teresa. I wondered what she'd be like. Would she fit in with the rest of the family? Ben had certainly taken to her, as had our Sheila. What else would this year bring for us all? Relaxed and feeling loved, I closed my eyes and let sleep take me.

Chapter Forty

Rachel

The nice nurse smiled as she took Joe's blood pressure. I read the monitor. 110/70. 'Is that normal,' I asked. 'Is he fit to leave?'

'Perfectly normal. He's doing well. I hear you've lined up some convalescence.'

'Yes, it's literally on the seafront. Our bags are packed and ready in the boot so we're all set for the off once he gets the go ahead.'

'Doctor shouldn't be long. And looking at his chart I don't think he'll have a problem.' She glanced to the right. 'Isn't that your mam and dad coming down the ward?'

I turned to look. 'It is.'

Joe blinked. 'Didn't you tell them I was going home with you?'

'Yes.' I looked to each of them. 'We weren't expecting you.'

'I know, sorry' – Peggy sank into the green chair by the bed and rested her handbag on her lap – 'I hope you don't mind, Joe, but we wanted to see you before setting off on your journey.'

'I'm fine, Mam, as you can see.' He leaned across and kissed Peggy on the cheek. 'You don't need to worry. I'm in good hands with Rach.'

'We know, son' – Adam rested his hand on Peggy's shoulder – 'but you know what your mam's like. She had to see for herself.

Also, I wanted to check whether you've made your statement to the police about the beating you took at Christmas.'

'Aye. All done. Police came in this morning and I told them everything. Rachel's made her statement too. With a bit of luck, the whole rotten shower will get locked up.' Joe ran his hand through his freshly washed hair. 'I can't say I'm looking forward to the hearing.'

'Me neither,' I said.

'Well don't worry about that now.' Adam passed Joe a motorcycle magazine. 'Some light reading for while you're away. You two have a good time, and Joe, come back well. I can't see the blighters getting bail, so with any luck they'll be locked up for a long time.'

I gripped Joe's hand. 'I'd throw away the key.'

'Exactly.' Adam checked his watch. 'We should be going in a minute, Peg. Only I still have an MOT to do before knocking off this evening.'

Peggy fiddled with the buttons on her coat. 'Can't we wait a little longer? Just until the doctor gets here.'

'As long as he comes soon.' Adam turned to me. 'Where did you say you were going, Rachel?'

'Southport. Well, just outside to be precise.'

'But that's so far away.' Peggy rubbed her eyes.

'Not really.' I squeezed her hand. 'I promise I'll look after him and there's nothing to stop you lot visiting for the day on a weekend. If you wanted?'

'Really?' Her face lit up. 'Did you hear that, Adam? We can visit. You'd better give me the address.' She opened her handbag and pulled out a red address book. 'Write it in here? Oh, you'll need a pen.' She rooted again and passed me a biro.

I scribbled the details down. 'The bungalow has a phone so I've written the number down too. And it's not that far away.

Only about an hour and half drive and positioned right on the seafront.'

'It's really kind of Rach's boss to let us have it,' Joe said as a doctor in his thirties came to his bed.

'How are you feeling, Mr Davies?'

'Ready to go home.' Joe smiled.

'Nurse, Mr Davies' chart please.'

'Certainly, doctor.' She passed him Joe's file. 'All his vitals are looking good.'

'Excellent.' The doctor studied the paperwork. 'It looks like we can release you, Mr Davies, but remember not to exert yourself and allow time to recover.'

'I will.' Joe beamed. 'Does that mean I can go now?'

'Yes. As soon as you're ready.'

'Thank you.' Joe grinned.

Adam shook the doctor's hand. 'Yes, thank you.'

The nice nurse pushed Joe in a wheelchair out to the front of the hospital where I'd parked the car.

Joe looked left to right. 'Where's your Mini?'

'Another surprise.' Adam grinned. 'I managed to get Rachel a good deal from the garage using the Mini as a part exchange.'

Joe furrowed his eyebrows. 'Are you okay with this, Rach?'

'Sure, it was my idea. I was worried about you struggling to get in and out of my little Mini. Anyway, I've always wanted a Triumph Toledo, and this gorgeous maroon colour is perfect.'

'Thanks for your help, Dad' – Joe shook Adam's hand – 'and take care of Mam,' he whispered.

'Don't worry, son. I will.'

'Bye, darling.' Peggy bent down and squeezed Joe close. 'Have a lovely time and get better soon.'

'I will, Mam.'

'You all set?' the nurse said.

'Yeah. Thanks for everything.' Joe pulled himself up from the wheelchair with the aid of the nurse and got into the passenger seat of the Toledo.

I climbed into the car. 'Give me a ring, Peggy, when you want to come down.'

'I will.' She wiped a handkerchief across her eyes.

Joe fiddled around in the glove compartment, and ran his fingers across the dashboard. 'Not bad. What year is it?'

'Ninety seventy-four. So still quite new.' I put the key in the ignition.

Peggy tapped on the window so I wound it down. 'What's wrong?'

'Nothing.' She sniffled. 'Ring us when you get there.'

'Will do.' I wound the window back up and turned to Joe. 'Ready?'

'Yep, let's go.'

I started the engine. Adam and Peggy waved us off and I drove out of the parking space, turned right into a side street and left onto the main road.

Joe reached out to touch my hand. 'For a time there I thought the universe was trying to stop us being together.'

'I know what you mean.' I switched on the windscreen wipers. 'Let's hope this rain doesn't come to much.'

Joe turned on the radio and 'You Light Up my Life' sang out.

'You light up mine too.' I smiled. At least a month on our own, with the exception of Peggy and Adam popping down for a day. But all that time alone and close to the sea was going to be idyllic.

The traffic lights turned red. 'Bit hilly here,' I said but got no answer and when I glanced at Joe I saw he was sleeping. He was going to need a lot of rest after the trauma he'd been through. I put the handbrake on and switched into neutral. When the lights changed to green I stuck the car into first gear, released the brake and did a hill start. Even now I loathed doing those things. I turned left towards the seafront but Joe was still fast asleep. Next, I took a right into a little cobbled street and pulled onto the drive at number seven Coastal Lane. Our picturesque home for the next few weeks. I turned off the engine. 'We're here, sleepyhead.'

'What?' Joe tossed his head. 'Where are we?'

'We've arrived.' I touched his lips with mine. 'Stay here while I get the stuff inside and I'll be back for you in a minute.' After getting out of the car, I took the bags from the boot and headed for the blue front door. I turned the key in the lock, pushed the door open and the warmth instantly hit me when I stepped inside. *Wow*. Mr Strange had asked his cleaner to get the place ready for us, she'd done a brilliant job. A fire burned in the grate. She must've lit it for us. How kind of her and how kind of Mr Strange. He'd gone out of his way so much to help me. I strolled into the kitchen and found a grocery hamper on the worktop. I picked through it. A loaf of bread, potatoes, teabags, a jar of Nescafé, cornflakes, and a cake box containing two doughnuts and two pink iced buns.

I opened the fridge and discovered a pint of gold-top milk, a dozen eggs, a block of Anchor butter, and a slab of cheddar cheese. Tucked in the side of the door was a bottle of Blue

Nun wine and four cans of lager. This woman had thought of everything.

I grinned. This was a perfect hideaway where Joe could get strong again. I made my way back into the sitting area and on the round teak table a terracotta flowerpot filled with purple violas had a little note next to it.

If there's anything you need, I'm just next door.
Eileen.

I hurried out to Joe and opened the passenger door. 'Wait until you see it. It's perfect.'

He leaned on me as he climbed out. 'I'm sorry, babe, but I don't think I'll be able to carry you over the threshold.'

I chuckled. 'So long as you don't expect me to carry you. Let's get inside as it's freezing but roasty toasty in there.'

Joe stepped inside. 'This is superb. Fancy your boss having this little sanctuary.'

'Yeah, Betty said he'd bought it as a getaway for weekends and his retirement in the long term.'

'What's he going to do while we're here?' Joe eased himself down on the sofa.

I shrugged. 'He told me not to worry about it. And he wouldn't take a penny off us for staying here. And he's paid for coal, and loads of groceries in the kitchen. He must've had to pay the cleaning lady too.' I slumped down next to Joe. 'This is comfy.'

'Let's hope the bed is too. Have you looked in there yet?'

'Nope.'

A tap came on the door. Joe and I glanced at each other. No one knew we were here and Miranda's family certainly wouldn't be knocking, they'd just barge in. 'I should get that.' I headed for the door.

'Sorry to disturb you, lass, I'm Eileen by the way. As it's such a cold day I thought you might like this.' She passed me a Pyrex dish. 'Chicken casserole. Heat in the oven on six for around half an hour and it'll be ready to eat.'

'Thank you, that's very kind of you. I'm Rachel. I work for Mr Strange. Thank you for lighting the fire, and all the groceries.'

'Just doing what the boss asked me.' Eileen smiled. 'Right, Rachel, I'm only next door if you need me.' She patted my hand.

'Thank you.' I closed the door. 'It was the lady from next door. And look, she's made us dinner. How kind is that?'

'Very.' Tears ran down Joe's cheeks.

'Hey. It's all right.'

'I don't know what's the matter with me. Crying for god's sake. It's a good job my old man can't see me.'

'Shh.' I put the casserole dish down on the table. 'I won't tell anyone.' I dabbed my hanky across his damp cheek. 'After what you've been through, you're entitled to have a bit of a boo. Are you hungry?'

His stomach rumbled. 'I think I am.'

'Right, I'll heat this up and then we can eat.' I picked up the dish and took it through to the kitchen and put it inside the oven. Gas. How the hell did a gas oven work? Matches. I opened a drawer and found not only a box of Swan Vesta but an instruction manual for the New World cooker. After deciphering the instructions, I pressed a button which ignited the pilot and suddenly the oven sprang into flame.

I took one of the cans of lager from the fridge, poured it into two tumblers and carried them through. 'Cheers.' I passed a glass to Joe.

'Awesome. They've thought of everything. Cheers, babe.' He patted the cushion next to him. 'Come and sit down.'

'Yep, I will in a minute, but first I'll stoke up the fire.' I gave the embers a bit of a poke, and used the tongs to add a couple of pieces of coal. 'Want the telly on?'

'Go on then, if you like?'

I switched it on. '*Crossroads*. Do you fancy that?'

'Go on then. I know you like it.'

⋆

I served the hot casserole onto two glass dinner plates and placed them on the dining table. 'Dinner's ready,' I said sitting down. 'There's a bottle of wine in the fridge. Do you fancy that?'

'I'm fine with the lager.' Joe got up and took a seat opposite me. 'We can keep the wine for tomorrow if you like?'

'Okay.' I tasted the stew. 'Yummy, this is delicious. This Eileen's a wonder woman. Great cook, great cleaner, great shopper. I wonder whether there's anything she's not good at. Hey, do you reckon Eileen's Mr Strange's fancy piece?'

'Might be, although I thought you said...'

'I know but I reckon John was winding me up. He can be a bit like that.'

Joe munched on the chicken. 'This is tasty. You know, Rach, we should get this Eileen a present before we leave. Flowers, chocolates or something. What do you reckon?'

'Fab idea. We should take Mr Strange something back too. Maybe a bottle of Scotch. What do you think?'

'Yeah. Didn't you say he smoked cigars?'

'I did. We could get some of them too.'

After putting the spark guard up in front of the dying fire, I went into the bedroom where Joe was standing at the window. 'Come and look at this, Rach.'

I joined him to look outside and he put his arm around me. The garden had a small patio with two chairs and a table, and a three-foot wooden gate at the bottom led to the sea where a full moon reflected on the waves. 'This is a spectacular view.' I lifted my face to kiss Joe. 'Imagine this place in the summer when we could sit outside and watch the waves and sky'.

'We still could if we bundled up. Get our coats and we'll wrap the quilt around us.'

'I don't want you to get cold.'

'I won't.'

'All right.' I hurried out to the hallway and grabbed our coats. By the time I got back to the bedroom, Joe had the French doors unlocked and the quilt off the bed. He opened the doors and we stepped outside, pulling the chairs next to each other and sitting down with the quilt across us.

'That's Orion's belt.' I pointed. 'I really must learn what the other constellations are. Fancy taking up astronomy?'

'Sure, if that's what you'd like. This is so romantic. The waves look like they've swallowed the moon. I wonder if it's a special moon with it being so big and bright.' He turned me to him and held my chin as he kissed me. 'There's only ever been you, Rach. I'm sorry I caused all this trouble with Miranda. If I hadn't married her then there would've been none of this mess. None of me getting beaten up, none of me getting stabbed, and none of you being threatened with a knife by her crazy brother.' He kissed me again. 'I'm sorry.'

'You have nothing to be sorry for. Like me, you were grieving, and searching for something or someone to take away the pain. You thought it was her. You weren't to know.' I gently rubbed his chest under the quilt. 'Are you still in pain?'

'It's not too bad. The painkillers help.'

'I never thought, should you have been drinking?'

'I only had half a lager, Rach. I'm sure that's fine. Let's go back inside. I want to see your gorgeous hair flowing over my pillow.'

'You prefer it longer?'

'I do, but you looked stunning with it short too. But you're my Rach with it long. Come on, babe. Take me to bed.'

I lifted the quilt and carried it inside and laid it back across the bed. Joe followed me in and perched on the bedcovers. I locked up the French doors but left the curtains open so we could watch the moonlight and hear the rushing waves through the glass. I lowered myself down next to Joe and stroked his neck, lifted his T-shirt over his head, and caressed his chest, smothering him in kisses. Joe unzipped his jeans. I unbuttoned my blouse, letting it fall from my shoulders, and slipped out of my trousers. 'There's something I want from you.' I nuzzled up to Joe and let him make the next move.

He dropped his black jeans to the floor and carried on kissing me while his hands expertly unfastened my bra and caressed my shoulders.

'Are you sure you're up to this?' I asked, 'I don't want you to hurt yourself.'

'Just be gentle with me.'

He was smothering my breasts in kisses when he pulled away, holding his chest.

'Are you okay?'

'Um, no, sorry, Rach, I don't think I'm quite as ready as I thought.'

'That's all right, darling, we've got the rest of our lives. I'll get you some painkillers.' Slithering off the bed, I made for the kitchen and took two tablets from the prescription bottle on the worktop. I filled a glass with water from the tap before padding back into the bedroom. 'Here take these.' I passed him the medicine and glass.

He sat up, popped a tablet in his mouth and tilted his head back swallowing each of the tablets in turn. 'Thanks, babe.' He passed the glass back to me and I put it down on the bedside cabinet before plumping up his pillows.

He crawled under the quilt, lay down and turned over on his side.

'I'm just nipping to the bathroom.' I brushed my lips against his, picked up the glass and took it into the kitchen. Afterwards I nipped to the loo and by the time I got back into the bedroom Joe had already drifted off to sleep. I slid under the covers next to him listening to his soft wheeze.

This was what it was all about. I'd fallen in love with Joe from that first day in March back in nineteen seventy-one when he was working as a waiter in Elmo's. He'd gazed at me with those twinkling chocolate eyes making my pulse rush and a few months later when he'd asked me to marry him, I was the happiest girl alive. But all our hopes and dreams had been crushed when we discovered we were half-siblings. Over six years wasted but now we were finally together and soon we'd move into our new home. Piece of paper or not, I'd go by the name of Mrs Rachel Davies. Would I go the next step and contact my real parents? I'd see how I felt once Joe and I were settled in our new house.

'Rach,' Joe murmured.

'Yes, darling.'

'Love you, babe.'

'I love you too.' And nothing or no one would ever stand in our way again. I snuggled into my soulmate as he breathed softly.

Acknowledgements

Special thanks to my friend Maureen Cullen. Not only for her perceptive and thoughtful editing in *The Woodhaerst Reunion* but her continuous support, encouragement and faith in me.

A big thank you to my fabulous beta readers for their invaluable feedback, and to Colin Ward for the cover design inasmanywords(.com).

Finally, a big thank you to my husband, children, family and friends for their continued support and faith in me.

About the author

Patricia M Osborne was born in Liverpool but now lives in West Sussex. She is married with grown-up children and grandchildren. In 2019 she graduated with an MA in Creative Writing. She is a published novelist, poet and short fiction writer. Her debut poetry pamphlet, *Taxus Baccata,* was nominated for the Michael Marks Pamphlet Award.

Patricia has a successful blog at Whitewingsbooks.com featuring other writers. When Patricia isn't working on her own writing, she enjoys sharing her knowledge, acting as a mentor to fellow writers.

You can find out more about Patricia by visiting her website, whitewingsbooks(.com).

Also by

House of Grace Family Saga Trilogy:

House of Grace (Book 1)
The Coal Miner's Son (Book 2)
The Granville Legacy (Book 3)

The Oath (*A Victorian era saga*)

The Woodhaerst Family Drama Trilogy:

The Woodhaerst Triangle (Book 1)
The Woodhaerst Reunion (Book 2)
The Woodhaerst Women (Book 3) To be published soon

Poetry Published by The Hedgehog Poetry Press

The Montefiore Bride

Taxus Baccata

Sherry & Sparkly

Symbiosis

Spirit Mother: Experience the Myth

Stickleback

Nature's Bookends

www.ingramcontent.com/pod-product-compliance
Lightning Source LLC
Chambersburg PA
CBHW030431010526
44118CB00011B/595